Wilde Style

Studies in Eighteenth and Nineteenth-Century Literature

General Editors
Andrew Sanders, Professor of English, University of Durham

Studies in Eighteenth and Nineteenth-Century Literature is an exciting
series of lively, original and authoritative critical studies at the student and
general reader. Each book takes as its subject an author, genre or a single
text. Some titles guide students through the perplexing cross-current of
critical debate by offering fresh and forthright reappraisals of their subject.
Others offer new and timely studies which are of importance and value to
the student. The series avoids critical identity or tight ideological approach,
allowing the authors to explore the subject in their own way, taking account
of recent changes in critical perspective.

Published titles

Forms of Speech in Victorian Fiction
Raymond Chapman

Henry Fielding: Authorship and Authority
Ian A. Bell

Utopian Imagination and Eighteenth-Century Fiction
Christine Rees

Robert Browning
John Woolford and Daniel Karlin

Wilde Style
The Plays and Prose of Oscar Wilde

Neil Sammells

An imprint of **Pearson Education**

Harlow, England · London · New York · Reading, Massachusetts · San Francisco
Toronto · Don Mills, Ontario · Sydney · Tokyo · Singapore · Hong Kong · Seoul
Taipei · Cape Town · Madrid · Mexico City · Amsterdam · Munich · Paris · Milan

Pearson Education Limited
Edinburgh Gate
Harlow
Essex CM20 2JE
England

and Associated Companies throughout the world

Visit us on the World Wide Web at:
www.pearsoneduc.com

First published 2000

ISBN 0–582–35759–4 PPR
ISBN 0–582–35760–8 CSD

British Library Cataloguing-in-Publication Data
A catalogue record for this book is available from the British Library

Library of Congress Cataloging-in-Publication Data
Sammells, Neil.
  Wilde style : the plays and prose of Oscar Wilde / Neil Sammells.
      p. cm. — (Studies in eighteenth- and nineteenth-century literature)
  Includes bibliographical references (p.) and index.
  ISBN 0–582–35759–4 (PPR) — ISBN 0–582–35760–8 (CSD)
    1. Wilde, Oscar, 1854–1900—Criticism and interpretation.   2. Wilde, Oscar,
  1854–1900—Literary style.   I. Title.   II. Series.
  PR5824.S29   2000
  828'.809—dc21   00–026032

Set in 11/13pt Minion by 35
Produced by Pearson Education Asia Pte Ltd

Transferred to digital print, 2007
Printed in Great Britain by CPI Antony Rowe, Eastbourne

ACKNOWLEDGEMENTS

I have benefited from conversations with many people over the years in thinking about this book. Ians Burton and Webb helped me think about style, in very different ways. Many others have provided interest and encouragement, as well as specific advice and knowledge: David Timms, Barrie Bullen, Ana Moya, Richard Haslam, Roberta Gefter Wondrich, Matt Campbell, Bruce Stewart, Colin Graham, Werner Huber, Barbara Suess, Clare Wallace, Claire Connolly to name but a few. My immediate colleagues in the Faculty of Humanities at Bath Spa University College (which provided financial help for me to complete the manuscript) have been both patient and supportive. Tessa Hadley pointed me to half-forgotten references in Henry James; Richard Kerridge was very influential on the sections dealing with Wilde and eco-criticism; Tracey Hill was typically combative on the subject of Postmodernism, and Jeff Rodman characteristically familiar with Potiphar's wife. I have been helped greatly by Terry Rodgers's detailed knowledge of the 1890s – and by the way, as Assistant Dean of Faculty, he has made sure I could balance this project with my other professional commitments. Jan Relf, Assistant Editor on *Irish Studies Review*, did invaluable work on the manuscript, and I am also grateful in this respect to my secretary Sara Kirkby. Paul Edwards acted above and beyond by reading every word; it is a better book because of the suggestions he made, and would, I sometimes suspect, have been better still if he'd written it. My greatest debt is to Barbara White, for not giving up on it.

For Alfred Cameron Sammells (1928–1995)

'One should always be a little improbable'

INTRODUCTION

In *De Profundis* Oscar Wilde declared that 'What the paradox was to me in the sphere of thought, perversity became to me in the sphere of passion.'[1] It is a characteristic combination of acute self-consciousness and self-narration. At this point in the love-letter to Lord Alfred Douglas, Wilde is sketching the trajectory of his career. He began, he says, with everything: 'genius, a distinguished name, high social position, brilliancy, intellectual daring.' His artistic achievements 'altered the minds of men and the colours of things: there was nothing that I said or did that did not make people wonder' (913). But – and here Douglas's culpability is hinted at – he allowed himself to be lured into a life of senseless pleasure: 'I amused myself with being a *flâneur*, a dandy, a man of fashion'. The pursuit of new sensations took him from the heights to the depths: 'Desire, at the end, was a malady, or madness, or both.' Now, in his horrible disgrace, in Reading Gaol, there is nothing left but absolute humility: 'just as there is only one thing for you, absolute Humility also. You had better come down into the dust and learn it beside me' (914).

Not much chance of Bosie agreeing to that, of course. Besides, it is a curious form of humility which Wilde is displaying. *De Profundis* provides Wilde with two starring roles: he swaps that of tragic hero for another and even more exalted. He argues that Christ is the type of the artist and hence the perfect individualist, while offering himself as the supreme modern example of both. He will, he assures Bosie, be Christ-like and humble in his frank acceptance of new experience. Acknowledging that people used to say that he was too individualistic, he believes that now, in his absolute humility, he needs to be 'far more of an individualist than I ever was' (937). So, humility is identified with its opposite: self-declaration and self-advertisement. This paradoxical method of argument, and self-fabrication, is entirely characteristic of Wilde as he moves through the proliferation of contradiction. The letter is not simple 'truth-telling' or penitent confessional. It is a strategy for survival in which Wilde tells more stories about himself, takes on new roles, summons his resources, in the hope of climbing from the depths and of moving forward. It is crucial that we read *De Profundis* in this way and not as Wilde's final judgement on himself, or as ours on him.

Nevertheless, what Wilde says about the importance to him of paradox and perversity is richly significant. He implies here, as he constructs his tragic narrative, that the passage from a concern with paradox to an obsession with perversity is symptomatic of the gathering pace of his self-destruction. However, what I want to emphasize is the degree to which Wilde recognizes that both are transgressive; and that this helps us to read his work against the pattern of compromise, failure and defeat into which Wilde himself appears to be organizing his life. Part of this book's project is to show how Wilde's paradoxes deconstruct oppositions we have come to see as self-evident and inevitable – as in the difference between nature and culture, for instance, or between male and female – and to demonstrate the potentially radical political implications of that process. Writing in the 1930s, Wyndham Lewis was vehemently dismissive of Wilde whom he described as a 'fat Dublin buffoon.' He lumped him in with other 'distinguished diabolists' such as Byron, Baudelaire, Huysmans and De Lautréamont, claiming that their insistent denial of the claims of morality was, paradoxically, no more than 'an excessive development of an ethical will: for by the simple expedient of reversing it, it can be converted into a first-class instrument of farcical self-display'.[2] Clearly suffering from a bad case of anxiety of influence, Lewis is working hard to distance himself from Wilde and his 'silly old "vice"'. Ironically, he is trying to define his own strident and iconoclastic Modernism by the same methods he is accusing Wilde of – by reversing what had preceded it, the Decadent Movement with which Wilde became so closely and calamitously identified (and which, for Lewis, was clearly the last gasp of a flagging Romanticism). I shall argue, however, that Wilde's reversals and paradoxes do not simply preserve the dominant ideological terms he engages with, but that they deconstruct them. Further, as my loaded use of 'deconstruct' suggests, I shall emphasize, in Chapter Two, the way Wilde anticipates some of the most important and influential cultural theories of our own day; and also suggest a formative role his ideas and example might play in the development of a specific emergent critical practice, ecocriticism. In this respect, as in others I shall highlight, he cannot be neatly consigned to the 'Naughty Nineties' as he is in Lewis's caricature of the period.[3] Wilde would, I hope, have enjoyed this; as one of his 'Phrases and Philosophies for the Use of the Young' would have it: 'To be premature is to be perfect' (1203).

Intriguingly, in his novel *Tarr* (1918), Lewis's hero sees himself as a mummy-case: 'Only he contained nothing but innumerable other painted cases inside, smaller and smaller ones. The smallest was not a substantial astral baby, however, or live core, but a painting like the rest. = His kernel was a painting. That was as it should be!'[4] As we shall see in Chapter Three, which examines lines of continuity between his aesthetic theories and his artistic practice which have not been generally recognized, *Dorian Gray* is Wilde's most extensive and explicit exploration of the nature of self. The novel deconstructs the surface/depth model of individual identity, which posits the 'real' self as the kernel in the nut, defining it instead in terms of multiformity. The self is all surface. Dorian's 'kernel' is, literally, a painting, his portrait: or, rather, he has no kernel at all. Wilde, in effect, anticipates both Lewis's ambivalent, Modernist rejection of the 'authentic' self (Tarr still thinks in terms of self-discovery through excavation, partially endorsing the surface/depth, appearance/substance dichotomies he wants to deny) and more radical postmodern versions of dispersed and decentred subjectivity. From this angle, Wilde can be seen performing an unlikely yet strangely elegant historical leap-frog.

Christopher Nassaar claimed in 1974 (in one of the first full-length studies of his writing) that Wilde was 'the last of the great Victorians'.[5] Lewis's remarks perhaps represent the nadir of Wilde's critical reputation; Nassaar's mark the beginning of a thorough reassessment of his work. However, Nassaar repeats Lewis's view that Wilde embodies the last spasm of a dying tradition, also seeing his roots in the Romantic period. To Edward Said, writing just a year later, though, he is a pivotal figure: 'Nearly every consciously innovative major writer since Oscar Wilde has repeatedly denied (or even denounced) the mimetic ambitions of writing.'[6] Since the mid-1980s it is precisely this sense of modernity which has become the focus for attention and which has sponsored the blossoming of Wilde's critical reputation, beyond somewhat scattered remarks like Said's. Much recent critical work has concentrated on Wilde as a professional writer in a recognizably modern commercial context, collaborating with other theatrical practitioners, polishing and revising his work through composition and performance. He is no longer an historical curio. In this book I want to explore that modernity in a specific sense, by examining the exact nature of Wilde's repudiation of 'the mimetic ambitions of writing' and by concentrating throughout on his major prose and plays, rather than the poetry which seems to me much less integrated with his innovative aesthetic theories, and is curiously inert as a consequence. In his poetry convention and genre deploy Wilde; in the prose and plays he deploys and transforms them. To understand the nature and function of these transformations we need to recognize that, despite orthodox approaches to his aestheticism which sum it up as 'art for art's sake', the dominant aesthetic category for Wilde is not art, but style.

Wilde replaces those mimetic ambitions with his own. Mimesis is based on the notion that art can be a window on the real, that it can in some sense be 'authentic' in its representation of the world. Art, for Wilde, must be self-conscious and deliberate in the ways it denies these pretensions to authenticity, and he couples this insistence with a radical erosion of Romantic and Humanist notions of the deep, integrated, authentic self which is discoverable beneath surface appearances and fluctuations. T.J. Clark traces Modernism's concern with significant surfaces to Manet and his followers, describing his famous *Un Bar aux Folies-Bergères* as 'a painting of surfaces: that verdict applies not just to the things in the world it seizes on as paintable – the gold foil, the girl's make-up, and the shine on the oranges – but to its insistence that painting is a surface and should admit the fact.'[7] Wilde's writing displays a similarly self-reflexive concern with its own surfaces (I describe his society comedies in Chapter Four as all surface) and a pervasive fascination with presenting identity as surface – hence indeterminate, slippery, reversible. Wilde creates 'flat' characters. Flatness, Clark claims, functions in Manet as a sign of modernity, 'with the surface meant to conjure up the mere two dimensions of posters, labels, fashion prints and photographs.'[8] The same might be said of Wilde as he too negotiates the shifting new relationship between art and image-making.

Wilde substitutes style for authenticity, and it is his fascination with style that marks him as our contemporary, as well as Manet's. Although in *De Profundis* he reproaches himself for becoming a dandy, in fact the dandy's sense of style and fashion does not detract from Wilde's artistic ambitions, it embodies them. In 'The Truth of Masks' Wilde declared that clothes are 'a most important, perhaps the most important, sign of the manners, customs and mode of life of each century' (1074), and the dandy's fine discriminating eye is evident in his own interest in dress reform for both men (like Baudelaire he objected to the ubiquity of funereal black) and women (believing women's clothes should be hung from the shoulders, Greek-style, rather than laced tightly to the waist as in the familiar Victorian female carapace). In reading clothes as signs, Wilde shows a keen, modern awareness of the semiotics of fashion; he is also aware of the way fashion can function as both a social code protecting exclusivity, and as a means by which such social exclusivity can be opened up and democratized. Style, though, for Wilde, embraces more than clothes and fashion – it involves 'attitude'. 'In aesthetic criticism' says Wilde at the end of 'The Truth of Masks', 'attitude is everything' (1078). In matters of style, for us too attitude is everything. Chapter Three argues for the importance of a particular playful and oppositional attitude, Camp, to our understanding of Wilde's work, and its resonance with aspects of contemporary taste. I draw a specific comparison with the films of Quentin Tarantino in the way both court notoriety, deploy popular forms, subvert the conventions of genre and resolutely aestheticize potentially 'dangerous' moral content. In Chapter Four I focus on his society comedies, which display greater and greater degrees of stylization, culminating in that most stylish, playful and political of his writings: *The Importance of Being Earnest*. The final chapter looks more closely at the political implications of the dandyism that Wilde develops principally from Baudelaire – and at his influence on dandyism in contemporary pop culture.

By closing with a discussion of Wilde's influence on pop culture, and of contemporary non-academic, sometimes 'creative' attempts to understand and appropriate him, I complete the frame. I start by examining in detail the recent flourishing of academic interest in Wilde, and, specifically, at the way he is currently being constructed as an Irish writer and as a gay writer. His apparent susceptibility to both approaches is fraught with danger – when they shade into attempts to fix and authenticate Wilde, they risk denying what this book argues is most challenging, contemporary and characteristic in him: *Wilde Style*.

REFERENCES

[1] *The Complete Works of Oscar Wilde*, Collins, London, new ed., 1966: 913. All further references to this edition will be included parenthetically in the text.

[2] Wyndham Lewis, *Men Without Art*, ed. Seamus Cooney, Black Sparrow Press, Santa Rosa, 1987: 143–4.

[3] *Men Without Art*: 148.

[4] Wyndham Lewis, *Tarr*, ed. Paul O'Keeffe, Black Sparrow Press, Santa Rosa, 1990: 58–9.

[5] Christopher S. Nassaar, *Into the Demon Universe*, Yale University Press, New Haven and London, 1974: xi.

[6] Edward Said, *Beginnings: Intention and Method*, Basic Books, New York, 1975: 11.

[7] T.J. Clark, *The Painting of Modern Life: Paris in the Art of Manet and his Followers*, Thames & Hudson, London 1985: 248.

[8] *The Painting of Modern Life*: 13.

1

ORIGIN AND TERMINUS

'Wilde' – as he is now variously constructed and, indeed, deconstructed – can tell us as much about ourselves as about the Victorians he was long thought of as simply entertaining or teasing. This is partly because, as Terry Eagleton puts it, his aesthetic theories and associated politics, prefigure to a sometimes astonishing degree 'the insights of contemporary cultural theory.'[1] In this respect, the recent efflorescence in critical discussions of Wilde can be explained in terms of a heightened sense of his 'relevance' to our own *fin de siècle* – as we examine ourselves in the mirror of another. Indeed, one of the aims of this book is to argue for the consistency between Wilde's aesthetic theories and his practice as a novelist and dramatist: a consistency which confirms the significance of his work for modern readers and audiences. However, before explaining and examining that particular relationship, I want to focus on the way in which contemporary versions of Wilde in academic discourse have become distributed across a number of current critical debates: stressing in particular the competing claims for the importance to our understanding of his life and work of his nationality and his sexuality. In both cases, this will involve scrutinizing related notions of 'authenticity' – notions which Wilde himself has already radically undermined.

An example of the way Wilde is now seen as centrally relevant to contemporary critical debate is Regenia Gagnier's introduction to a 1992 collection of reprinted essays (selected to represent state-of-the-art Wilde criticism as it appeared in the US) in which she claims that: 'Wilde means many things to our time. Most important among them, he means – whether in gay activism, social theory or interpretive margin or latitude – freedom and toleration.'[2] Despite confessing that her favourite among the biographies is Rupert Croft Cooke's *The Unrecorded Life of Oscar Wilde* (1972), which 'loved its data not wisely but too well', she goes on to quote Richard Ellmann approvingly: 'we inherit [Wilde's] struggle to create supreme fictions in art, to associate art with social change, to bring together individual and social impulse, to save what is eccentric and singular from being sanitized and standardized, to replace a morality of severity with one of sympathy.'[3] For Gagnier, her collection signals this *fin de siècle* paying tribute to the last, 'in the hope of freedom and necessity of toleration.'[4] In specific terms, she sees Wilde as peculiarly relevant to *fin de siècle* America; her introduction summons up his languid spectre as a potential corrective to a number of the ills of contemporary American society. *The Soul of Man under Socialism* is, she tells us, 'an essay for our time' in the lessons it can teach an American media which 'invariably equate capitalism with democracy and socialism with totalitarianism.'[5] The prison-letter *De Profundis* has especial urgency, 'as the United States has taken the lead of all nations in the proportion of its citizens incarcerated, as our number of prisoners has exceeded one million, as more and more Americans fall through the safety net, become homeless, and, as homeless, are incarcerated.'[6] Indeed, she even proposes Wildean wit as a possible antidote to a malady much commented upon 'in the popular press and pedagogical literature': Americans' increasing inability to comprehend irony.[7] Gagnier's collection, and the claims she makes for it, are, of course, testament to the extraordinary transformation that has taken place in Wilde's critical status since the mid-1980s: the variety of approaches to his work that she anthologizes is offered as representative of 'our collective critical moment'.[8] In other words, the totality of North American critical writing about Wilde is seen as state-of-the-art in every respect.

Whatever the importance of Wilde to contemporary America, there is no doubting the importance of America to Wilde. His 1882 lecture tour established him as a major media celebrity: his assiduous self-commodification as the proselyte of Aestheticism finding itself in conflict with discourses which were attempting – as Mary Warner Blanchard has argued – to reconstruct American masculinity in the wake of the Civil War.[9] Indeed, the inevitable clash of cultures Wilde engineered as he travelled westward has become important not just to academic constructions of Wilde, but to his place in American popular culture, as in Walter Satterthwaite's *Wilde West* (1991), in which Wilde solves a series of Ripper-style murders and comes to a sexual awakening at the hands of Doc Holliday, and in the 1950s television Western series *Have Gun Will Travel* (one episode features a knickerbockered Wilde held hostage by a band of desperadoes – his rescue finally effected by the star of the show, Richard Boone).[10] Richard Ellmann argues that an unexpected result of Wilde's tour was not that he discovered his sexuality (as in Satterthwaite's novel) but that he 'rediscovered himself as an Irishman.'[11] Before explaining how I think Wilde saw his own Irishness, and how we might read it in relation to his writing, I want to discuss the 'rediscovery' of his nationality by academic literary and cultural criticism, because it has been one of the most significant, if problematic, developments in recent attempts to understand him.

As recently as 1981, Alan Warner could claim – in a guide to 'Anglo-Irish literature' – that '[Wilde's] plays have no Irish dimension' and that we cannot think of Wilde as being moulded by influences that were moulding Ireland.[12] However, the rise of postcolonial criticism in Irish Studies over the last two decades – so that it is now in some respects the dominant critical practice in Irish literary and cultural studies – means that such an assertion now looks antedeluvian. Nevertheless, the nature of Wilde's 'Irishness' (and the relationship of his writing to Irish cultural, political and historical contexts) sets the editors of *The Field Day Anthology of Irish Writing* (1991) at odds with themselves and each other. In his introduction to the section dealing with drama from 1600 to 1800, Christopher Murray retreads what he knows is something of a cliché and identifies a characteristic Irish wit which he says is 'more subversive' than that of English writers; behind the mask of the laughing Irishman, he tells us, 'be it Farquhar or Goldsmith or Shaw or Wilde, lay the determined enemy of English falsity'. However, such subversive potential seems compromised; Murray also notes that 'from William Congreve to Oscar Wilde the profile of the expatriate Irish playwright is of the polished man of letters, as eager for social status in England as for literary fame. He wrote primarily to please the English arbiters of taste.' Murray makes Wilde's wit seem strangely anodyne and ornamental; political questions, he claims, 'hardly entered the picture at all before the arrival on the scene of W.B. Yeats.'[13] Murray's discussion is uneasy and self-contradictory; it seems more than a little coloured by Daniel Corkery's mechanically nationalistic analysis in *Synge and Anglo-Irish Literature* (1931) and his condemnation of expatriate writers like Wilde 'who did not labour for their own people', preferring to write 'not for their brothers and co-mates in exile' but 'for their kinsfolk in England'.[14] Echoing Corkery's insistence on the importance of 'land' to his construction of Irishness, Murray claims that Irish drama only became fully political – and by implication genuinely subversive – with the return of Yeats to Dublin and his founding of the Irish Literary Theatre in 1899. Murray is not alone among the editors of the anthology in finding Wilde's work compromised by his English context. Seamus Deane says of his poetry that it is vulgar in its facility of feeling and rhythmic automatism; as in all of Wilde's work, Deane continues, 'the subversive, even radical critique of society that is implicit in what he has to say, finds no release within the linguistic conventions which he mocked but by which he remained imprisoned.'[15] (Seamus Heaney gives this a different twist, describing *The Ballad of Reading Gaol* as a link in a chain connecting Wilde's poem with John Mitchel's *Jail Journal* (1854) and Brendan Behan's *The Quare Fellow* (1956): politically-motivated Irish prison-protest literature.[16]) John Wilson Foster's discussion of contemporary Irish fiction looks to its antecedents and compares the 'natural flight from provincialism to

London of Shaw, Wilde and Moore' with the later 'more painful and thought-out exile of Joyce.'[17] The charge, though implicit, is clear, and is the same as Murray's: Wilde concedes too readily – if understandably – to English arbiters of taste in his pursuit of metropolitan success. As we shall see, this narrative of compromise shading into a betrayal of his national roots is mirrored in some accounts of Wilde's sexuality.

However, the comments of Declan Kiberd and W.J. MacCormack take a different tack. MacCormack claims of *The Canterville Ghost* that it is a parodic reworking of the gothic mode in Irish fiction which suggests that 'an invasion of manners is no less an invasion than the Norman conquest: Wilde is as much a political writer as Maria Edgeworth and, like her, he understands that style is a miniature politics.' Nevertheless, the possibility that the playful manner might obscure the subversive potential of the writing is hinted at. Wilde's politics, he concludes, 'were consistently, if not always evidently, radical.'[18] Wilde's radicalism is amplified by Declan Kiberd who insists that he 'was, to the end of his days, a militant republican'. Indeed, Kiberd revises the analyses of some of his colleagues by seeing Wilde's expatriate status not as a compromise but as a confrontation: he and Shaw 'challenged, by personal behaviour as well as by artistic skill, the prevailing stereotypes of the Irish in Britain.' On the question, though, of Wilde's relationship with English arbiters of taste and, in particular, with the linguistic conventions which Deane thinks confounded Wilde, Kiberd is less decisive. He says that Wilde and Shaw 'tried, with much success, to liberate the enemy language from its historic freight of meaning for an Irish person'.[19] However, in an excerpt from a 1984 Field Day pamphlet which is itself anthologized, and which touches on Wilde's contemporary relevance, Kiberd sees this success as crucially qualified: 'the forces which neutralised the subversive paradoxes of Wilde and Shaw are no less potent in the 1980s than they were in the 1880s.'[20]

So, the compilers of the new postcolonial canon shift uneasily in their attempts to describe the nature of Wilde's Irishness and for the effect it has upon his work. For Murray and Deane, in particular, Wilde's is a story of compromise, of metaphorical imprisonment in English literary convention anticipating literal incarceration in Reading Gaol. Kiberd's analysis is more stimulating in this respect; his is not a narrative of contamination, invoking an Irish essence which cannot survive its English environment. This is the key. The Irish Wilde is, in my view, best understood not in essentialist terms nor best explained in terms of personal and artistic defeat. We can see this, I think, by focusing on a group of texts which – despite the usefulness of Wilde's self-critical commentary upon them – have been relatively neglected by academic critics: the fairy tales. As I shall show, attempts to account for them by recourse to notions of cultural authenticity do not do justice to the complexity of their deployment of both Irish and English material and analogues.

Until quite recently such little critical attention as had been paid to Wilde's fairy tales regarded them principally as a quarry for biographical speculation. For instance, Ellmann – although he has little to say about the stories in his 1987 biography – introduced Wilde's *Selected Writings* in 1961 by noting that 'the fairy tale was a natural form for him to write in, and perhaps all his creative work belongs to this genre'; in these fantasies he could cancel 'his nightmare of being found out with light-hearted dreams of pardon and transfiguration'.[21] Similarly, Christopher Nassaar has argued that they are Wilde's attempt to remain within the 'charmed circle of his children, innocent and safe from evil' and to assert 'the primacy of his family life and to reject the siren call of homosexuality.'[22] Such a critical approach reached its nadir in Robert K. Martin's reading of 'The Happy Prince' as Wilde's covert celebration of his newly discovered homosexuality over the heterosexual life he had lived before. Martin says of the relationship between the swallow and the reed: 'A good deal of Oscar's experience with Constance undoubtedly went into this passage: she, although attractive, was hardly literary and was intellectually incapable of sharing her husband's life.'[23] However, that biography might give place to politics in a more stimulating analysis of the fairy tales had been noticed by George Woodcock in 1949, who claimed of 'The Young King' that it was 'a parable on the capitalist system of exploitation as severe as anything in William Morris' and that its depiction of the horrors of labour could 'stand beside the grimmest passages of Marx'.[24] Apparently taking her cue from Woodcock, Jerusha MacCormack insists that the fairy tales are to be read 'from the perspective of the poor, the colonised, the disreputable and dispossessed.'[25] I want to concentrate, though, less on the tales as political commentary than on the implications of Wilde's decision to use this particular form, a choice which – if Ellmann is right in describing it as natural – would be perhaps the only natural thing that Wilde ever did.

The Happy Prince and Other Tales (1888) and *The House of Pomegranates* (1891) are contemporaneous with the composition and publication of 'The Decay of Lying' and 'The Critic as Artist', essays in which Wilde expounded his anti-naturalistic aesthetic theories, and which I shall examine in detail later. It is thus reasonable to suppose that these fairy tales might bear the same self-conscious relationship to those theories as does *The Picture of Dorian Gray*, first published in 1890. Indeed, Wilde talks about the fairy tales in much the same terms. In defending *Dorian Gray* against the charge of immorality, Wilde described it as 'an essay on decorative art. It reacts against the brutality of plain realism.'[26] In a letter to Leonard Smithers (July 1888) he says that 'The Happy Prince' is 'a reaction against the purely imitative treatment of modern art – and now that literature has taken to blowing loud trumpets I cannot but be pleased that some ear has cared to listen to the low music of a little reed.'[27] In defending Charles Ricketts's cover-design for *The House of Pomegranates* against the questionable taste of the reviewer of the *Speaker*, Wilde made the link with his novel explicit. The reviewer had objected to Ricketts's abstract design, claiming to discern in what Wilde called 'the delicate tracing, arabesques, and massing of many coral-red lines on a ground of white ivory' an Indian club with a house-painter's brush on top of it. Wilde was imperious in his dismissal: 'Now, I do not for a moment dispute that these are the real impressions your critic received. It is the spectator, and the mind of the spectator, as I pointed out in the preface to *The Picture of Dorian Gray,* that art really mirrors.' According to Wilde, Ricketts had managed to orchestrate a colour-effect culminating in 'high gilt-notes' – 'what the gilt notes suggest, what imitative parallel may be found to them in the chaos that is termed Nature, is a matter of no importance.'[28] Characteristically, Wilde collapses the distinction between surface and depth, form and content, and outlines the aesthetic strategies of the stories by theorizing the pleasures to be had from the designs they are bound with. That the fairy tales generally were for Wilde, at an important level, experiments in form is confirmed by his comments to Thomas Hutchinson on 'The Nightingale and the Rose': 'I like to think that there may be many meanings to the Tale – for in writing it . . . I did not start with the idea and clothe it in form, but began with a form and strove to make it beautiful enough to have many secrets and many answers.'[29] Wilde said that 'all fine imaginative work is self-conscious and deliberate' (1020), and his aesthetic choice to employ the fairy tale is as self-conscious and deliberate as any he made as a writer. In this respect, the fairy tales deserve to be considered as specific and important examples of those anti-realist strategies which Declan Kiberd – in *Inventing Ireland* (1995) – has associated so closely with Wilde's republican and anti-imperialist sympathies.[30]

Kiberd's *Inventing Ireland* mounts a much more thorough endorsement of Wilde's postcolonialist credentials than he is allowed anywhere in the *Field Day Anthology*. Kiberd draws heavily on the work of Ashis Nandy and his influential psychology of colonialism; Nandy claims that Wilde was 'an unself-aware, but more or less complete critic of the political culture which sired colonialism.'[31] Paradoxically, however, a reading of the fairy tales grounded in Nandy's work could be used to contradict Kiberd's claims for the political efficacy of Wilde's writings. Such a reading would, as Deane argues of the poetry, see the political commentary of the fairy tales as compromised by the genre Wilde chooses to work in. Nandy notes that one of the principal strategies of imperialism is to construct a fantasy of hyper-masculinity on the part of the colonizers, and the projection of childishness and effeminacy onto the colonized. Poignantly enough, it is Lord Alfred Douglas who expresses this identification most succinctly in his belligerently entitled *Without Apology* (1938): 'Unless you understand that Wilde is an Irishman through and through, you will never get an idea of what his real nature is. In many ways he is as simple and innocent as a child.'[32] In utilizing the fairy tale then, Wilde is treading a dangerous line: laying himself open to the accusation that he has internalized the child-like qualities and awareness projected onto the Irish by a Celticism as much in the service of the imperial masters as of the cultural nationalists. Indeed, Micheál MacLiámóir, one of Wilde's most celebrated interpreters – and, curiously, an Englishman re-inventing himself as Irish – speaks of *The Happy Prince and Other Tales* in symptomatic terms: 'Are these stories really intended for children? To me they seem to have been written for everybody who is or has ever been a child in the complete sense of the word, and who is fortunate enough, or wise enough, to have preserved something of what, in Childhood itself, is fortunate, wise and eternal.'[33] For MacLiámóir, then, being 'in touch' with the child within is not simply a measure of his ability to appreciate the fairy stories, it is a way of self-fashioning an Irishness which is both overperformed and overdetermined. Predictably, Wilde has it both ways on the question of intended audience. He sent a copy of *The Happy Prince* to Gladstone, coupling a declaration of his own 'Celtic blood' with the shy-sounding claim that his book 'is really meant for children'.[34] Indeed, Wilde anticipates MacLiámóir in a letter to G.H. Kersley, describing the stories as 'meant partly for children, and partly for those who have kept the childlike faculties of wonder and joy, and who find in simplicity a strange subtleness.'[35] Elsewhere he chooses an entirely different tack. He responded to a review of *The House of Pomegranates* in the *Pall Mall Gazette* by declaring that no 'fairly educated' person could really believe his stories were meant for children: 'I had as much intention of pleasing the British child as I had of pleasing the British public. Mamilius is as delightful as Caliban is entirely detestable, but neither the standard of Mamilius nor the standard of Caliban is my standard.'[36] Nandy sees Wilde's homosexuality as a politico-pathological statement against imperialism, one shared with the likes of his fellow Irishman George Moore, and such Bloomsbury luminaries as Lytton Strachey, J.M. Keynes, Virginia Woolf, and E.M. Forster – but he emphasizes constantly the lack of self-awareness in these 'chaotic, individuated' protests.[37] What I want to suggest is that it is precisely the self-consciousness with which Wilde employs the fairy tale form which allows us to defend him against the accusation that his anti-imperialism is compromised by genre. After all, his identification of the British public with Caliban the slave is a sly inversion whereby the distinction between the colonizer and Prospero's colonized subject is collapsed. Wilde does not internalize childhood and childishness, he stylizes them – and gets his retaliation in first. Later, I shall look more closely at the nature and importance of stylization in Wilde's arch and knowing redeployment of genre.

Norbert Kohl argues that the political edge to 'The Young King' is blunted by the way Wilde's descriptions of poverty and exploitation move from the realistic to the allegorical, as the eponymous hero encounters Avarice, Fever, Plague and Death. For Kohl, this stylistic slippage is redolent of a socialism more interested in aesthetic effect than political propaganda. Allegory, in fact, occupies a privileged position in that postcolonial criticism which, when it attributes a specific mode to a text, is convinced – erroneously according to Kevin Barry – 'that it has defined logically the politics of that text.'[38] Barry's critique of these assumptions focuses on the work of David Lloyd and Luke Gibbons. According to both, Barry argues, allegory and metonymy – the trope of difference because it leaves things casually side by side – 'throw the weight of authority and influence behind insurgent social groups which oppose or have opposed the nation-state'. Opposed to allegory and metonymy are symbol and metaphor which – to put it crudely – force things together: 'metaphor and symbol erase differences, of economy, social class and gender, in the supposed interest of a higher but fully existent unity.'[39] Allegory emerges as the aesthetic of dissent, symbolism as the aesthetic of union. Barry discusses Gibbons's analysis of the allegorical oaths of nineteenth century Irish secret societies, such as the Whiteboys, dedicated to agrarian violence,[40] and Lloyd's contention that in allegorizing the landscape around Coole Park, with a superb indifference to fact, Yeats expresses a recalcitrance towards the homogenizing impulses of the nation-state.[41] (In Barry's view, Lloyd's analysis is based on a simple misreading of an Ordnance Survey map.) Although Owen Dudley Edwards would no doubt balk at his own methods of scholarship and analysis being described as postcolonial, such an approach is echoed in his reading of 'The Selfish Giant'. Patrick Pearse, Dudley Edwards claims, drew heavily on both 'The Selfish Giant' and 'The Happy Prince' for his own Gaelic tales, translating them back not just into the Irish language but into an Irish setting: 'He set the stories in the Connaught where the Wildes had worked and played. "The Selfish Giant" in particular suggests not just a peasant context, where Pearse put it, but the Giant as owner of the Big House with the little children as peasants and, presumably, Catholics.'[42] In other words, Wilde's political point in the fairy story – that repressive authority can be both subverted and transformed from below – is refracted through the allegorical mode of representation which, according to Lloyd and Gibbons, correlates to the oppressed and dissident Irish social groups struggling to effect that transformation.

A less theoretically inflected, more positivist, postcolonial criticism than Lloyd's or Gibbons's, however, attempts a direct recuperation of Wilde for the native culture endangered and silenced by the colonizers. Jerusha MacCormack introduces the essays she has collected as *Wilde the Irishman* (1998) by saying that they seek to 'reinstate his spirit back in its own haunting grounds: to relocate its origins and its effects in its native Ireland and in that spiritual territory that Wilde himself understood as home to the collective unconscious of his race.'[43] In this context, the most revealing essay is by Deirdre Toomey in which she argues that Wilde's fairy tales stem from the tradition of Irish story-telling – pointing out that many of his stories were not written down but recorded by acquaintances like André Gide, Charles Ricketts, Jean Lorrain and Guillot de Saix, who were present at their improvisation but did not have the Irish context in which to appreciate them.[44] Toomey's starting-point is Yeats's contention that Wilde's fairy tales become less original and accomplished the further they go from improvisation and a sense of particular audience, an aesthetic judgement, she points out, which is also 'a mark of an Irish cultural valuing of the oral over the written.'[45] I would add that Yeats's comments, from his introduction to a 1923 edition of *The Happy Prince and Other Tales*, now read like a retrospective attempt to reclaim Wilde from the discredited Decadent movement of which he was widely seen as the High Priest. Paul Bourget had argued, for instance, in his *Essais de psychologie contemporaine* (1883–85) that 'a decadent literature sequesters the reader from a shared reality, and the high artifice of the style deepens the divide between spoken and written language, which Mallarmé had opened.'[46] In this respect, as Peter Nicholls notes, decadent writing could be seen to perpetrate a kind of Barthesian violence against spoken language and the forms of social cohesion it should promote and embody.[47] By emphasizing Wilde's 'orality', Yeats and Toomey implicitly relocate him in an organic community which has yet to succumb to the modernist fragmentation of its social structures, sense of identity and modes of representation.

Inevitably, then, such a recuperation of Wilde – relocating '[his]origins and [his] effects back in [his] native Ireland' – is undertaken not just in the name of cultural authenticity, but for an authentic culture, or a culture imagined as authentic; and its tone veers constantly toward the elegiac. Toomey, for instance, says of Wilde's much-admired oral tale 'The Poet' that it is, in effect, an Irish folk tale inverted: 'a product of that dying oral culture to which Wilde was tied by what Yeats called his "half-civilised blood", the culture of those who listened to spoken tales undivided by book culture – "friend by friend, lover by lover" '.[48] Indeed, the temptation to see Wilde as somehow tied to these origins is strong: Owen Dudley Edwards decides that Oscar Fingal O'Flahertie Wilde was 'a hostage to Irish cultural identity.'[49] One of the principal aims of this book is to establish the dangers inherent in applying notions of authenticity to our understanding of Wilde's

life and work – particularly notions of cultural, national and sexual authenticity. Interestingly, Toomey's emphasis on the importance of the element of
performance in Wilde's story-telling suggests an escape from conclusions
which are otherwise limiting and nostalgic. She claims that the

> cardinal sins of literacy are the cardinal virtues of orality. Originality in an
> oral culture consists not in inventing an absolutely new story but in stitching
> together the familiar in a manner suitable to a certain audience, or by intro-
> ducing new elements into an old story. The persistent charge of plagiarism
> seems oxymoronic in an oral culture.[50]

Wilde, of course, would claim that the charge of plagiarism – so often
levelled against him and, publicly, as early as 1881 when the Oxford Union
refused his gift of *Poems* on these grounds[51] – was oxymoronic in a print-
culture too: 'It is only the unimaginative who ever invents. The true artist is
known by the use of what he annexes, and he annexes everything.'[52] In a
fashion that might be recognized as characteristically postmodern, Wilde –
as I shall argue in more detail later – 'samples' his pre-texts and refuses the
distinction between 'high' and 'low' culture. Recognizing the equivalence of
all objects, he was prepared to praise a buttonhole or a teacup in much the
same terms as he would a sculpture or a painting. According to Susan Sontag,
such a 'hypertrophy of appetite for culture'[53] lends Wilde's writing a fundamentally democratic esprit. It also, in my view, signals that – for Wilde – his
Irishness (despite dramatic declarations of his 'Celtic blood', as in the letter
to Gladstone) is a form of discursive play and performance: national identity becomes a theatrical 'liminal space'[54] in which Irishness and Englishness
encounter and collapse into each other. The playwright Frank McGuinness
writes memorably of *De Profundis* that it is a fucking of Bosie by verbal force
– and goes on to identify the characteristically Wildean drama that the letter
enacts:

> Whatever is written can be published, and whatever is published is performed.
> *De Profundis* is not the meditation of the penitent at prayer. It is the act of a
> penitent as performer. It is a histrionic defiance of the histrionic judgement
> passed against Wilde at his trial, a theatrical explosion to break the silence
> that his prison sentence demanded: it is a play.[55]

Such a reading not only prevents us from accepting that the 'penitent' Wilde
of *De Profundis* is in some sense the authentic Wilde – cornered, finally, in
the misery of the prison-cell. It also reminds us of Wilde's other theatrical
performances, including his starring-role as an Irishman in late-Victorian
English society. Wilde's Irishness is not a compromised position. It is a

wilfully **compromising** one: a dramatic posture he can adopt in order to confront and transform the very Englishness he needs for his theatrical effects. That nationality was histrionic for Wilde is evidenced by his reaction to the banning of *Salome*: 'I am not English. I am Irish, which is quite another thing,' he claimed – simultaneously announcing his intention to take up French citizenship.[56] Interestingly, another version of this remark in an interview for *Le Gaulois* is even more telling: 'I am not at present an Englishman. I am an Irishman, which is by no means the same thing'.[57]

Even allowing for the vagaries of translation and transcription, the notion of nationality as a transitory, shifting position is an intriguing one. What I am not suggesting is that seeing Wilde's Irishness as in some way per-formed diminishes the significance of his nationalist politics – as voiced, for instance, in his damning review of J.P. Mahaffy's *Greek Life and Thought: From the Age of Alexander to the Roman Conquest* and what he regards as its anti-democratic and anti-nationalist reading of ancient and contemporary history.[58] As is clear from his praise for Wilfred Scawen Blunt – who was an Irish nationalist, though English by birth, and was imprisoned in Galway Gaol for his attachment to the 'noble cause'[59] – Wilde recognized that nationalism could be a self-conscious and deliberate political choice rather than determined exclusively by nationality and notions of 'blood ties'. We should see Wilde's nationalism as part of a nexus of radical political sym-pathies which help to characterize his work, and not as atavistic in any sense. In effect, it is a style of 'being Irish' and, as we know, for Wilde, in matters of great importance, style, not sincerity, is the vital thing. Wilde's national-ism is 'A Study in Green'. This is the subtitle of his essay on the artist, forger and serial killer Thomas Griffiths Wainewright, 'Pen, Pencil and Poison', in which he claims that a fondness for green – the national colour – denotes an artistic temperament in individuals and is said in nations to denote a laxity of morals (996). Green, in other words, is the colour of the artist, the decad-ent, the subversive, the **Irish**. This series of sliding identifications is crucial to our understanding of the importance to Wilde of both his nationalism and his nationality. His penchant for the green carnation buttonhole is symp-tomatic: it is the badge of a homosexual coterie, a demonstration of the self-consciously modern and refined taste which prefers the artificial to the natural, and a declaration of national allegiance which refracts and politi-cizes both. It is, in effect, a languidly insistent and coded declaration of **difference**: a multiform, hybrid signifier.[60]

To return to the fairy tales: what I want to suggest is that they are best understood as cultural hybrids. Isobel Murray, for instance, sees analogues for Wilde's parables of art and industry not in Irish material but in William Morris's *News from Nowhere* and Tennyson's *The Palace of Art*, and believes that he plundered Matthew Arnold's poems for the details which flesh-out the exotic orientalism of 'The Fisherman and his Soul'.[61] This is, then, a complex cultural exchange: Irish and non-Irish elements are transformed, as borders and boundaries blur and collapse. To appreciate fully the complexity of these stories, we need to recognize the limitations of any approach which seeks to 'naturalize' them, either by denying the artfulness of Wilde's aesthetic choices, or by authenticating them – tracing them back to Celtic origins. Indeed, Wilde himself is instructive on this point: 'The Celtic element in literature is extremely valuable, but there is absolutely no excuse for shrieking "Shillelagh!" and "O'Gorrah!"'.[62]

'I don't know whether Wilde was sincere,' the actor Stephen Fry who played him in the film *Wilde* (1997) told the *Irish Times*, 'but I do feel he was authentic. I think this is important. It also cost him dearly.'[63] Of course, what Fry clearly has in mind is Wilde's sexual authenticity, the 'real' homosexual hiding behind the public mask: an authenticity which, in the end, cannot be denied. Characteristic of approaches to Wilde which seek to emphasize the importance to his writing of his sexuality, is the attempt to authenticate his work by uncovering its hidden homosexual content: a 'queer' narrative either outs itself, or is outed by the diligent critic. Lytton Strachey's facetious commentary on a 1907 revival of *A Woman of No Importance* is paradigmatic in this respect. Describing the play as 'The queerest mixture!', Strachey identifies an Ortonesque narrative in which 'a wicked Lord' determines to bugger one of the guests at a country house. The guest, of course, turns out to be his own son: 'It seems an odd plot, doesn't it? But it required all my penetration to find out that this was the plot, as you may imagine.'[64] The penetrative abilities of more recent critics have frequently been similarly employed. Kate Millett, for instance, in her pioneering *Sexual Politics* (1977), strips away what she sees as the misogynistic fears of *Salome* to lay bare the homosexual subtext beneath. Salome herself, according to Millett, is not exclusively or even fundamentally female: she is Wilde too, and the play is a drama of homosexual guilt and rejection followed by revenge. The play's homosexual imagery is disguised and elusive, she admits, but is evident most clearly in Salome's arias of desire for Jokanaan: 'The kiss she courted, the ivory knife cutting the pomegranate, the scarlet band on a tower of ivory – all are images of anal penetration or fellatio.'[65] The notion that anal penetration and fellatio are practices exclusive to male homosexuals is indeed a queer one. Nevertheless, Millett's comments are useful as examples of a fundamentally positivist approach to Wilde's sexuality and its presence in his writing: one which relies on the traditional strategy of 'close reading' as its principal method of analysis. The conviction that a homosexual narrative and expressions of homosexual desire can be uncovered by close attention to the linguistic complexities of Wilde's texts similarly underpins Christopher Craft's pyrotechnic essay 'Alias Bunbury' (1994), which locates an authentic, hidden meaning in the multifarious puns which, he claims, abound in *The Importance of Being Earnest.*[66]

However, 'gay' readings of Wilde's texts are not homogeneous, and much recent, theoretically inflected, criticism is concerned to interrogate not just the idea that they can be reduced to an authentic homosexual meaning, but also the notion of authentic sexual identity itself. Jonathan Dollimore, for instance, in describing what he calls Wilde's 'transgressive aesthetic', insists that 'for Wilde, although desire is deeply at odds with society in its existing forms, it does not exist as a presocial authenticity; it is always within, and informed by, the very culture which it also transgresses.'[67] This is a crucial insight because it begins to account for the complexities in any notion of Wilde as an authentic 'gay martyr', and, insofar as it suggests the degree to which Wilde's sexual 'revolt' was mediated, for some of the ambivalences in the reactions to his work of critics and readers with a gay agenda. Alan Sinfield, for instance, while dubbing this *The Wilde Century* (1994) and offering us an image of Wilde in a unique sartorial combination of subfusc and a 'Queer as Fuck' t-shirt, refuses to reduce the texts to a homosexual meaning or narrative, partly – he claims – because homosexuality as we understand it did not preexist Wilde and his trials, so Wilde could not have had a sense of himself as 'authentically' homosexual. Wilde and his writings look 'queer', according to Sinfield, because our stereotypical notion of male homosexuality derives from Wilde, and our ideas about him. So, for instance, Wilde's 'The Portrait of Mr W.H.', which offers a fantasized male original for the love-object of Shakespeare's sonnets, cannot be read unproblematically: 'Wilde, whatever his wishes, could not simply discover a queer precursor in Willie Hughes, because "Mr W.H.", the plays, the trials, and the whole package we call "Oscar Wilde", were key sites upon which a modern queer identity has been constructed.'[68] In effect, according to Sinfield, Wilde is implicated in a process of stereotyping which has helped to fix and oppress male homosexuals. After the trials, he argues 'the entire, vaguely disconcerting nexus of effeminacy, leisure, idleness, immorality, luxury, insouciance, decadence and aestheticism, which Wilde was perceived variously as instanciating, was transformed into a brilliantly precise image.'[69]

Elsewhere, Sinfield argues that as a gay icon Wilde leaves a lot to be desired. For a start, 'His writings do not celebrate gay love', and, when given the opportunity to martyr himself in the dock, 'he denied everything sexual – in his writing, with Lord Alfred Douglas, with the young men he had picked up.' To this is added the charge that his legacy 'includes elements of snobbery, misogyny, class and intergenerational exploitation.' Sinfield sums up Wilde's ambivalence for gay men in a memorable phrase: 'As well as our Christ, then, Wilde was our Judas.'[70] Neil Bartlett's extraordinary *Who Was That Man? A Present for Mr Oscar Wilde* (1989) does not share Sinfield's 'constructionist' approach to gay criticism (constructionist in the sense that Sinfield does not believe sexualities to be 'natural' or 'essential', but socially and culturally constructed) but it is equally vehement in both its celebration and condemnation of Wilde. Bartlett's book is partly an exercise in recuperation: an attempt to recover the forgotten history of nineteenth-century gay life in London, and to listen again to its silenced voices. It is also part sexual fantasy: Bartlett imagines picking up Wilde on Hampstead Heath and taking him back for sex. He also addresses two imaginary letters to Wilde. The first begins and ends: 'Darling, it's all for you. We're doing all this for you'.[71] The second angrily denounces him as a fat bitch and an old queen. Central to Bartlett's condemnation of Wilde is the sense of betrayal he feels, believing Wilde complicitous in the imposition of silence on a thriving but threatening gay subculture:

> The question was, and is, who speaks, and when, and for whom, and why. As the perverse pantomime of the trial was enacted, the power of speech was taken away from us and given to our judges. Wilde never spoke out; he only answered questions. The evidence of our lives was placed under their control. They assigned us meanings.[72]

Bartlett's Wilde, then, is betraying his sexual roots and acting out another narrative of compromise and defeat.

Inevitably, the trials are the centre-piece of any attempt to understand and assign significance to Wilde's sexuality: for Sinfield they are the historical moment in which modern homosexuality is constructed, for Bartlett a fateful verdict upon and silencing of an already flourishingly self-conscious way of life. Sinfield's constructionist approach is clearly indebted to Foucault, who argues that it was only in the late nineteenth century, and in the work of early sexologists such as Max Nordau, Richard von Krafft-Ebing and Havelock Ellis, that sexual behaviour was categorized in an attempt to define sexual identity, and homosexuality and heterosexuality were established as binary opposites.[73] Michael Foldy argues, however, that more than simply the impulse to medicalize, define, discipline and punish sexual 'deviancy' was at work at the Old Bailey. Wilde – he claims – came to be seen as a potent threat to the 'health' of Britain at a crucial moment in its history (a moment of acute anxiety about its imperial role), and that his trials and imprisonment were a concerted effort by society to cure a debilitating 'sickness' and thus affirm the existing moral and political order. Foldy also offers an intriguing political reading of Wilde's 'sodomitical' practices. Drawing on the work of David Halperin, he argues that Wilde's own Hellenistic models are instructive: for the ancient Athenians, he claims, sex, *per se*, was penetrative, implying that only the active partner had 'sex'. Penetration connoted activity, which conferred agency, which in turn conferred 'being'. Conversely, receptivity was considered passive, which conferred an onto-logical status next to non-existence. The proper sexual targets of adult male citizens in Athens were women, boys, foreigners and slaves: the disenfranch-ised. So, as long as the Athenian male retained what Foldy inelegantly terms the 'insertive' role with someone from a lower social category he was 'politically correct' in terms of his sexuality – whether he was inserting himself into a woman, a boy, a foreigner or a slave. 'Wilde's gender role was masculine', announces Foldy with mysterious confidence, 'and his phallocentric protocol was, as far as we know, insertive.'[74] In stylistic terms, this last sentence is hardly Foldy's finest moment – but equally maladroit is his insistence that we know what Wilde always did with his genitals. Foldy also takes at face-value the shame, humiliation and remorse concerning their roles as accomplices in the various enactments of Wilde's sexual fantas-ies professed by trial-witnesses Charles Parker and Alfred Wood – using their self-declared victim-status to bolster his conclusion that 'Wilde's sexual relations with young men were more than just sexual acts between will-ing partners. They were political acts as well, which reproduced patriarchal norms and reinforced conventions of class privilege.'[75] This is a typically new-historicist conclusion: Wilde's sexuality – his 'feasting with panthers', the pleasure he clearly took in the dangers of sexual slumming – only looks transgressive; in fact it is both contained and defined by the sexual and political order he appears to be challenging. In effect, Wilde's apparently subversive lifestyle merely allowed power the opportunity to assert and dis-play itself in legal, visual, dramatic terms at the Old Bailey. As in most new-historicist critique, resistance – paradoxically – proves its own worst enemy: provoking and maintaining the power that will crush it.

Sinfield has acknowledged that 'I am sometimes accused of hijacking Wilde for gay culture' and says his reply is to point out that English heterosexism did this by persecuting him. Nevertheless, the defensive tone is symptomatic of his recognition that Wilde is at the centre of a critical tug-of-love. Writing in 1995 – during the centenary commemorations of Wilde's trials, which crystallized popular images of him as multiform martyr and victim, and which gave added impetus to the new Wilde industry – he declared his willingness to 'share him with the Irish people'.[76] Sinfield, in what he clearly sees as a conciliatory gesture, proposes an articulation of Wilde's Irishness and gayness. In so doing, he would, I suggest, be unlikely to draw the same conclusions as G.J. Renier who – in a 1933 biography – claimed that although Wilde's homosexual temperament was present to a fairly marked degree it was not enough to prevent marriage and procrea-tion, but 'upon this temperament was imposed a lack of self-control due to his nationality.'[77] What is clear is that Wilde is a problematic, shifting, challenging and contested figure for those on both sides of the tug-of-love: and that any attempt to authenticate him by exclusive reference to either his nationality or his sexuality will open up fault lines in the approach itself, as well as the 'Wilde' it is trying to construct.

In fact, as Renier's sinister example shows (he goes on to suggest that 'it is not through persecution but through science that the mass production of homosexuals will be averted'[78]) the articulation of Wilde's Irishness and his gayness has proceeded without Sinfield – and has frequently taken as its subject the complex interrelation of the two in the way Wilde was seen and described. Michael Foldy, for instance, suggests that the threat Wilde was perceived as posing at the time of his celebrity was not simply a matter of his 'sexual deviancy': he came to symbolize the 'very antithesis of Englishness'[79] as his sexuality and his nationality coalesced in the discourses of 'healthy' late-Victorian society. Adrian Frazier argues that such a coalescence – at this historical juncture – was understandable in the sense that Irish men and gay men empathized with each other: 'It was hard work for an Irish author to get accepted in England, though not as hard as for a homosexual.' The demand to meet an alien standard, he continues, amounted to an accusation against one's manhood; 'one wasn't, if Irish, a man of quite the right type. So it was attractive to enter into a cabal with men equally estranged, with the aim of interrogating the justice of the whole manly military rule of Ireland.'[80] Owen Dudley Edwards has suggested that Wilde's Irishness was on trial at the Old Bailey as much as his sexual deviancy and that his compatriot, Edward Carson, cracked Wilde's English facade when, during cross-examination, he invited 'very Irish responses to his heavy-handed questions about alleged immorality in Wilde's writings.' The press made the connection by alluding to 'the Irish QC'. As Dudley Edwards puts it: 'Come down to the Old Bailey and watch the Paddies whack.'[81] Terry Eagleton says in the preface to his *Saint Oscar* (1988) that he was concerned not to write a 'gay' play about Wilde – though he acknowledges that Wilde's homosexuality was 'on any account at the heart of what he was' – but to 'put that ambiguity or doubleness back in the context of a much wider span of ambivalences.'[82] Part of that wider span of ambivalences is his Irishness: in the dock Eagleton's Wilde announces that he objects to the trial on the grounds that 'no Irishman can receive a fair hearing in an English court because the Irish are figments of the English imagination. I am not really here; I am just one of your racial fantasies.' Interestingly, Eagleton's fictional Wilde conceives of his 'doubleness' in terms which align him with real Irish 'traitors' such as Casement and William Joyce: he is, he says, a fifth columnist, 'a spy, a changeling, an alien smuggled into the upper class to corrupt their offspring.'[83] John Banville's novel *The Untouchable* (1997) explores this concatenation of Irishness, homosexuality and treachery in explicit terms:

the real Sir Anthony Blunt – Keeper of the Queen's Pictures and spy for the Russians – is transmogrified into the Irish Victor Maskell. Wilde is clearly one of the models for this 'Queer Irish Spy':[84] aesthete, classical scholar, married gay predator, outsider/insider, man of many masks.[85]

Wilde himself claimed in 'Pen, Pencil and Poison' that a mask can tell us more than a face (995). In proclaiming the truth of masks, and the falsity of the 'authentic', Wilde sounds clearly our contemporary. As Jonathan Dollimore puts it:

> Wilde's transgressive aesthetic suggests that certain aspects of what post/ modern theory finds so very contemporary about itself – anti-essentialism, especially, and the critique of the depth model of identity and culture – are not so new, having been developed as subversive and defensive strategies in subcultures before more recent manifestations in the intellectual main stream.[86]

Wilde is being made and remade by current critical practice. Far from being perceived as simply one of the most celebrated victims of Victorian morality and hypocrisy, he is now someone worth fighting over, his life and work are enlisted to define two of the cornerstones of modernity: national and sexual identity. Part of this book's project is to explore the series of self-conscious and deliberate stylistic choices by which Wilde maintains that shifting complexity which successively and successfully eludes all attempts to fix and authenticate him. I shall concentrate on trying to define Wilde Style, and on tracing the way it operates in his writing, rather than on seeking to locate the 'real' or 'essential' Wilde – to scrape away the accretions of Englishness, for instance, to get at the Celtic core. Indeed, Wilde provides his own warning to those who would wish to define him in terms of national, cultural or sexual authenticity. When Lady Bracknell hears that Jack Worthing's provenance is Victoria Station, she tells him he is the first person she has ever met whose origin is a terminus.

REFERENCES

[1]   Terry Eagleton, *Saint Oscar*, Field Day, Derry, 1989: vii.
[2]   Regenia Gagnier, ed., *Critical Essays on Oscar Wilde*, G.K. Hall, New York, 1992: 2.
[3]   Richard Ellmann, *Oscar Wilde*, Hamilton, London, 1987: 553.
[4]   Gagnier, ed., *Critical Essays*: 2.
[5]   *Critical Essays*: 6.
[6]   *Critical Essays*: 17–18.
[7]   *Critical Essays*: 15.

[8] *Critical Essays*: 2.

[9] See Mary Warner Blanchard, *Oscar Wilde's America: Counterculture in the Gilded Age*, Yale University Press, London and New Haven, 1998. Blanchard argues that the American aesthetic movement (partly inspired by Wilde, but largely carried forward by women artists and writers) was a brief interlude of cultural expansion and experimentation, cut off by Wilde's fall in 1895 and superseded by the resurgence of a culture of war and virility – exemplified by the rise of Teddy Roosevelt and the imperialist adventures of the late 1890s.

[10] Fintan O'Toole argues, intriguingly, for the close association in the American popular imagination, between Wilde and outlaws. Noting the death of Jesse James in April 1882, he says that 'Just as versions of Jesse James, and of Billy the Kid, were being "sighted" all over America, Wilde himself became a transferable icon, an image of dandified civility which was the other side of the coin of the image of the outlaw derring-do which attached itself to the notorious desperadoes.' See 'Venus in Blue Jeans: Oscar Wilde, Jesse James, Crime and Fame' in Jerusha MacCormack, ed., *Wilde the Irishman*, Yale University Press, London and New Haven, 1998: 72.

[11] Ellmann, *Oscar Wilde*: 185.

[12] Alan Warner, *A Guide to Anglo-Irish Literature*, Gill & Macmillan, Dublin, 1981: 5.

[13] Seamus Deane. ed., *The Field Day Anthology of Irish Writing*, Field Day, Derry, 1991, vol. 1: 506–7, 502, 507.

[14] *Field Day Anthology*, vol. 2: 1008.

[15] *Field Day Anthology*, vol. 2: 721.

[16] Seamus Heaney, introduction to RTE broadcast of *The Ballad of Reading Gaol*, 1992. I am grateful to Ana Moya for pointing me to this connection.

[17] *Field Day Anthology*, vol. 3: 940.

[18] *Field Day Anthology*, vol. 2: 846.

[19] *Field Day Anthology*, vol. 2: 373, 372.

[20] *Field Day Anthology*, vol. 2: 639.

[21] Richard Ellmann, ed., *Selected Writings of Oscar Wilde*, Oxford University Press, Oxford, 1961: xii.

[22] Christopher Nassaar, *Into the Demon Universe: a Literary Exploration of Oscar Wilde*, Yale University Press, Yale, 1974: 5–6.

[23] Robert K. Martin, 'Oscar Wilde and the Fairy Tale: The Happy Prince as self-dramatization', *Studies in Victorian Fiction*, vol. 16, 1979: 74–77. Norbert Kohl summarizes the similarly biographical approaches to 'The Fisherman and his Soul', 'The Birthday of the Infanta' and 'The Star-Child' of Leon Lemonnier and Robert Merle. See Kohl, *Oscar Wilde: The Works of a Conformist Rebel*, trans. David Henry Wilson, Cambridge University Press, Cambridge, 1989: 49–50. See also Michael C. Kotzin, ' "The Selfish Giant" as Literary Fairy Tale', *Studies in Short Fiction*, vol. 16, 1979: 301–9; Kotzin argues that 'The Selfish Giant' turns out to be about a sinner who is forgiven, 'as Wilde the sinner hoped that he himself would be'.

[24] George A. Woodcock, *The Paradox of Oscar Wilde*, T.V. Boardman, London, 1949: 148–49.

[25] Jerusha MacCormack, 'Wilde's Fiction(s)' in Peter Raby, ed., *The Cambridge Companion to Oscar Wilde*, Cambridge University Press, Cambridge, 1997: 102.

[26] *Daily Chronicle,* 30 June 1890.

[27] Rupert Hart-Davis, ed., *The Letters of Oscar Wilde,* Hart-Davis, London, 1962: 221.

[28] *Letters:* 301.

[29] *Letters:* 218.

[30] See Declan Kiberd, *Inventing Ireland: The Literature of the Modern Nation,* Jonathan Cape, London, 1995: 33–50.

[31] Ashis Nandy, *The Intimate Enemy: Loss and Recovery of Self under Colonialism,* Oxford University Press, Oxford, 1988: 45.

[32] Lord Alfred Douglas, *Without Apology,* Martin Secker, New York, 1938: 75.

[33] Micheál MacLiámóir, *The Happy Prince and Other Stories,* Puffin Books, London, 1962: 9. For a discussion of the significance of Alfred Willmore's self-fashioning as Micheál MacLiámóir, see Eibhear Walshe, 'Sodom and Begorrah, or Game to the Last: Inventing Micheal MacLiammoir', in Eibhear Walshe, ed., *Sex, Nation and Dissent in Irish Writing,* Cork University Press, Cork, 1997: 150–169.

[34] *Letters:* 218.

[35] *Letters:* 219.

[36] *Letters:* 302.

[37] Nandy, *The Intimate Enemy:* 36.

[38] Kevin Barry, 'Critical Notes on Post-colonial Aesthetics', *Irish Studies Review,* 14, Spring 1996: 2–3.

[39] 'Critical Notes': 2.

[40] See Luke Gibbons, 'Identity Without a Centre: Allegory, History and Irish Nationalism', *Cultural Studies,* vol. VI, no. 3, 1992: 358–75.

[41] See David Lloyd, *Anomolous States: Irish Writing and the Post-Colonial Moment,* Lilliput, Dublin, 1993: 65–79.

[42] Owen Dudley Edwards, 'Impressions of an Irish Sphinx', in MacCormack, ed., *Wilde the Irishman:* 59.

[43] Jerusha MacCormack, 'Introduction', *Wilde the Irishman:* 5.

[44] Deirdre Toomey, 'The Story-Teller at Fault: Oscar Wilde and Irish Orality', *Wilde the Irishman:* 24–35.

[45] 'The Story-Teller at Fault': 25.

[46] Quoted in Peter Nicholls, 'A Dying Fall? Nineteenth century Decadence and its Legacies' in Tracey Hill, ed., *Decadence and Danger: Writing, History and the Fin de Siècle,* Sulis Press, Bath, 1998: 18.

[47] 'A Dying Fall?': 18–19.

[48] Toomey, 'The Story-Teller at Fault': 35.

[49] Dudley Edwards, 'Impressions of an Irish Sphinx': 58.

[50] Toomey, 'The Story-Teller at Fault': 28.

[51] For a detailed account of this incident, see Sandra F. Siegal, 'Oscar Wilde's Gift and Oxford's "Coarse Impertinence"', in Tadhg Foley and Sean Ryder, eds, *Ideology and Ireland in the Nineteenth Century,* Four Courts Press, Dublin, 1998: 69–78.

[52] *Dramatic Review,* 30 May 1885: 278. Quoted by Sos Eltis, *Revising Wilde: Society and Subversion in the Plays of Oscar Wilde,* Clarendon Press, Oxford, 1996: 55.

[53] Susan Sontag, *A Susan Sontag Reader,* ed. Elizabeth Hardwick, Penguin, Harmondsworth, 1983: 235.

[54] For a discussion of 'liminality' in related contexts, see Colin Graham, '"Liminal Spaces": Post-Colonial Theories and Irish Culture', *Irish Review* 16, 1994: 33.

[55] Frank McGuinness, 'The Spirit of Play in *De Profundis*', in MacCormack, ed., *Wilde the Irishman*: 141.

[56] 'The Censure of *Salome*', *Pall Mall Budget* XL, 30 June 1892: 947; also in E.H. Mikhail, ed., *Oscar Wilde: Interviews and Recollections*, Macmillan, London, 1979, vol. 1: 188.

[57] Maurice Sisley, 'La Salome de M. Oscar Wilde', *Le Gaulois*, 29 June 1892: 1; and Mikhail, ed., *Interviews and Recollections*: 190. I am very grateful to Richard Haslam for pointing me to the significance of this remark.

[58] See Richard Ellmann, ed., *The Artist as Critic: Critical Writings of Oscar Wilde*, W.H. Allen, London, 1973: 80–4.

[59] *The Artist as Critic*: 115.

[60] Wilde was once asked, having distributed buttonholes on the opening night of *Lady Windermere's Fan*, what the green carnation meant. 'Nothing whatever,' he replied, 'but that is just what nobody will guess.' (See W. Graham Robertson, *Time Was*, Hamish Hamilton, London, 1931: 135). This studied attempt to supply both an excess and a nullity of meaning – to keep the signifier floating free of any anchoring signified – is, of course, confronted head on by Robert Hichens. He caricatures Wilde as Esme Amarinthe (who has a somewhat sinister interest in choirboys) in his novel *The Green Carnation* (1894).

[61] See Isobel Murray, ed., *Oscar Wilde: Complete Shorter Fiction*, OUP, Oxford, 1980: 9–14.

[62] Review of *Pictures in the Fire* by George Dalziel, *Pall Mall Gazette*, 20 January 1888.

[63] In an interview with Eileen Battersby, 'Big Fry', *Irish Times*, 30 October 1997.

[64] Quoted by Ellmann, *Oscar Wilde*: 357.

[65] Kate Millett, *Sexual Politics*, Virago, London, 1977: 154.

[66] See Christopher Craft, *Another Kind of Love: Male Homosexual Desire in English Discourse, 1850–1920*, University of California Press, Berkeley, 1994. 'Alias Bunbury' is reprinted in Regenia Gagnier, ed., *Critical Essays on Oscar Wilde*: 119–137.

[67] Jonathan Dollimore, *Sexual Dissidence: Augustine to Wilde, Freud to Foucault*, Oxford University Press, Oxford, 1991: 11.

[68] Alan Sinfield, *The Wilde Century*, Cassell, London, 1994: 20–1.

[69] *The Wilde Century*: 3. For a similar argument, see Ed Cohen, *Talk on the Wilde Side: Towards a Genealogy of Discourse on Male Sexualities*, Routledge, New York, 1993.

[70] Alan Sinfield, 'Wilde and the Queer Moment', *Irish Studies Review* 11, Summer 1995: 48. For a similarly critical view of Wilde's legacy, see Hugh David, *On Queer Street: A Social History of British Homosexuality, 1895–1995*, HarperCollins, London, 1997.

[71] Neil Bartlett, *Who Was That Man? A Present for Mr Oscar Wilde*, Serpent's Tail, London, 1988: 211.

[72] *Who Was That Man?*: 149.

[73] The first English edition of Nordau's *Degeneration* appeared in February 1895, the same month as Queensbury's calling-card precipitated the Wilde trials. Nordau

cited Wilde as an example of the 'degenerate' aesthetic temperament which was symptomatic of a generalized cultural crisis and, Stephen Arata has argued, his book was used to frame sensationalist press accounts of the trials. See Stephen Arata, *Fictions of Loss in the Victorian Fin de Siècle*, Cambridge University Press, Cambridge, 1996.

[74] Michael S. Foldy, *The Trials of Oscar Wilde: Deviance, Morality and Late-Victorian Society*, Yale University Press, New Haven and London, 1997: 121.

[75] *The Trials of Oscar Wilde*: 121. Interestingly, Joseph Bristow focuses on Wilde's interest in Classical models of 'same-sex' relationships to draw entirely opposite conclusions. Wilde, he argues, adhered to the 'higher' Socratic ethos of Oxonian Hellenism; this allows Bristow to claim that there is a sexual morality underpinning *The Picture of Dorian Gray*. Lord Henry Wotton shows a lamentable disregard for the consequences of the influence he exerts over Dorian and other young men: 'Nothing could be more distant from the democratic spirit enshrined in the Socratic ethos that sought to strengthen emotional and physical bonds between men. Little wonder the picture of Dorian Gray undergoes the most appalling kinds of disfiguration, as he becomes tyrannised by passions that need to be disciplined – not exploited – by the care and attention constituting *paederastia*.' See Joseph Bristow, '"A Complex multiform creature": Wilde's sexual identities' in Peter Raby, ed., *The Cambridge Companion*: 213.

[76] Sinfield, 'Wilde and the Queer Moment': 48.

[77] G.J. Renier, *Oscar Wilde*, Nelson, London, 1933: 4.

[78] Renier, *Oscar Wilde*: 96.

[79] Foldy, *The Trials of Oscar Wilde*: xv.

[80] Adrian Frazier, 'Queering the Irish Renaissance: The Masculinities of Moore, Martyn and Yeats' in Anthony Bradley and Maryann Gialanella Valiulis, eds, *Gender and Sexuality in Modern Ireland*, University of Massachusetts Press, Amherst, 1997: 33.

[81] Owen Dudley Edwards, 'Oscar Wilde: The Soul of Man under Hibernicism', *Irish Studies Review*, 11, Summer, 1995: 12. Wilde's contemporary Frank Harris made the same point about the trials: 'I had seen enough of English justice and English judges and English journals to convince me that Oscar Wilde had no more chance of a fair trial than if he had been an Irish "Invincible"'. See Frank Harris, *Oscar Wilde: His Life and Confessions*, Panther, London, 1965: 167.

[82] Terry Eagleton, *Saint Oscar*, Field Day, Derry, 1989: xi.

[83] *Saint Oscar*: 23.

[84] John Banville, *The Untouchable*, Picador, London, 1997.

[85] Thomas Kilroy's play *Double Cross*, 1986 about Willam Joyce ('Lord Haw-Haw') and Brendan Bracken is similarly concerned with exploring the connections between Irishness, role-playing and treachery. Bracken was born in County Tipperary, was a republican sympathizer in his youth, went to Sedburgh public school in England, was widely assumed to be Churchill's son when he started to make his way in English politics, and served as both a Conservative MP and Churchill's Minister of Information during the war. Kilroy describes him as 'an actor loose in the world of English politics and what used to be called Society.'

Kilroy's Bracken justifies himself in familiar terms: 'I used to subscribe to the Wildean notion that one must make of one's life a work of art. We're given pretty dismal material to start with. One must shape it into significance. I believe that's what's meant by salvation.' Reprinted in Seamus Deane, ed., *The Field Day Anthology*, vol. 3: 1282.

[86] Dollimore, *Sexual Dissidence*: 25.

2

THEORIZING STYLE: THE ESSAYS

In a poignant moment of self-congratulation and self-torment, Wilde – prisoner of Reading Gaol – described himself as 'a man who stood in symbolic relations to the art and culture of my age' (912). I want to argue that Wilde the theorist is janus-faced. His aesthetic theories as outlined in the 1880s and 1890s look back to Baudelaire, Gautier, Poe, as well as to more recent influences and predecessors such as Ruskin, Whistler and Pater; he is also very much our contemporary. In a sense, then, Wilde's double-face is indeed symbolic of his *fin de siècle*: he looks back deep into his own century and forward into ours. Richard Ellmann recognized as much when he announced that 'Wilde is one of us.' However, Ellmann also discerns a discontinuity between Wilde's theories and his practice: 'While the ultimate virtue in Wilde's essays is make-believe, the denouement of his dramas and narratives is that masks have to go. We must acknowledge what we are.'[1] Despite the fact that in 'The Decay of Lying' Wilde dismisses 'the dullard and the doctrinaire' who pursue their principles to 'the bitter end of action, to the *reductio ad absurdum* of practice' (971), I want to question this notion of discontinuity, arguing for a consistency between the theoretical essays and his practice as a novelist and playwright. In order to do that I need first to examine those theories themselves, suggesting that although they have always been seen as proclaiming the supremacy of Art, Wilde's dominant category is, in fact, Style. I shall look first primarily at 'The Decay of Lying' which is Wilde as Theorist as Dandy and in which, like Lord Henry Wotton in *The Picture of Dorian Gray,* he plays with ideas and wings them with paradox, living up to the dandy's dictum: '"To test Reality we must see it on the tight-rope. When the Verities become acrobats, we can judge them"'(43).

Wilde claimed in 'Pen, Pencil and Poison' that most artificial people have a great love of nature (1002). This wry paradox neatly collapses that binary opposition between Nature and Culture which postmodernism has laboured (is perhaps still labouring) so indefatigably to deny. When Wilde declares in 'The Decay of Lying' that 'Art is our spirited protest, our gallant attempt to teach Nature her proper place'(970), he is voicing, as Terry Eagleton points out, a hostility to 'oppressive normativity' which he shares with Roland Barthes and Michel Foucault, a normativity which they also identify with constructions of Nature and the 'natural'.[2] This elevation of the constructed, the artificial, the specious above the given, the natural, the authentic is at the theoretical centre of the essays collected as *Intentions* in 1891: 'The Decay of Lying', 'The Critic as Artist', 'Pen, Pencil and Poison' and 'The Truth of Masks'. In *The Environmental Imagination* (1995), an eco-critical survey of representations of the natural world, Lawrence Buell suggests that the 'long-lost world of nineteenth-century realism' has been twice displaced, first by high modernism and then by contemporary cultural theory.[3] In fact, this model of displacement is deceptive. As an examination of Wilde's critical theories – and the influence upon them of earlier critics – will show, the foundations of the 'prison-house of realism' were being undermined before the edifice was built; such an examination is important because it helps to prevent the spurious notion of a Victorian monolith being overturned by the innovations of modernity. Wilde's case shows that we should perhaps be thinking in terms of Victorianisms rather than Victorianism.[4]

In reviewing 'The Salon of 1856', for instance, Baudelaire bewailed the corrupting influence of a new technology – photography – and the fact that 'Each day art further diminishes its self-respect by bowing down before the external reality; each day the painter becomes more and more given to painting not what he dreams but what he sees.' He went on to describe the imagination as the Queen of Faculties and to declare that 'As it has created the world [. . .] it is proper that it should govern it.'[5] Wilde's mouthpiece in 'The Decay of Lying' – the insouciant iconoclast Vivian – has clearly read his Baudelaire. He dismisses the infinite variety of Nature as pure myth: 'It is not to be found in Nature herself. It resides in the imagination, or fancy, or cultivated blindness of the man who looks at her' (970).[6] Through Vivian's pyrotechnic argumentation and the grudging responses of the stolid Cyril, Wilde repeats Baudelaire's insistence that artistic perception is both active and creative: art does not reflect, or photograph, it constructs. Vivian seals his point by enlisting Shakespeare, claiming that the 'unfortunate aphorism about Art holding up a mirror to nature is deliberately said by Hamlet in order to convince bystanders of his absolute insanity in all art-matters' (981). Such crucial distinctions Wilde would also have encountered in Whistler (whom he called that 'miniature Mephistopheles mocking the majority'[7]) and in Walter Pater's enormously influential *Studies in the History of the Renaissance* (1873). For Whistler, according to Wilde,

There is nothing of which the ordinary English painter more needs to be reminded than that the true artist does not wait for life to be made picturesque

for him, but se' s life under picturesque conditions always – under conditions,
that is to say, v/hich are at once new and beautiful.[8]

Pater's version of the same idea involves comparing Giotto and Masaccio
unfavourably with Botticelli because they 'merely transcribed the outward
image' and were 'almost passive spectators of the action before them.'[9]

However, in crowning the imagination, Baudelaire was careful to distance
himself from the 'ruins of the old romanticism' which he found in a painter
like Boulanger, who seemed to adhere to the accepted notion that 'inspiration is enough and takes the place of everything else.'[10] Baudelaire would
have encountered the same rejection of the primacy of 'inspiration' in Edgar
Allan Poe, particularly in his 1846 essay on The Philosophy of Composition
which emphasized the calculated effects of composition. Poe described his
'The Raven' as proceeding 'step by step to its completion with the preci-
sion and rigid consequence of a mathematical problem.'[11] (Indeed, Walter
Benjamin criticizes Baudelaire's theory of art for its overdependence on Poe,
'down to its formulation'[12].) Wilde – who as we have seen regarded all fine
imaginative work as necessarily self-conscious and deliberate – echoes both
sentiments in a letter to the American actress Marie Prescott in 1883: 'Success is a science,' he announces, 'if you have the conditions, you get the
result. Art is the mathematical result of the emotional desire for beauty. If it
is not thought out, it is nothing.'[13] Given that the success Wilde is talking
about is that which he expects to attend his disastrous play Vera, or the
Nihilists, it is difficult not to remark that, in this instance, his confidence is
misplaced. Nevertheless, the point is clear: Wilde follows Baudelaire and
Poe in ascribing to the imagination the qualities of self-consciousness and
deliberation and – in so doing – he neatly trumps Plato whose Republic
would have had no place for artists on the grounds that by copying Nature
they neglected the Ideal and thus engaged in a process of continued decep-
tion (copying a copy):

> People have a careless way of talking about a 'born liar', just as they talk about
> a born poet. But in both cases they are wrong. Lying and poetry are arts – arts
> as Plato saw, not unconnected with each other – and they require the most
> careful study, the most disinterested devotion.

(972)

For Vivian, lying 'is an art, a science, and a social pleasure'(972). In using
the rhetoric of scientism to dispense with the notion of inspiration, Wilde
signals that his approach is not just anti-naturalistic, it is anti-Romantic too:

and sides with Aristotle's treatment of art from the aesthetic point of view, rather than with Plato's relentlessly ethical emphasis.

Once again, Wilde is also following the example of Pater (Harold Bloom describes Wilde as 'brilliantly vulgarizing' his former Oxford tutor[14]). 'The Renaissance' adopted a similar strategy, with Pater striking a self-consciously modern and contentious note with his use of scientific and materialist analogies to describe artistic creation. For him, few artists were capable of casting off all debris, 'leaving us only with what the heat of their imagination has fused and transformed.' Wordsworth is a case in point: 'the heat of his genius, entering into the substance of his work, has crystallised a part, but only a part of it'; similarly, Pater employed the language of the laboratory to describe the activity of the aesthetic critic who was exhorted to note down the virtues of the art-object in the manner of a chemist analysing an element.[15] Geoffrey Monsman points out that Pater's grasp of scientific theory was very much that of a layman, but recognizes that his use of the rhetoric of scientism was an important aspect of his delight in the intellectual risqué, its materialism a provocative challenge to Oxford orthodoxy.[16] In 'The Decay of Lying' Wilde echoes Baudelaire in dismissing the Romantic notion that art is inspiration (as embodied in the Wordsworthian definition of poetry as the spontaneous overflow of powerful feelings), that it is in some sense 'natural' – or authentic – rather than constructed: 'make-believe' in Ellmann's phrase. He also takes as his principal target the Naturalistic aesthetics of Emile Zola. Writing in the 1870s, Zola had claimed that the literary artist had no real choice but to swim with the scientific current of the time: art should aim at direct observation, exact anatomy, the acceptance and depicting of what is.[17] Lawrence Danson notes that Wilde worked on 'The Decay of Lying' during the controversy surrounding the English translation of Zola's novel La terre in 1889, which saw the publisher indicted for obscene libel and imprisoned for three months.[18] Nevertheless, it is important to understand the Aristotelian, rather than Platonic, terms in which Wilde condemns Zola: 'his work is entirely wrong from beginning to end, and wrong not on the ground of morals, but on the ground of art'. 'We have,' explains Vivian, 'no sympathy at all with the moral indignation of our time against M. Zola. It is simply the indignation of Tartuffe on being exposed'(974). Wilde's essay dismisses Zola's central notion of art as a 'window on the real', yet, while countering it with his own claim for the primacy of the imagination over the natural world, he turns paradoxically to Pateresque materialism, making a 'scientific' appeal to Aristotle to justify Vivian's claim that the basis of life is merely the desire for expression (985). Wilde is here in no sense endorsing Zola's call for a 'scientific realism' that is based on scrupulous observation and reproduction. The rhetorical strategy is self-consciously sophisticated: by writing a degree of understanding and observation of the natural world and its 'elements' into his anti-naturalistic aesthetic theories, Wilde claims for his ideas the determined modernity on which Zola had prided himself two decades before.

'For what is Nature?' asks Vivian: 'Nature is no great mother who has borne us. She is our creation. It is in our brain that she quickens to life. Things are because we see them, and what we see, and how we see it, depends on the Arts that have influenced us' (986). Without wishing to bring to bear upon Wilde anachronistic notions of political correctness (he, of course, would have recoiled from the attempt to describe him as correct in any sense), Wilde's protofeminism might be glimpsed in this qualified denial of the familiar and venerable trope by which the feminine is figured as natural, in some sense instinctive, at best prerational and, like a wild and untended plot, in need of husbandry. Wilde is pitting Mind against Nature. 'Nothing,' opines Vivian, 'is more evident than that Nature hates Mind. Thinking is the most unhealthy thing in the world, and people die of it just as they die of any other disease' (971). 'The Decay of Lying' thus champions an art which is unnatural, unhealthy and untruthful: in effect, an art which is subversive of all political, cultural and social institutions and discourses which solidify or ossify into the 'natural' state of affairs. As Terry Eagleton succinctly puts it, in aligning Wilde with Barthes and Foucault and, consequently, with a postmodern preoccupation with the nature of power: 'Nature is the family, heterosexuality, stock notions, social conventions; and Wilde had only to be presented with a convention to feel the irresistible urge to violate it.'[19] Wilde's irresistible urges content themselves in this instance with a provocative displacement of the natural by the aesthetic: 'Life imitates art far more than Art imitates life' (982).

Baudelaire had made the same point in his essay on Constantin Guys: 'The Painter of Modern Life' (1863). Here Baudelaire – in the course of what is a seminal discussion of nineteenth-century dandyism – says of fashion plates that they construct an ideal of beauty which affects the individual: 'it ruffles or stiffens his coat, gives curves or straight lines to his gestures and even, in the process of time, subtly penetrates the very features of his face.'[20] This is a crucial insight. In addition to recognizing the way art can provide forms for self-realization, teaching us how to see ourselves and others (Wilde's version of this in 'The Decay of Lying', of course, is his reference to the ubiquity of Pre-Raphaelite women), Baudelaire effectively cancels the distinction between 'High Art' and other cultural forms. The imagery of advertising is as powerful and worthy of note and analysis as the 'masterpieces' in the salons. (In this respect, Baudelaire had again been anticipated by Poe, who wrote in 1840 on *The Philosophy of Furniture*, and who could remark that 'A judge at common law may be an ordinary man; a good judge of a

carpet *must* be a genius'.[21] Interestingly, Vivian seems determined to establish his own genius by exercizing himself on the subject of the aesthetic value
of carpets (979–80).) Wilde's familiarity with Baudelaire's formulation is
explicit; he refers, in a review, to a 'charming article' by Baudelaire on 'the
artistic value of frock-coats' using it to answer a reckless critic who once
asked of Reynolds how he could paint 'these ugly three-cornered hats'.[22]
For the Baudelairean *flâneur*, the self-possessed idler languidly cruising the
Parisian arcades, 'the shiny, enamelled signs of businesses are', according to
Benjamin, 'at least as good a wall ornament as an oil painting is to a bour-
geois in his salon'.[23] This cancellation of the distinction between 'High Art'
and the seductively ephemeral products of Benjamin's 'era of high capitalism' is as marked in Wilde as it is in Baudelaire. It informs Wilde's proselyt-
izing for the House Beautiful and his continued interest in dress reform (for
both women and men) and is perhaps most neatly expressed in his undergraduate aim of living up to his blue china. Wilde's modish taste for Japanese art and design is another example. In the 1880s and 1890s, the fashion
for the 'Japanesque' could be seen, for instance, in 'Tokio Toothpowder',
Worcester Pottery, Whistler's paintings and the erotic prints which influenced Aubrey Beardsley.[24] For Wilde, Japan – with its 'rejection of imitation,
its love of artistic convention, its dislike of the actual representation of any
object in Nature' (979) – exercizes some of the fascination that the oriental
'Empire of Signs' does for Roland Barthes. In its avoidance of perspective,
pictorial depth, Japanese drawing and painting presents itself as all surface.
Wilde claimed a desire to wander in Japan, 'where I shall pass my youth,
sitting under an almond tree in white blossom, drinking amber tea out of a
white cup, and looking at a landscape without perspective.'[25] The reference
to youth is characteristically disingenuous – Wilde was 27 at the time – but
the comments are revealing. Wilde imagines himself into the design of his
china, the reverie is of an escape into artifice. 'Japan' functions as a sign for
the triumph of the elegantly anti-natural, discovered in the amber depths of
a tea-cup.

In 'The Decay of Lying', Wilde's Barthesian and postmodern-looking
emphasis on the significant ephemera of fashion, and his inversion of conventional notions of *mimesis* intersect in his critique of contemporary painting. The women Vivian encounters in the artistic *beau-monde* are the creations
of the Pre-Raphaelites. Further, Nature itself, for the urbane Londoner of
the 1890s, is simply the product of a particular, fashionable school of painting. 'Where', asks Vivian, 'if not from the Impressionists, do we get those
wonderful brown fogs that come creeping down our streets, blurring the
gas-lamps and changing the houses into monstrous shadows?'(986). Crucially, Vivian counsels against delighting uncritically in such powers. 'Now,
it must be admitted, fogs are carried to excess. They have become the mere

mannerism of a clique, and the exaggerated realism of their method gives
dull people bronchitis. Where the cultured catch an effect, the uncultured
catch cold' (986). Art can fog our perception as well as clear it: shades again
of Pater here and his almost Beckettian assertion that 'failure is to form
habits'.[26] The kind of art Wilde advocates will perform something akin to
the Russian Formalist function of *ostranenie*; by 'making things strange' it
will teach us to see them anew, freeing us from the trammels of habit. Such
art will meet Baudelaire's definition of the beautiful, which demands the
unexpected, the 'slightly distorted'.[27] (The imagination, Baudelaire claims,
'creates a new world, it produces a sensation of newness.'[28]) As Vivian notes,
'To look at a thing is very different from seeing a thing. One does not see a
thing until one sees its beauty' (986). In *The Picture of Dorian Gray*, Lord
Henry Wotton says to his pupil that,

> You may fancy yourself safe, and think yourself strong. But a chance tone of
> colour in a room or a morning sky, a particular perfume that you had once
> loved and that brings subtle memories with it, a line from a forgotten poem
> that you had come across again, a cadence from a piece of music that you had
> ceased to play – I tell you, Dorian, that it is on things like this that our lives
> depend.

> (162)

This is a Proustian summmation of the power of involuntary memory, those
rare and dangerous moments in which, according to Beckett, habit breaks
down and sensation, knowledge, insight, suffering rush in.[29] Wilde knows
that art can be an agent of such change.

The best example of Wilde putting into practice his principles regarding
the representation of the natural world is in the opening paragraphs of *The
Picture of Dorian Gray*.[30] Wilde toys with the distinction between Nature
and Culture: acknowledging it only to collapse it. Basil Hallward's artist's
studio is 'filled with the rich odour of roses, and when the light summer
wind stirred amidst the trees of the garden, there came through the open
door the heavy scent of the lilac or the more delicate perfume of the pink-
flowering thorn' (18). In effect, the two realms are melding: the garden
(Nature) is infiltrating the studio. This transgressive movement transforms
both sides of the opposition: 'odour' becomes 'scent' which becomes 'perfume'. The natural world, in other words, appears as cultivated (the garden)
and smells like a 'fragrance', contrived by a fashionable *parfumier*; the world
of *couture*, on the other hand, is offered as simply an intensification of
'natural' odours. Wilde artfully employs synaesthetic effects to heighten the
impression of boundaries being crossed and distinctions dissolved: different senses are appealed to, simultaneously. For instance, the blossoms of a

laburnum are 'honey-sweet' and 'honey-coloured'. (We are told, also, with characteristically alliterative insistence, that the laburnum's branches seemed 'hardly able to bear the burden of a beauty so flamelike as theirs.' Few of Wilde's readers would have missed this thinly veiled reference to the celebrated Conclusion of Pater's 'Renaissance' and its contention that the purpose of life was to surrender to sensation, to burn with a hard, gemlike flame.) In the studio itself 'the fantastic shadows of birds in flight flitted across the long, tussore-silk curtains that were stretched in front of the huge window'(18). Are these 'real' birds outside, or silk patterns inside? Wilde leaves the question unanswered, and in so doing further blurs the distinction between 'inner' and 'outer', between the room and the garden. This confusion produces a 'momentary Japanese effect' and makes Lord Henry Wotton 'think of those pallid, jade-faced painters of Tokio, who, through the medium of an art that is necessarily immobile, seek to convey the sense of swiftness and motion'(18). Wilde's prose attempts to emulate this ability of Japanese artists to deny difference: the stillness of the garden is heightened by the tiny movements of bees; the dusty woodbine has 'gilt' horns; the 'dim roar' of London sounds like 'the bourdon note of a distant organ' (18).

Wilde gives us an environment that is emphatically **written**: the aestheticization of the Natural, and the naturalization of the Cultural, is consistently foregrounded. If 'The Decay of Lying' displays the Nature-Culture split in order to invert it – raising the bogus above the real – *Dorian Gray* gives fictional form to the collapsing of the distinction between the two terms that this theoretical inversion is a prelude to. At the centre of Basil's studio is the quintessential art-object: the picture of Dorian Gray. Vivian says that 'the only portraits in which one believes are portraits in which there is very little of the sitter and a great deal of the artist' (989). As this implies, this portrait is not in any sense a mirror held up to its ostensible subject. The relationship between Dorian and his portrait precisely enacts that collapsing of the binary opposition between Nature and Culture, or art and life, which Wilde's opening to the novel – partly by foregrounding the complexity and artifice of the prose – both describes and embodies. By staying eternally young Dorian acquires the immutability of the art-object; by growing old his image is ravaged by the natural processes of decay. Life imitates art and art imitates life. (In his masterpiece, *The Importance of Being Earnest,* Wilde burlesques this confusion in the story of Miss Prism (misprision?) who cannot distinguish the two: she puts her three-volume novel of 'more than usually revolting sentimentality' into a bassinette, and a baby in a handbag.) So, Wilde evokes the natural world at the beginning of *The Picture of Dorian Gray* not simply as a means of setting the scene, but in order to signal the transgressive and subversive strategies which will structure the novel itself.

Towards the end of *De Profundis* Wilde tells Bosie of his 'strange longing
for the great simple primeval things, such as the Sea, to me no less of a
mother than the Earth.' He declares his desire to seek purification in ele-
mental forces (954). Nature will also be a sanctuary for the outcast: 'Society,
as we have constituted it, will have no place for me, has none to offer; but
Nature, whose sweet rains fall on unjust and just alike, will have clefts
in rocks where I may hide, and secret valleys in whose silence I may weep
undisturbed' (955). This is a self-conscious palinode: a deliberate reversal of
the way Nature has been constructed and deployed in his previous work.
However, this explicit declaration of the consolatory authenticity of Nature,
its great primeval simplicity, is simultaneously undercut. First, the artfully
overwrought prose operates in characteristic fashion, enculturing the natural world. Wilde looks forward to release from Reading Gaol, when he will
seek out the lilac blossom which will 'toss the pale purple of its plumes' and
transform his humdrum surroundings: 'all the air shall be Arabia for me'
(954). He also claims that 'there is not a single colour hidden away in the
chalice of a flower' (955) to which his nature does not answer. Secondly, as
the use of 'chalice' suggests, Nature has been enlisted to play a part in
Wilde's penitential drama: it provides both stage-set and stage-props. I have
already warned against reading *De Profundis* simplistically as Wilde's final
judgement on himself, or of adopting it as ours on him. As a strategy for
survival the letter allows him to summon his resources through performance, to remake himself through role-play. Wilde appears to be turning to
Nature as a refuge from a corrupt and hostile society. He is also demonstrating his capacity for self-renewal by adopting, with theatrical aplomb, a
Romantic rhetoric. It is his method of preparing for another role, that of
Sebastian Melmoth, the wanderer. This paean to Nature is thus deeply paradoxical: a celebration of the simple and the authentic, of Wilde's new-found
'integrity', which turns surreptitiously into its opposite.

Lawrence Buell says of literary representations of the natural world
grounded in the traditions of *mimesis* – those claiming, in effect, to hold a
mirror up to Nature – that 'environmental facticity in any era might be felt
to smack of acquiescence, fatalism, even death. Sooner or later, the implacable *thereness* of the external world is found to represent the adversary. No
matter how resolutely cheerful or stoic one's temperament, in some moods
or phases nature will metamorphose from possibility into fate, as for the
aging Emerson.'[31] Wilde's 'enculturation' of the natural world, his anti-
naturalistic theory and practice, is of course a conscious disavowal of facticity; and Nature is thus brought – because constructed rather than given –
into the realm of human action, responsibility and choice. By denying the
'implacable thereness of the external world' Wilde enacts an aesthetic version
of his own political choices; Wilde the radical socialist affirms an optimistic

belief in the possibility of human agency and change. He also prevents Nature being annexed simply for human use. This is evident in the ironies of 'Pen, Pencil and Poison', where he points out the 'ruins of the old romanticism'[32] in a series of witty asides at the expense of Wordsworth and his propensity for turning the natural world into a kind of moral gymnasium. We are told that Griffiths Wainewright was brought up at Linden House in Turnham Green and that to 'its lovely gardens and well-timbered park he owed that simple and impassioned love of nature which never left him all through his life, and which made him so peculiarly susceptible to the spiritual influences of Wordsworth's poetry' (1003). The Seer of Grasmere would, I think, have been somewhat perplexed to find himself credited with so influential a part in the moral and spiritual education of a serial poisoner who gave as his reason for dispatching one of his victims that she had thick ankles. Wilde claims that Griffiths Wainewright was always reticent on the subject of his 'strange sin' and his 'terrible experiments and methods', preferring to speak of Wordsworth's 'The Excursion' and 'Poems Founded on the Affections'(1003). In 'The Decay of Lying', Vivian is more explicit in condemning Wordsworthian narcissism:

> Wordsworth went to the lakes, but he was never a lake poet. He found in sermons the stones he had already hidden there. He went moralizing about the district, but his good work was produced not when he went to Nature but to Poetry. Poetry gave him 'Laodamia' and his fine sonnets, and the great Ode, such as it is. Nature gave him 'Martha Ray' and 'Peter Bell', and the address to Mr. Wilkinson's spade.

(977–8)

By a curious irony, Wilde shows more 'respect for nature' than Wordsworth: to aestheticize Nature is to affirm its beauty and otherness; to turn it into a moral exercise-yard is sanctimonious, egotistical and ugly.

Part of the Wordsworthian project is to define the moral and social self by anchoring it in a natural world that is definable, fixed, stable. Wilde's paradoxical dissolution and reinvention of nature as encultured, fabricated, written, entails a concomitant freeing up of notions of human subjectivity. In effect, denying to Nature its authenticity entails denying it to the human subject also. Instead of the narratives of moral and spiritual growth offered by Wordsworth, Wilde gives us multiplicity, discontinuity, flux: as he says in *The Soul of Man Under Socialism*, all we know of human nature is that it changes, 'change is the one quality we can predicate of it' (1101). Dorian Gray, for instance, is a murderer and a drug-addict; he is also Prince Charming and the most fashionable and desirable man in London. His are multiple personalities simultaneously maintained, just as Lord Goring in *An Ideal Husband*, is a personal combination of antitheses: while displaying 'all the delicate fopperies of fashion' and enjoying the *flâneur*'s life of languid ease and detachment, he also takes responsibility for intervening in the disastrous private life of his politician friend, Sir Robert Chiltern, and is, Wilde claims, 'the first well-dressed philosopher in the history of thought' (522). Dorian himself, Wilde tells us,

> used to wonder at the shallow psychology of those who conceive the Ego in a man as a thing simple, permanent, reliable, and of one essence. To him, man was a being with myriad lives and myriad sensations, a complex, multiform creature that bore within itself strange legacies of thought and passion . . .

(112)

In *The Importance of Being Earnest* complexity and multiformity are given a comic twist in the way the young lovers make a virtue of their changeability: 'If you are not too long,' Gwendolen tells Jack, 'I will wait for you all my life'(379). 'What people call insincerity,' says Gilbert in 'The Critic as Artist', 'is simply a method by which we can multiply our personalities'(1048); this multiplication of identity is clearly central to Wilde's interest in Thomas Griffiths Wainewright, whose masks and pseudonyms (Janus Weathercock, Van Vinkwooms, Egomet Bonmot), we are told, intensified rather than diffused his personality (995). When Griffiths Wainewright was finally arraigned for forgery, Wilde claims that he offered as a *circonstance attenuante* the fact that the crime had been committed thirteen years before. Wilde notes that 'the permanence of personality is a very subtle metaphysical problem and certainly the English law solves the question in a very rough-and-ready manner' (1006). Given that Wilde was himself maintaining contradictory personalities, Bunburying, in effect, at the time of writing this essay, it is impossible not to acknowledge the prophetic irony in this statement: Wilde was soon to become subject, in the dock at the Old Bailey, to the roughness and readiness of the English law.

Once again we see Wilde refusing the limiting and oppressive notion of authenticity: denying the 'naturalness' of individual identity. Multiple selves are slippery selves; deprived of an anchorage in a natural world which has the brooding facticity of fate, which is instead fashioned by the human agent rather than for the human subject, the individual personality is free-floating, self-fashioning, supremely and stylishly indifferent to a hostile normativity. Wilde's Nature is not a place for dwelling, or for the legitimation and authentication of communities, nations or races who dwell in a specific

landscape, an owned and owning place. (We have already seen how important the notion of 'land' can be to essentialist notions of Irish identity, for
instance – as in Daniel Corkery's political and literary critique of those
'Irish' writers like Wilde who deserted their national, cultural and racial
'roots'.) It is in this respect that Wilde's anti-naturalistic theory and practice
can open up a radical political landscape which contemporary eco-criticism
might occupy: one not defined by organicist metaphors and assumptions,
and an associated conservative political agenda.[33] Indeed, the socialist utopia
Wilde imagines is one in which man will be 'in harmony with himself and
his environment' (1104). What Wilde replaces authenticity with is style –
with a series of deliberate aesthetic choices governing the ways we see the
world, the ways we represent it, and the ways we present ourselves to it; and,
as 'The Decay of Lying' tells us, 'It is style that makes us believe in a thing –
nothing but style' (989).

Style becomes the central theoretical term for Wilde. In 'The Decay of
Lying' Vivian insists that 'Truth is entirely and absolutely a matter of style'
(981) and Gilbert says, in 'The Critic as Artist', the second of the Socratic
dialogues collected in *Intentions*, that 'there is no art where there is no style'
(1020). In 'The Portrait of Mr W.H.' Wilde used Shakespeare as evidence
that 'Sincerity itself, the ardent, momentary sincerity of the artist, is often
the unconscious result of style' (1186): another example of his repeated
insistence that content does not dictate form but is derived from it. The real
artist, Gilbert tells us, is 'he who proceeds not from feeling to form, but
from form to thought and passion' (1052). In effect, the central importance
of style is subsumed under one of Wilde's most important – and modern-
looking – formulations: 'The Critic as Artist' intensifies the theoretical thrust
of the 'The Decay of Lying' by claiming that language is 'the parent and not
the child of thought' (1023). This appears to anticipate structuralist concerns with language as a sign-system which **creates** meanings, rather than
one which is created **by** meaning. ('Mere words!', we hear in *Dorian Gray*,
'Was there anything so real as words?' (30).) However, Wilde is even more
markedly our contemporary than this suggests: his ideas are closer to
poststructuralism than to 'classical' structuralism because he is not merely
content to display the structures of signification, he wants to deconstruct
them.

The editors of the notebooks Wilde kept at Oxford as an undergraduate
claim that he was heavily influenced by Max Müller, the comparative philo-
logist he studied under during his first year. Müller believed that language
was 'the one great barrier between the brute and Man: Man speaks and no
brute has ever uttered a word. Language is our Rubicon and no brute will
dare to cross it.'[34] Certainly this finds an echo in 'The Critic as Artist': 'There
is no mode of action, no form of emotion, that we do not share with the

lower animals. It is only by language that we rise above them, or above each other' (1023). However, Wilde's view of language and, equally importantly, the way he deploys it, has more in common with influential poststructuralist critics such as Lacan, Derrida and de Man than it has with his Victorian contemporaries such as Müller and his 'golden age' theory of language, with its etymological emphasis on 'roots' as authentic expression.[35] For Lacan, language cannot be traced back to 'roots', because it has none: rewriting Freud with the help of Saussure, he sees the entry into language as the entry into a relational system, or structure, which defines the human subject (language as the parent, not the child, of subjectivity). Derrida draws attention to the need in Western thought and philosophy for 'centres' which guarantee meaning and presence: which fix, stabilize and authenticate. We discriminate, he claims, between speech and writing because speech is seen as immediate, present, authentic: emanating from a physical body we can identify. Writing, on the other hand, is – according to this 'phonocentric' view – contaminated speech, removed from the 'originating' thought. Writing is reproducible, reinterpretable, slippery, multiple, lacking in authenticity and presence. This notion of contamination is important to de Man too, who (and he draws heavily on Nietzsche here) sees the referential pretensions of language as always contaminated by its figurality: it is not a 'window on the real' but a figuration of it. What unites these variously subversive views of the way language operates is the deconstruction of the human subject as the *fons et origo* of meaning; indeed, the subject is effectively dispersed and decentred by the processes of signification which simultaneously bring it into being. From this perspective, Wilde's emphasis on the multiformity of the subject, and on the way the most apparently private, internal and authentic responses are styled by language and literary form, is fundamentally anti-humanist.

For Derrida, the distinction assiduously maintained between speech and writing does not operate on the horizontal but on the vertical: it is, in effect, a value-structure – or what he calls, evocatively, a 'violent hierarchy', where one of the two terms effectively governs and polices the other. 'Classical' structuralism was content to identify the binary opposition: poststructuralism performs a political act by demonstrating the instability, arbitrariness, collapsibility of the binary opposition, helping a literary text to unravel itself and expose its ideological underpinnings. In Derridean deconstruction the first act is an inversion whereby the 'lower' term is elevated above the 'higher'. We have already seen this in 'The Decay of Lying' where the bogus is elevated above the real. However, deconstruction needs to go further – to dissolve the binary opposition itself, not simply to invert it (otherwise one power-structure is simply replaced by another). Wilde does this in his collapsing of the distinction between the natural and the cultural in *Dorian*

Gray. In 'The Critic as Artist' the same strategy is at work, as he unpicks the difference between artistic creation and art-criticism. The ominously-named Ernest begins by wondering aloud why artists cannot simply be left alone by critics, thus implying a neat distinction between the imagination, which he privileges, and analysis and self-consciousness, which he clearly does not. Gilbert's response is to deny this violent hierarchy, but – in a rhetorical reworking of Derridean procedure – begins by collapsing creation and criticism into each other: 'The antithesis between them is entirely arbitrary' (1020). The rhetorical force of his argument is to drive toward a climactic inversion: 'Criticism, being the purest form of personal impression, is in its way more creative than creation' (1027).[36] Nevertheless, the point of the argument is to show that what we expect to find on one side of any binary opposition will also turn up on the other:

> Criticism is itself an art. And just as creation implies the working of the critical faculty, and, indeed, without it cannot be said to exist at all, so criticism is really creative in the highest sense of the word. Criticism is, in fact, both creative and independent.

(1026)

As we have seen, in 'The Decay of Lying' Wilde deploys a similar paradox by both inverting and denying the relationship between Life and Art as the qualities we attribute exclusively to one turn out to be equally present in the other: Life imitates, Art creates. In Dorian Gray the paradox is even clearer: the picture ages, Dorian stays the same.

Gilbert's argument is shaped by a series of sliding identifications: all fine imaginative work is self-conscious and deliberate, self-consciousness and the critical spirit are one, therefore art and criticism are one and the same. The result of this is to define style in specific terms: there is no art without style, therefore style is self-conscious, deliberate, critical. It is form seen under certain conditions, performing specific functions. Gilbert says 'An age that has no criticism is either an age in which art is immobile, hieratic, and confined to the reproduction of formal types, or an age that possesses no art at all' (1021). Style, in other words, is dynamic, corrosive of hierarchies, order and power, formally innovative. And style is as important to contemporary practitioners of deconstruction as it was to Wilde: both as a subject of analysis and as a method of argumentation. Indeed, John Schad says that French poststructuralists consistently advertise their work as a 'tissue of metaphors' which asks to be read poetically. He cites Cixous as proudly confessing that she lets herself be carried off by the poetic word, Foucault saying that he never wrote anything but fictions, and Derrida's insistence that deconstruction is itself a literary text to be read like other literary texts.[37] Similarly, Christopher Norris claims of the Yale Deconstructionist Geoffrey Hartman that he 'makes a virtue and even a vocation of pushing his critical style to the very edge of self-indulgence'. This self-conscious 'overwriting' – an attempt to foreground the very artifice of critical language – embodies a fundamental dislike of the view of criticism as 'at best a humble handmaid to creative endeavour'.[38] 'The Critic as Artist' clearly associates this view with what Hartman calls the 'Arnoldian concordat': Matthew Arnold's insistence that the function of criticism is simply to see and describe the art-object as in itself it really is. For Gilbert, the 'independence' of criticism means that it must see the object as in itself it really is not: remaking it under new conditions. Once again, Pater is a clear influence here, with Gilbert using his refabrication of the Mona Lisa in 'critical' prose as an example of how criticism can restyle its apparent subject (1028). (In other words, true criticism should not be any more mimetic than true art.) Wilde, then, is clearly anticipating one of the central characteristics of postmodern culture: the determined 'cross-over' of criticism into literature, and of critics (such as Umberto Eco, John Barth, Julia Kristeva, David Lodge, Malcolm Bradbury, Terry Eagleton) into novelists and playwrights. In a sense, 'The Decay of Lying' and 'The Critic as Artist' are formal archetypes: their playful, semi-dramatic structures signalling the 'performed' and stylized nature of Wilde's ideas.

Of course, a criticism as obsessed with its own style as that of its apparent subject cannot be judged by conventional notions of fairness. As Gilbert says, with characteristic *hauteur*, 'It is only an auctioneer who can equally and impartially admire all schools of Art. No; fairness is not one of the qualities of the true critic' (1047). He, like Vivian, has clearly been reading his Baudelaire, who declared that criticism should be 'partial, passionate and political'.[39] What I want to argue is that Wilde's use of language – his stylization of English – lives up to this dictum as a self-consciously critical and political gambit. Rebecca West said in 1912, that, coming from Ireland, Wilde was probably used to hearing 'good, clean English' and that he and his *Yellow Book* followers 'set about imposing style on English literature.'[40] Wilde described his project in similar terms. In his lecture 'The Irish Poets of '48', which he gave in San Francisco in April 1882, he claimed that 'The Saxon took our lands from us and left them desolate – we took their language and added new beauties to it.'[41] From a postcolonial perspective, Wilde's predicament is that of a colonial subject operating within the discourses of his imperial masters. Other Irish playwrights have solved this problem in their own way. Synge, for instance, in his dramas of Irish rural life, attempts to 'unenglish' English, bending it to the rhythms and cadences of Irish to express his mocking denial of authority in all forms.[42] O'Casey follows a similar path in creating a dramatic dialogue which blends realism with a heightened, poetic fantasy. Wilde, on the other hand, 'outenglishes' English. His characters speak with a style, an elegance and an almost extra-territorial perfection which exploits English to its own destruction, to the point where it describes only a void: 'Miss Fairfax,' says Jack nervously in *The Importance of Being Earnest*, as his speech curls back around emptiness, 'ever since I met you I have admired you more than any girl . . . I have ever met since . . . I met you' (329). In a sense, Wilde's consciousness of his foreignness – his 'otherness' and 'difference' – informs his stylistic engagement with language. As an Anglo-Irishman he contrives to 'distance himself' within English, thus registering his paradoxical position in the colonial power-structure between England and Ireland. As a member of the Anglo-Irish Ascendancy, and an Irish Nationalist, Wilde is implicated in English domination yet contemptuous of it – a contradiction enacted in his precise deployment, and disarming, of the language itself. A modern parallel is helpful here, and can be found in the opening sentence of Julia Kristeva's *Séméotiké* (1969). She signals her own status as an alien working both in and on French in the following way: 'To work on language, to labour on the *materiality* of that which society regards as a means of contact and understanding, isn't that at one stroke to declare oneself a stranger to language?'[43]

Raman Selden has claimed that, whereas structuralism was heroic in its desire to master the world of man-made signs, deconstruction is comic and anti-heroic in its refusal to take such claims seriously.[44] It is a neat and useful distinction – shedding much light on Wilde's comic dismantling of the pretensions of discourse; but it does less than justice to the political implications of his subversive wit and style. Of course, poststructuralism – as the symptomatic postmodern critical practice – has frequently been criticized for its apparent lack of a political agenda: a lack which, from a Marxist perspective in particular, smacks of a willingness to acquiesce in the political status quo.[45] However, once again Wilde's example is instructive: the recognisably 'postmodern' manner of his theoretical essays – playful, pervasively ironic, self-advertising – is not inimical to, but stylishly constitutive of, a radical politics. In *The Soul of Man Under Socialism* the political implications of *Intentions* receive forceful and explicit, if characteristically paradoxical, articulation. Peter Ackroyd's ventriloquism has Wilde remarking of his involvement in Ruskin's ill-fated attempt to enlist his Oxford undergraduates in the communitarian project of building a road to the village of Ferry Hinksey: 'I learned so much about the body of man under socialism that afterwards I cared only to write about the soul'.[46] At the risk of sounding humourless – or, worse, **earnest** – it's not a bad joke, but it underestimates both Wilde and the essay.

Inevitably, style makes a crucial appearance in *The Soul of Man Under Socialism*. Wilde claims that in order to be popular

> the artist would have to do violence to his temperament, would have to write not for the artistic joy of writing, but for the amusement of half-educated people, and so would have to suppress his individualism, forget his culture, annihilate his style, and surrender everything that is valuable in him.

(1091)

The statement is worth unpacking because it is more than simply a declaration of the superiority of the artist's to popular taste, and of the need – already insisted upon in 'The Decay of Lying' – for the artist to teach his or her public how to see. Wilde again carefully establishes his position by collapsing apparent opposites. The artist's temperament – or 'nature' – is the same as his 'culture', and his characteristic 'style' (conventionally associated with surfaces, with performance, manner, artifice, decoration) is identified with 'everything that is valuable in him'. In other words, Wilde is again deconstructing differences: between external and internal, between surface and depth, between the authentic and the contrived, between the essential and the inessential.

So crucial is the notion of style to Wilde's theoretical conjunction of aesthetics and politics that an alternative title for the essay might be 'The Style of Man Under Socialism'. 'Art,' Wilde declares, 'is the most intense mood of Individualism that the world has known' (1090). What *The Soul of Man* establishes is that Wilde is arguing for a certain style of individualism. He distinguishes between the individualism 'generated under conditions of private property', which is 'not always, or even as a rule, of a fine or wonderful type' (1081) and that individualism which is a form of art (and hence stylish – because, as we know, where there is no style there is no art). This stylish individualism is 'a disturbing and disintegrating force. Therein lies its immense value. For what it seeks to disturb is monotony of type, slavery of custom, tyranny of habit, and the reduction of man to the level of a machine' (1091). Again, style is defined implicitly in terms of the functions it performs. Wilde is restating the subversive potential of style outlined by Gilbert in 'The Critic as Artist', with its rejection of uncritical and styleless art which is 'immobile, hieratic, and confined to the reproduction of formal types'. For Wilde, style is disturbing, disintegrating and dangerous: radically subversive of ways of seeing and saying, and of those political structures they sustain. Wilde condemns 'unhealthy' art whose style is 'obvious, old-fashioned, and common' and whose subject 'is deliberately chosen, not because the artist has any pleasure in it, but because he thinks that the public will pay him for it' (1093–94). Here is another set of sliding identifications, with Wilde equating style with a Barthesian *jouissance*, with the writerly pleasures of a text which disturbs the reader's easy assumptions. Style, furthermore, is that which prevents art from becoming merely a commodity, bought and sold in the capitalist market-place. It is, for Wilde, radically incompatible with bourgeois culture, with the middle-class reading public and its addiction to the novel: 'no artist expects grace from the vulgar mind, or style from the suburban intellect' (1093).

For Wilde, the abolition of private property, marriage, the family, and of poverty will result in a utopian society in which – on socialist lines – the state withers away, allowing everyone to become an artist, relieved of the 'sordid necessity of living for others' (1079). The role of art in bringing about this revolution is vital: artists are types of the political agitator. Wilde recognizes the importance of ideology and the 'false consciousness' which allows the poor to accept their lot: 'no class is ever really conscious of its own suffering. They have to be told of it by other people, and they often entirely disbelieve them' (1082). Style thus performs an ideological function; it remakes consciousness, laying bare the power structures and exploitative nature of a society which rests precariously on the acquiescence of the poor. Wilde is characteristically acute on the complicity of Christianity in the maintenance of capitalist ideology, offering consolation as it does to the 'virtuous poor'. He restyles Christ (along the lines suggested by Renan in his *The Life of Jesus*) as a revolutionary, a proto-socialist with the message ' "You should give up private property. It hinders you from realising your perfection" ' (1085). Wilde was undoubtedly influenced by George Bernard Shaw's fabian socialism in targeting Christianity in this way.[47] Furthermore, *The Soul of Man* may have been fed back into Shaw's preface to *Major Barbara* (1907) with its savage attack on 'Crosstianity' and the seven deadly virtues; Shaw certainly attempts a series of Wildean paradoxes in his championing of socialism, based on 'the universal regard for money' which he claims is 'the one hopeful fact in our civilization, the one sound spot in our social conscience'.[48]

Baudelaire – who appears in the essay as an example of the elite who have, under existing conditions, 'been able to realise their personality more or less completely' (1083) – is again a clear and strong influence. His defence of individualism involves condemning capitalist commerce as 'shameful' because conceived of as 'natural' and therefore somehow immutable and irresistible.[49] (However, as we shall see in the final chapter, Baudelaire's vehement anti-bourgeois stance issues in a reactionary politics which Wilde rejects.) Interestingly, *The Soul of Man* again deploys the idea of Nature subversively. Wilde uses explicitly organicist similes to describe the progress of society toward full individualism: 'It will be a marvellous thing – the true personality of man – when we see it. It will grow naturally, and simply, flower-like, or as a tree grows' (1084). The editors of his Oxford notebooks argue that Wilde believed in Spencerian evolutionary theory and in progress towards 'differentiation and specialization of function, toward more freedom and more individualism'.[50] In this context, then, the organicist comparisons seem self-consciously 'scientific' rather than romantic. Robbie Ross made a telling point in his preface to a 1912 reprint of *The Soul of Man*: 'It may interest some of the author's admirers to note that in this essay he acknowledges what in his previous writings he pretended to ignore – the potentialities of science'.[51] Indeed, Wilde appears to collapse the distinction between the artist and the scientist in a direct analogy: both challenge received notions, and the artist can no more strive to be popular than the scientist can worry about hurting the sensibilities of people who know nothing about science (1090). (In 'Pen, Pencil and Poison', Wilde draws another, and clearly related, comparison: 'neither art nor science knows anything of moral approval or disapproval' (1008).) The crux of the matter, though, is that Wilde recognizes the important part science must play in realizing his socialist utopia. The future he imagines is one in which machines will do all the dirty work. As John Wilson Foster has argued, it is misleading to credit Wilde with a simplistic rejection of science in favour of art; 'Through Hellenism, Wilde associated science not with pessimism or glum materialism but with optimism and progress'.[52] In effect, then, Wilde is enlisting Nature, and its scientific study, in the cause of art. *The Soul of Man* explicitly links Nature not with the given, the immutable and the irresistible, but with progress – with change. 'Under Individualism', he claims, 'people will be quite natural and absolutely unselfish' (1101). It is a deliberately loaded phrase, redefining Nature not as 'red in tooth and claw' but as a style of being: one which all true artists must adopt. 'Pleasure,' he continues, 'is Nature's true test, her sign of approval' (1104). Pleasure, for the artist, is the pleasure of the new, the critical, the stylish and the subversive; it is to be found in the fissures art opens up in the 'natural' state of affairs. To return to Lawrence Buell: in *The Soul of Man*, Nature is metamorphosed not from possibility into fate, but from fate into potential.

Regenia Gagnier has argued that one of Wilde's major aims in *The Soul of Man* is to rescue words from the stylistic distortions of journalism, and to return them to their genuine, authentic meanings.[53] This is to take at face value the rhetorical flourish with which Wilde condemns authority in all forms; the authority of government, of public taste, of the 'classics', of journalism: 'It has been pointed out that one of the results of the extraordinary tyranny of authority is that words are absolutely distorted from their proper and simple meaning, and are used to express the obverse of their right signification' (1101). Wilde deploys the notions of 'simple meaning' and 'right signification' with tactical acumen, to drive home the polemical force of his attack on journalism. However, as we have seen, the larger strategy of the essay is to complicate meaning rather than to simplify it: to work on the materiality of language by shaking words free of the significations they have become bound to by the operations of ideology. His redefinition of the meanings of 'immoral', 'unintelligible', 'exotic', 'unhealthy', 'morbid' – the jargon of journalistic art criticism – is not so much an attempt to stabilize the processes of signification, as to appropriate them: to seize the means of definition and dissemination. That the essay has an immediate and specific polemical purpose in attacking journalism is similarly claimed by Owen Dudley Edwards. For him, *The Soul of Man* is as clearly evidence of Wilde's Irish nationalism as it is of his socialism: it is a 'furious denunciation of the British press and its destruction of Parnell'.[54] Parnell is the central absent presence in the argument, according to Dudley Edwards, and Wilde's failure to mention him by name was not a matter of deliberate concealment: 'he simply seems to have been in so white a heat that he failed to allow for a life for his essay beyond the date of its magazine.'[55] (The essay was originally published in the *Fortnightly Review* in February 1891.) Nevertheless, it is, according to Dudley Edwards, obviously the topical example of the leader of the Irish Home Rulers being publicly destroyed by a divorce case which lies behind Wilde's condemnation of the way 'serious, earnest, thoughtful' journalists nail their ears to the keyhole and 'drag before the eyes of the public some incident in the private life of a statesman, of a man who is a leader of political thought as he is a creator of political force, and invite the public to discuss the incident, to exercise authority in the matter' (1095). (There is no need here to reinforce the degree to which Wilde anticipates criticism of contemporary tabloid journalism; suffice it to say that his wry comments on the very different French attitude to the sex lives of politicians, has a more than familiar ring.) Dudley Edwards is right to point out this specific and urgent context because it reminds us that we cannot simply dismiss the socialism of *The Soul of Man* as abstract and wilfully impracticable; it is intimately connected with a larger radical agenda which embraces Wilde's nationalism and his feminism. In addition to Baudelaire, Shaw and Renan, Wilde draws heavily upon William Morris, the Taoist philosophy of self-culture, and European Anarchist thinkers such as Kropotkin; but we should not let the characteristic eclecticism of the essay detract from the secure and sophisticated theoretical underpinnings of that radicalism.[56]

Nevertheless, Wilde's political sympathies have always evinced a sceptical response. Frank Harris is a case in point. For him *Vera, or the Nihilists* – which folded after a week's run in New York in 1883 – was a piece of characteristic opportunism. He says Wilde 'seized occasion by the forelock' in order to exploit the topicality of revolutionary violence in Russia, coming up with a drama 'impregnated with popular English liberal sentiment.' (In reality, Vera was an accidental victim of that topicality. The London production, planned for 1881, had to be cancelled because of the assassinations of Tsar Alexander II and President Garfield.) Harris insists that Wilde's republicanism was not even skin-deep, that his political beliefs and prejudices were those of the English governing class 'and were all in favour of individual freedom, or anarchy under the protection of the policeman'.[57] (It may be worth noting that this tells us as much about Harris's opportunism as Wilde's: he managed to crush his doubts about the sincerity of Wilde's politics long enough to publish *The Soul of Man* in his *Fortnightly Review*.) Recent scholarship, though, has challenged Harris's judgement. Sos Eltis, for instance, has usefully documented Wilde's personal contact with the world of the émigré radicals and anarchists in the London of the 1880s and 1890s: the world he satirized as radical chic in *Lord Arthur Savile's Crime*. He tried to organize a petition in support of the Chicago Anarchists in 1886, was a friend of S.M. Stepnyak, who had assassinated the chief of the Russian secret police, and stood bail for the young John Barlas, who signalled his anarchism by firing a pistol outside the Houses of Parliament in 1891.[58] He was also personally acquainted with a number of well-known members of the French artistic avant-garde who were prominent in revolutionary and anarchist politics: such as Félix Fénéon and Adolphe Retté. Eltis also emphasizes the seriousness of Wilde's feminism, claiming that he was a consistent champion of women's rights and supported all the primary demands of late nineteenth-century feminism – in particular the campaigns for women's suffrage and greater access to higher education.[59] Central to this claim is Wilde's editorship of *Woman's World*. Eltis describes how he transformed the magazine when he took it over in 1887, signalling his 'womanly' rather than 'feminine' agenda by changing the name from *Lady's World*. As editor Wilde introduced a 'high intellectual content' and 'radical tone', dropping articles on 'Pastimes for Ladies' and giving space instead to those arguing for women's right to equality of treatment with men and to a greater role in public and political life.[60] Eltis insists that the brevity of Wilde's tenure as editor – he quickly tired of the day-to-day routine of running the magazine – should not detract from his commitment to the cause.[61]

The Soul of Man was published in the same issue of the *Fortnightly Review* as 'The Celt in English Art' by the influential anthropologist, Darwinist, essayist and novelist Grant Allen. Drawing, like Wilde in his treatment of Christ, on Renan, Allen argued that the conquered Celts would eventually overturn English dominance and emerge as political as well as cultural leaders. He regarded the 'great and victorious aesthetic movement' as part of 'the general racial, political, and social return-wave', a Celtic reflux which would result in the triumph of Celtic ideals: 'imagination, fancy, decorative skill, artistic handicraft; free land, free speech, human equality, human brotherhood.' Allen emphasized what he saw as the connection between 'the decorative revival and the Celtic upheaval of radicalism and socialism', and pointed to William Morris and Wilde as exemplars of this aesthetico-political project.[62] We need not dwell on Allen's belief in the racial origins of aestheticism, or accept the view of some commentators that, because Wilde shared the pages of the *Fortnightly Review* with Allen, we can assume he shared the latter's belief in the desirability of eugenics.[63] What is crucial is Allen's intertwining of radicalism, aestheticism and socialism in the name of Celticism. As we have already seen, Celticism and Irishness were not for Wilde essentialist notions legitimating forms of authenticity but floating signifiers he could appropriate for his own tactical and strategic purposes: principally to define his own oppositional stance, his 'otherness', his rejection of authority. What I want to concentrate on now is not the degree to which Wilde's political statements can be seen as 'sincere' or otherwise (trying to distinguish between style and substance, an opposition Wilde is at pains to deny) but the consistency with which his politically charged theories inform his aesthetic practice. To do this I shall return to the centrality of style.

REFERENCES

[1] Ellmann, *Oscar Wilde*: xiv.

[2] Terry Eagleton, *Heathcliff and the Great Hunger: Studies in Irish Culture*, Verso, London, 1995: 334.

[3] Lawrence Buell, *The Environmental Imagination: Thoreau, Nature Writing and the Formation of American Culture*, Harvard University Press, Cambridge, Mass., 1995: 88.

[4] A related point is made by Peter Nicholls, who argues that, in its persistent ghosting of modernism – and, indeed, postmodernism – Wildean 'Decadence' should be seen 'more as a mode than an epoch, more as a sort of limit-case of modern writing, than as the terminal point of an exhausted tradition.' See 'A Dying Fall?', in *Decadence and Danger*, ed. Hill: 24.

[5] Charles Baudelaire, *Art in Paris 1845–1862*, ed. and trans. Jonathan Mayne, Clarendon Press, Oxford, 1981: 154, 156.

[6] There are distinct echoes of Poe here. In his 1849 essay 'The Veil of the Soul' he claimed that 'The mere imitation, however accurate, of what is in nature, entitles no man to the sacred name of "Artist".' He then goes on to prefigure Wilde's 'cultivated blindness': 'We can, at any time, double the true beauty of an actual landscape by half-closing our eyes as we look at it.' In David Galloway, ed., *Edgar Allan Poe: Selected Writings*, Penguin, Harmondsworth, 1967: 498.

[7] In Ellmann, ed., *The Artist as Critic*: 14.

[8] *The Artist as Critic*: 17.

[9] Harold Bloom, ed., *Selected Writings of Walter Pater*, Signet, New York, 1974: 25.

[10] Baudelaire, *Art in Paris*: 13.

[11] Poe, *Selected Writings*: 482.

[12] Walter Benjamin, *Charles Baudelaire; A Lyric Poet in the Era of High Capitalism*, trans. Harry Zohn, New Left Books, London, 1973: 82.

[13] *Selected Letters*: 50.

[14] Bloom, ed., *Selected Writings of Walter Pater*: viii.

[15] *Selected Writings of Walter Pater*: 18, 19.

[16] Geoffrey Monsman, *Walter Pater*, G.K.Hall, Boston, 1977: 29.

[17] See Emile Zola, 'The Experimental Novel and Other Essays' in *Dramatic Theory and Criticism: Greeks to Grotowski,* ed., Bernard Dukore, Holt, Rinehart and Winston, London, 1974: 705.

[18] Lawrence Danson, 'Wilde as Critic and Theorist' in Raby, ed., *The Cambridge Companion*: 82.

[19] Eagleton, *Heathcliff and the Great Hunger*: 334.

[20] *Baudelaire; Selected Writings on Art and the Artist*, trans. P. Charvet, Cambridge University Press, Cambridge, 1972: 391.

[21] Poe, *Selected Writings*: 415–16.

[22] Ellmann, ed., *The Artist as Critic*: 17.

[23] Benjamin, *Charles Baudelaire*: 37.

[24] See Wolf Von Eckhardt, Sander L. Gilman and J. Edward Chamberlin, *Oscar Wilde's London*, Anchor Press, New York, 1987: 34.

[25] *Selected Letters*: 41.

[26] *Selected Writings of Walter Pater*: 60.

[27] Baudelaire, *Intimate Journals*, trans. Christopher Isherwood, City Lights, San Francisco, 1983: 31.

[28] Baudelaire, *Art in Paris*: 156.

[29] See Samuel Beckett, *Proust and Three Dialogues with Georges Duthuit*, Calder, London, 1965.

[30] Curiously, George Woodcock compared these opening paragraphs unfavourably with similar 'descriptive' passages in Pater's *Marius The Epicurean*. He called it 'a particularly slipshod piece of prose which shows Wilde at his worst'. *The Paradox of Oscar Wilde*: 49.

[31] Buell, *The Environmental Imagination*: 111.

[32] Baudelaire, *Art in Paris*: 13.

[33] For a discussion of contemporary eco-criticism, and some of the political fissures and tensions which define it, see Richard Kerridge and Neil Sammells, eds, *Writing the Environment*, Zed Books, London, 1997.

[34] Max Müller, *Lectures on the Science of Language* (1868), quoted in Philip E. Smith II and Michael S. Helfand, eds, *Oscar Wilde's Oxford Notebooks: A Portrait of a Mind in the Making*, Oxford University Press, Oxford, 1989: 9.

[35] Wilde is dismissive of Müller, for instance, in 'The Truth of Masks', when he says that 'archaeology is only really delightful when transfused into some form of art.

I have no desire to underrate the services of laborious scholars, but I feel that the use Keats made of Lemprière's dictionary is of far more value to us than Professor Max Müller's treatment of the same mythology as a disease of language' (1068).

[36] Baudelaire also explicitly emphasizes the creative dimension to criticism, claiming that 'the best account of a picture may well be a sonnet or an elegy.' *Art in Paris*: 44.

[37] See John Schad, *Victorians in Theory: from Derrida to Browning*, Manchester University Press, Manchester, 1999: 2–3.

[38] Christopher Norris, *Deconstruction: Theory and Practice*, Methuen, London, 1982: 87.

[39] *Art in Paris*: 44.

[40] Rebecca West, 'English Literature, 1880–1895' in *The Young Rebecca: Writings of Rebecca West 1911–1917*, ed. Jane Marcus, Virago, London, 1983: 51. I am grateful to Terry Rodgers for pointing me to these comments.

[41] Quoted in Montgomery Hyde, *Oscar Wilde*: 85.

[42] See Seamus Deane, *A Short History of Irish Literature*, Hutchinson, London, 1986: 149–54.

[43] Quoted in Toril Moi, *Sexual/Textual Politics*, Methuen, London, 1985: 150.

[44] Raman Selden, *A Reader's Guide to Contemporary Literary Theory*, Harvester, Brighton, 1985: 72.

[45] See, for instance, Christopher Norris, *What's Wrong with Postmodernism: Critical Theory and the Ends of Philosophy*, Harvester, Brighton, 1991; Alex Callinicos, *Against Postmodernism: A Marxist Critique*, Polity Press, Cambridge, 1989; Fredric Jameson, 'The Politics of Theory: ideological positions in the postmodern debate' in David Lodge, ed., *Modern Criticism and Theory: A Reader*, Longman, London, 1988: 373–83; Terry Eagleton, 'Capitalism, Modernism and Postmodernism', *Modern Criticism and Theory*: 385–398. For an attempt at a rapprochement between poststructuralism and radical politics, see Catherine Belsey, 'Literature, History, Politics', *Modern Criticism and Theory*: 400–10.

[46] Peter Ackroyd, *The Last Testament of Oscar Wilde*, Abacus, London, 1984: 34.

[47] Ellmann says that Wilde was 'probably stimulated' by a lecture by Shaw (*Oscar Wilde*: 328), while Lawrence Danson suggests that Wilde's decision to write on socialism was somewhat pragmatically influenced by the success of *Fabian Essays* – to which Shaw had contributed – in 1890 ('Wilde as critic and theorist': 93). Ellmann no doubt has in mind Shaw's contribution to a series of Fabian Society lectures on 'Socialism in Contemporary Literature' in the summer of 1890. The lecture was later expanded and published as *The Quintessence of Ibsenism* (1891).

[48] George Bernard Shaw, *Major Barbara*, Penguin, Harmondsworth, 1945: 21.

[49] See, for instance, *Intimate Journals*: 89–95.

[50] Smith and Helfand, *The Oxford Notebooks*: 70.

[51] *The Soul of Man Under Socialism*, Arthur L. Humphreys, London, 1912: viii. Ross attempts his own stylistic homage to this aspect of Wilde by using a scientific analogy; '"The Soul of Man", like its author, has many facts, and illustrates the well-known principle that the angle of incident is equal to the angle of reflexion' (x).

[52] John Wilson Foster, 'Against Nature? Science and Oscar Wilde' in MacCormack, ed., *Wilde the Irishman*: 113–26.

[53] Regenia Gagnier, *Idylls of the Marketplace: Oscar Wilde and the Victorian Public*, Scolar Press, Aldershot, 1987: 29–30.

[54] Owen Dudley Edwards, 'Oscar Wilde: the Soul of Man under Hibernicism': 11.

[55] 'The Soul of Man under Hibernicism': 11.

[56] Interestingly, George Woodcock, one of the first critics really to take Wilde's politics seriously, emphasized his 'anarchism' at the expense of his nationalism: 'Oscar was never a very outspoken or extreme Irish Nationalist. His ideas and tastes were too cosmopolitan to be bounded by any parochial creed.' *The Paradox of Oscar Wilde*: 27.

[57] Frank Harris, *Oscar Wilde*: 52, 66. Harris's memoir was first published in 1938.

[58] See Eltis, *Revising Wilde*: 17–18.

[59] *Revising Wilde*: 7.

[60] *Revising Wilde*: 6–13.

[61] Others have argued that Wilde's actual contribution to feminism was, at best, equivocal. Sally Ledger, for example, describes his editorial policy at *Woman's World* as self-contradictory, though she admits, rather grudgingly, that he did have 'one or two feminist credentials'. For Ledger, Wilde's downfall had a damaging effect on the New Woman because of the moral and political rearguard action which followed the Wilde trials: decadence and feminism being closely associated in the public mind. Ledger, though, is sympathetic enough to admit that Wilde was 'a lot more generous to the feminist movement than the feminist movement was to him.' See Sally Ledger, 'Oscar Wilde and the "Daughters of Decadence"', Hill, ed., *Decadence and Danger*: 109–118.

[62] Grant Allen, 'The Celt in English Art', *Fortnightly Review*, 1 February 1891: 267–77.

[63] See Smith and Helfand, *Oscar Wilde's Oxford Notebooks*: 80–6.

3
THEORY INTO PRACTICE:
DORIAN GRAY AND SALOME

Susan Sontag's 1964 essay 'Notes on Camp' and its companion 'On Style' – published a year later – remain among the best brief introductions to Wilde's work. For Sontag, Camp is a precise mode of aestheticism, one which sees the world 'not in terms of beauty, but in terms of the degree of artifice, of stylization'. While she says that, ultimately, Camp is not the most satisfying kind of art and regards it as apolitical, she nevertheless mounts an acute and staunch defence of its frivolousness, its theatricality and its resolute undermining of habitually ethical valuations of art and people: 'Camp is a solvent of morality. It neutralizes moral indignation, sponsors playfulness'.[1] Central to this defence is her refusal of the 'violent hierarchy' of the aesthetic and the ethical. She says in 'On Style' that the problem of art versus morality is a pseudo-problem: 'The distinction itself is a trap; its continued plausibility rests on not putting the ethical into question, but only the aesthetic'.[2] Sontag traces this distinction back to Plato, and in denying it she is aware that she is presenting an oblique challenge to some of the basic metaphysical assumptions of Western thought. Wilde's defence of *The Picture of Dorian Gray* – that 'tale spawned from the leprous literature of the French Décadents'[3] – similarly deconstructs the opposition between ethics and aesthetics, is entirely consistent with his theoretical construction of style as the dominant aesthetic category, and has radical implications for the ways we read his novel.

Responding to an attack on *Dorian Gray*, in a letter to the editor of the *St James's Gazette* on 25 June 1890, Wilde declared his inability to understand how a work of art could be criticized from a moral standpoint: 'the sphere of art and the sphere of ethics are absolutely distinct and separate'.[4] This echoes the famous art-for-art's sake doctrine of Gautier's preface to *Mademoiselle de Maupin* (1836) and Baudelaire on the subject of *Les Fleurs du Mal* (1857): 'I have never thought of literature and the arts as having any aim other than disconnected with morality, and [. . .] the beauty of the idea and the style are enough for me.'[5] It also anticipates the Paterese of the preface Wilde added to *Dorian Gray* when it was issued in extended, volume-form in 1891 (having first appeared in *Lippincott's Monthly* the

previous year); it is in his preface that we find the famous claims that
'All Art is quite useless' and that 'There is no such thing as a moral or an
immoral book. Books are well written, or badly written. That is all' (17).
Wilde followed up his opening salvo the following day in another letter to
the same magazine, noting that 'Good people belonging as they do to the
normal, and so commonplace, type, are artistically uninteresting. Bad people are, from the point of view of art, fascinating studies. They represent
colour, variety and strangeness. Good people exasperate one's reason; bad
people stir one's imagination'.[6] He compounds this resolutely aesthetic
approach by turning the tables on his critics with great dexterity: 'The poor
public, hearing from an authority so high as your own, that this is a wicked
book that should be coerced and suppressed by a Tory government, will, no
doubt, rush to it and read it'. However, he continues with an unexpected
twist by claiming that readers in search of forbidden thrills will be dis-
appointed: 'But, alas! They will find that it is a story with a moral. And the
moral is this; All excess, as well as all renunciation, brings its own punishment'.[7] He goes on to explain how the Dorian–Lord Henry–Basil triangle
illustrates this and ends with another apparent *volte face*: 'Is this an artistic
error? I fear it is. It is the only error in the book.'[8] Wilde's tactics are deliberately puzzling and apparently self-contradictory. He begins by denying
the applicability of ethical judgements to an aesthetic object or experience,
then claims that his own book has a moral,[9] defines that in self-cancelling
terms by collapsing the difference between excess and renunciation (they
amount, in the end, to the same thing), then returns to his original position
by claiming that the presence of a moral, however unconventional, is an
aesthetic flaw because it brings together separate spheres.

Four days later, in a letter to the *Daily Chronicle*, Wilde explained that in
taking over the Faustian myth he had, from an aesthetic point of view, failed
to keep the moral 'in its proper secondary place'.[10] (In this respect, the
preface might be seen as a self-conscious attempt to redress the balance, to
act as an 'amoral' corrective to the 'moral' shape of the borrowed narrative
that follows. In effect, Wilde sets up a deconstructive dynamic between the
preface and the narrative it purports to introduce: in so doing, he anticipates Derrida on the way prefaces subvert and deconstruct the authority of
the 'text'.[11]) However, the letter continues, 'this moral is so far artistically
and deliberately suppressed that it does not enunciate its law as a general
principle, but realises itself purely in the lives of individuals, and so becomes
simply a dramatic element in a work of art, and not the object of the work of
art itself.'[12] In effect, Wilde is aestheticizing – stylizing – the 'moral content'
of his narrative. In an incisive subversion of accepted categories, Wilde defines
the moral content of *Dorian Gray* as an element of its aesthetic design, 'a
dramatic element in a work of art'. This refusal of antithesis is behind the

loaded phrasing of another letter, this time to the *Scots Observer* (13 August 1890): 'You ask me, Sir, why I should care to have the ethical beauty of my story recognised. I answer, simply because it exists, because the thing is there'.[13] There we have it: **ethical beauty**.

'All art,' Wilde announces in the preface to *Dorian Gray*, 'is at once surface and symbol. Those who go beneath the surface do so at their peril. Those who read the symbol do so at their peril' (17). This statement is a characteristic denial of the surface-depth model by which meaning is located **inside** the text and the narrative can be authenticated by returning it to an originary 'moral': reading as cracking the code. Conrad's *Heart of Darkness* (1902) provides an instructive parallel here. A comparison is drawn between the yarns of sailors which have a 'direct simplicity, the whole meaning of which lies within the shell of a cracked nut' and the technique of the narrator, Marlowe, in telling Kurtz's story: 'to him the meaning of an episode was not inside like a kernel, but outside, enveloping the tale which brought it out only as a glow brings out a haze'.[14] Wilde's 'moral' is not the kernel to the nut; it is defined not as the shaping presence, but as the presence of shape, of style. In effect, Dorian's 'come-uppance' – shaped as he is by the Faustian narrative – provides readers with a sense of closure that is ethically beautiful and beautifully ethical: it invokes the satisfactions of design. Lord Henry articulates this belief in the primacy of aesthetic design when he announces that 'I should like to write a novel certainly; a novel that would be as lovely as a Persian carpet, and as unreal' (45). Henry James was no great admirer of Wilde (referring to him as 'an unclean beast', a 'fatuous fool' and a 'tenth-rate cad'[15]), but Lord Henry's comparison is directly echoed in his short story, 'The Figure in the Carpet', when the meaning of a narrative is described not as hidden and interior but as something 'in the primal plan, something like a complex figure in a Persian carpet.'[16] As Stephen Arata has persuasively argued, Wilde's defence of his novel is a challenge to conventional ways of reading, which are premised, we might add, on a 'direct simplicity' Wilde so elegantly and insistently denies. Arata further claims that Edward Carson's cross-examination of Wilde shows these opposed ways of reading in direct and fateful conflict. *Dorian Gray* was adduced as evidence by Carson of Wilde's 'deviance' and, hence, of the accuracy of Queensberry's claim that in 'posing as a somdomite' (*sic*) he was merely and theatrically declaring the truth about himself. The novel could be read with 'direct simplicity': the kernel in the nut was Wilde's criminal sexuality. 'Carson's common reader,' says Arata, 'knew that language was transparent; that a work of literature expressed the personality of its author; that fiction would be a vehicle of either good or evil depending on the nature of the influence it exercised.' As we have seen, Wilde spent a great deal of intellectual energy in trying to disarm these ideas but, Arata notes, 'in court his objections to such dreary (and, as it proved, dangerous) literal-mindedness were largely ineffectual'. Carson attempted to authenticate *Dorian Gray*, to crack it open and reveal the rotting kernel and, in so doing, to authenticate Wilde. Arata points to an intriguing parallel: *Lord Arthur Savile's Crime*, he says, parodies the kinds of reading Carson proposed. Lord Arthur is 'read' as a murderer by the palmist, and proceeds to try and construct himself accordingly, internalizing the processes by which self becomes subject: Carson read the signs and practised on Wilde 'a form of cheiromancy akin to Septimus Podgers's.' [17] For Wilde, however, *Dorian Gray* was an opportunity, not for self-authentication, but for self-dramatization and self-styling, in which he distributed himself across the narrative in a series of poses. If the novel were to express the personality of the author, it would emphasize not simplicity but multiplicity: 'I am so glad you like that strange many coloured book of mine: it contains much of me in it. Basil Hallward is what I think I am: Lord Henry what the world thinks me: Dorian what I would like to be – in other ages, perhaps.' [18]

What is clear is that Wilde, in his defence of the novel, is anticipating some crucial notions in contemporary, postmodern narrative theory. In the preface he attempts to disarm moralistic readings of *Dorian Gray* by shifting the onus of responsibility: 'Those who find ugly meanings in beautiful things are corrupt without being charming. This is a fault. Those who find beautiful meanings in beautiful things are the cultivated. For these there is hope' (17). In so doing, he foreshadows what Mark Currie sees as a poststructuralist shift away 'from the assumed transparency of the narratological analysis towards a recognition that the reading, however objective and scientific, constructed its object.' [19] Wilde appropriates and reframes the notion of mimesis to clinch his point: in this respect it is 'the spectator [reader], and not life, that art really mirrors' (17). Similarly, Wilde's comments on the process of self-styling (by which, as Lord Henry, Basil and Dorian, he becomes simultaneously Dandy, Dowdy and Debauchee), deconstruct essentialist notions of identity, substituting instead the idea that, as Currie puts it, 'identity is not within us because it exists only as a narrative.' By this Currie means that we learn to 'self-narrate' from the outside (rather than discover ourselves as the kernel in the nut); through other stories we learn to tell the story of ourselves. [20] What Wilde presents us with then, is a narrative of radical indeterminacy, which attempts to short-circuit readings which are exclusively moralistic and those which, conversely, ignore the importance of morality to the complexity of its aesthetic design.

Wilde's short-story, 'The Portrait of Mr W.H.', written during 1887 and published the following year in *Blackwood's* is something of a dry-run for *Dorian Gray* insofar as it explores the erotics of influence between men: the narrator; the older Erskine; and Cyril Graham who concocts the theory that

Shakespeare's sonnets were inspired by and dedicated to a beautiful young boy-actor, Willie Hughes. The story is also a parody of what we might call the hermeneutics of authenticity. Cyril develops an obsession with tracing the sonnets back to their originary meaning (Shakespeare's love for the 'somewhat effeminate' seventeen year-old), and produces a fake portrait of Hughes in order to provide Erskine with the independent evidence that he existed: 'Here was an authentic portrait of Mr W.H. with his hand resting on the dedicatory page of the Sonnets' (1159). The narrator becomes caught up in this obsession and finally convinces Erskine of its validity at the very point he stops believing in it himself. Graham shoots himself as a 'sacrifice to the secret of the Sonnets' (1160) and Erskine seeks to prove his own new-found faith in the theory by committing suicide himself. In fact, he is simply matching Cyril Graham's forgery with one of his own: he dies of consumption, not by his own hand. This reading of the sonnets constructs its own object (and fabricates its own evidence) in the relentless search for a kernel of meaning, and the fate of Graham and Erskine foreshadows that of Dorian and Salome: they seek self-authentication but find only self-extinction.

'The Portrait of Mr W.H.' is also notable for the way it combines this comic deconstruction of the hermeneutics of authenticity with an entirely sceptical attitude to the notion of the authentic, stable, homogeneous self. The obscure object of desire, Willie Hughes, turns out to be a forgery, his personality multifariously constructed by an erotically charged inventiveness. When the narrator finally writes his theory down, with all the assembled evidence, he finds he no longer believes it. This moment of doubt embraces his sense of who he is. 'Was there no permanence in personality?' he asks, 'Did things come and go through the brain, silently, swiftly, and without footprints, like shadows through a mirror? Were we at the mercy of such impressions as Art or Life chose to give us? It seemed to me to be so' (1196–7). Identity is thus seen in terms of surface, fluctuation, dispersal, rather than depth, stability and integration. The mirror-image anticipates those which Wilde uses to affirm Dorian's growing recognition of his polymorphous self as it is multiplied through sensation.

All this has great significance for the ways in which we 'read' Dorian. To go beneath the surface is to do so at one's peril. Dorian is Wilde's most thorough evocation of the elusive, multiform, inauthentic personality. A conventional reading of his character – and of Wilde's narrative – would see the portrait as registering the 'real', the authentic Dorian: the ugliness beneath the surface beauty, the index of his moral decline.[21] However, Dorian is described consistently in terms which deny the existence of authentic 'depths' beneath illusory surface. Basil Hallward insists that it is 'merely' Dorian's 'visible presence' which has had such a profound effect upon him and on his painting: 'he defines for me the lines of a fresh school, a school that is to have in it all the passion of the romantic spirit, all the perfection of the spirit that is Greek' (24). In effect, Dorian collapses together surface beauty and 'inner' character as 'visible presence' and 'personality' become one. 'His personality has suggested to me,' says Basil, 'an entirely new manner in art, an entirely new mode of style. I see things differently, I think of them differently. I can now recreate life in a way that was hidden from me before' (24). This is a crucial statement: Dorian is associated squarely with the renewing, subversive, revelatory possibilities of style. Indeed, he even transforms the 'natural' world for Basil, helping him to see its artistic possibilities: 'for the first time in my life I saw in the plain woodland the wonder I had looked for' (24). (As we have seen, for Wilde that means enculturing Nature, seeing the stylish 'green lacquer leaves' the narrator mentions moments later (26).) Dorian is himself a work of art: 'I see him in the curves of certain lines, in the loveliness and subtleties of certain colours,' says Basil. The point is not lost on Lord Henry, who, characteristically, turns it against Basil, with an elegant twist of the knife. 'Some day you will look at your friend,' he says 'and he will seem to you to be a little out of drawing, or you won't like his tone of colour, or something' (25). Dorian is created by Hallward's artistic skill and Lord Henry's theorizing ('To a large extent the lad was his own creation' (55)), which together deliberately bring him to the self-consciousness Wilde identifies with style.

When Dorian sees the portrait 'the sense of his own beauty came upon him like a revelation. He had not felt it before' (34). Surfaces encounter surfaces and the portrait becomes a mirror – as Arata would have it, a 'lacanian mirror',[22] and as Dorian describes it later a 'magical' mirror (88) – in which he 'recognised himself for the first time' (33). Thereafter Dorian maintains contradictory personalities, simultaneously: murderer, drug-addict, Prince Charming, the most desirable and fashionable man in London. (And, indeed, woman. He makes a stunning appearance in drag at a costume ball as Anne de Joyeuse.) After enlisting Alan Campbell to dispose of Hallward's body, Dorian is ushered into Lady Narborough's drawing-room by bowing servants, 'exquisitely dressed and wearing a large button-hole of Parma violets'. He wonders at his own calmness, and 'for a moment felt keenly the terrible pleasure of a double life' (134). Previously he had stared at the portraits of his ancestors in the 'gaunt cold picture-gallery of his country house' (112) and wondered at the characteristics he may have inherited from them, this sense of heredity as a determining factor in his personality being neatly cancelled by the self-styling at work in his choice of literary progenitors: 'one had ancestors in literature, as well as in one's own race, nearer perhaps in type and temperament, many of them, and certainly with an influence of which one was more absolutely conscious' (113).

Wilde says that Dorian is tormented throughout his life by an exagger-ated sense of conscience, and Arata points out that the portrait itself is seen only by Dorian and by Basil Hallward, 'the novel's principal spokesman for conventional morality.' In this respect, the 'grotesque stigmata' do not sig-nify Dorian's 'deviance' but rather 'they symbolize his conformity to bour-geois morality. In best Foucauldian fashion, Dorian is disciplined to an ideology that teaches him to read himself as criminal'.[23] By slashing the portrait with the knife that killed Basil, Dorian attempts to go beneath the surface – with fatal consequences. (Lord Henry had previously tried to defuse these ethical responses. When Dorian told him that he could not bear the thought of his soul becoming hideous, his mentor had seized upon the ambivalence of the phrase to cancel the ethical with the aesthetic: 'A very charming artistic basis for ethics, Dorian! I congratulate you on it!' (82).) Interestingly, Basil speaks about the portrait as if it might one day authenti-cate him, become evidence against him, just as *Dorian Gray* was to be turned against Wilde: 'every portrait that is painted with feeling is the portrait of the artist, not of the sitter. The sitter is merely the accident, the occasion. It is not he who is revealed by the painter; it is rather the painter who, on the coloured canvas, reveals himself. The reason I will not exhibit this picture is that I am afraid I have shown in it the secret of my soul' (21). Without wishing to sound as if I am trying to authenticate the novel by appealing to biography, it is hard not to note that Wilde came, in Reading Gaol, to read himself in much the same way as Dorian. In what is perhaps his most poignant letter, he petitioned the Home Secretary, Sir Matthew White Ridley, for his early release. Wilde pointed to Max Nordau's *Degeneration* in which he was adduced as an example of the artistic temperament and its proximity to madness; he attempts to excuse himself on the grounds that during the 'most brilliant years of his life' (referring to himself in the third person, as 'the petitioner', narrating himself, in effect, from the outside) he was suffer-ing from 'the most horrible form of erotomania.'[24] It is, he says, the fear of madness which now makes him plead for an end to his torment. Had Wilde really been disciplined to read himself as deviant, or is this another perform-ance for calculated effect, an attempt to deploy rather than subvert the language of power and authority? In truth, it hardly matters: the alternatives are equally painful and humiliating. It is in this letter, rather than in *De Profundis* (where he rallies himself by taking on new, histrionic roles), that, if he ever does, Wilde speaks from the depths.

In fact, it is precisely the complexity of Dorian's multiple personalities which so fascinates Lord Henry (this sense of multiplicity is reinforced by a plethora of classical allusions as Dorian is compared to Adonis, Narcissus, Antinous, Adrian). And style is the dominant category in Lord Henry's aesthetic, just as it is in Wilde's: 'It often happens that the real tragedies of life occur in such an inartistic manner that they hurt us by their crude violence, their absolute incoherence, their absurd lack of style' (84). He teaches Dorian to see things, and himself, with style: 'Suddenly we find that we are no longer the actors, but the spectators of the play. We watch ourselves, and the mere wonder of the spectacle enthrals us' (84). His function is not simply to act as a counterweight to Basil Hallward's ethical misgivings about the life Dorian is leading, but to emphasize repeatedly the potential for inauthenticity, for transforming oneself, and others, into a liberating theatrical spectacle: 'being natural is simply a pose, and the most irritating pose I know' (20). When he hears of Dorian's engagement to Sybil Vane, he reacts with characteristic insouciance, despite Basil's histrionic worries. While declaring that the drawback to marriage is that it makes one unselfish ('And unselfish people are colourless' (66)) he also acknowledges that there are certain temperaments which 'marriage makes more complex'. Such as Dorian 'retain their egotism, and add to it many other egos. They are forced to have more than one life. They become more highly organised, and to be highly organised is, I should fancy, the object of man's existence' (66). Sybil is of interest, both to Lord Henry and to Dorian, only insofar as her abilities as an actress allow her many roles and personalities. She is an object of desire because of her 'lack' of a 'real', stable, graspable identity. When Sybil attempts to authenticate herself through love the results are disastrous and foreshadow what happens to her Prince Charming. In some respect, *Dorian Gray* is a peculiarly Wildean parody of the nineteenth-century *Bildungsroman*: Dorian does not learn through experience who he is (like other literary 'orphans' before him, such as David Copperfield and Oliver Twist), rather he tries to act out a narrative of self-definition, but ends by living one of self-destruction. When he 'kills conscience',[25] as Wilde would have it, and attacks the portrait he is, in effect, trying to reduce multiplicity and complexity: to simplify the aesthetic sophistication and organisation of his own design, to return himself to monochrome.

However, it would be misleading to see Lord Henry as simply Wilde's spokesman, the unproblematic mouthpiece for an aesthetic credo which the novel sets out to put into fictive practice. Though Lord Henry is – in Wilde's words – 'an excellent corrective of the tedious ideal shadowed forth in the semi-theological novels of our age',[26] Wilde is also clear that he and Basil cancel each other out, and that self-cancelling is part of the narrative's indeterminacy. Basil becomes too involved with Dorian and pays the penalty; Lord Henry knows little of the life Dorian leads at his prompting and is a strangely attenuated hedonist, insofar as his pleasure-seeking is a matter of abstraction, verbalization and voyeurism, rather than action. Basil finds this somewhat exasperating: 'You never say a moral thing, and you never do a wrong thing. Your cynicism is simply a pose' (20). As Wilde puts it: 'Lord Henry seeks to be merely the spectator of life. He finds that those who reject the battle are more deeply wounded than those who take part in it.'[27] When Tom Stoppard transported Lord Henry as Lord Malquist to 1960s London in his novel *Lord Malquist and Mr Moon* (1966) he had him announce his intention to withdraw with style from the chaos, and proclaim a change in the heroic posture from the man of action to 'that of the Stylist, the spectator as hero, the man of inaction who would not dare roll up his sleeve for fear of creasing the cuffs'.[28] Stoppard's dandy resigns himself to his fate as a martyr to the cause of hereditary privilege and, disdaining to outlive his wealth, lives a life of elegant suicide: 'Let it be said of me,' he announces from his bath, 'that I was born appalled, lived disaffected, and died in the height of fashion'.[29] Style, for Malquist – and the phrase is as neatly descriptive of Lord Henry's languidly aristocratic posture – is 'an aesthetic inbred and disengaged'.[30] The crucial point is that although style is Lord Henry's dominant aesthetic category, unlike for Wilde it is Style as Withdrawal rather than Style as Engagement. For Pater, Lord Henry's personal philosophy was a travesty, a 'dainty' Epicureanism merely, which – ironically – amounted to a withdrawal from the complexity of experience and personality he appeared to value: 'A true Epicureanism aims at a complete though harmonious development of man's entire organism. To lose the moral sense therefore, for instance, the sense of sin and righteousness, as Mr Wilde's heroes are bent on doing as speedily, as completely as they can, is to lose, or lower, organisation, to become less complex, to pass from a higher to a lower degree of development.'[31] (In terms of its complex organization of the moralistic and the aesthetic, Wilde's narrative could therefore be seen as achieving the Epicureanism its protagonists fail to.) As a personal philosophy for the supersophisticated, Style as Withdrawal allows Lord Henry a protective shell – but Wilde is concerned to extend our notion of style so that it becomes a means of engaging with, rather than turning away from, the 'vulgar' whether manifest in artistic forms and genres, or political realities. That engagement is partly enacted through the agency of Camp.

Sontag locates Wilde in a particular historical moment. His career, she claims, exemplifies a transitional phase in the history of dandyism when the 'old-style dandy' who hated vulgarity is displaced by the connoisseur of Camp: 'The dandy held a perfumed handkerchief to his nostrils and was liable to swoon; the connoisseur of camp sniffs the stink and prides himself on his strong nerves.'[32] For Sontag – despite her misgivings about the political efficacy of Camp – Wilde's recognition of the equivalence of all objects and their claim to aesthetic notice displays a fundamentally 'democratic *esprit*'. (In the dock, Wilde declared himself indifferent to matters of social class, claiming a democratic impulse to his 'feasting with panthers' at the

Café Royal: the delight he took in transgressing the boundaries between
'high, respectable' and 'low, rent-boy' culture.) Dorian himself can be seen
to combine these two aspects of dandyism: the connoisseur's appreciation of
jewels, precious perfumes, embroideries, ecclesiastical vestments, etc. (ex-
haustively catalogued in Chapter 11); and the less 'refined' delight in theatrical kitsch and slumming in the drug-dens of the East End. Dorian – himself
all style – holds these objects and experiences in a certain way, invests them
with a certain style. Sontag explores this process of stylization most clearly
in her comments on the films of Jean-Luc Godard. I want to dwell on them
because they help us to understand Wilde's own relationship to genre, and
the way in which he finds an unlikely contemporary successor in Hollywood
wunderkind Quentin Tarantino – as is demonstrated in his notorious *Reservoir Dogs* (1992) and comedy of murderous manners *Pulp Fiction* (1995).

In effect, although Sontag does not herself draw the comparison, Godard
takes up where Wilde left off, bringing a discriminating and transforming
eye to the artefacts of 'popular culture': and it is this which further links
Wilde to Tarantino and to important elements of contemporary taste. She
places Godard in good company here, claiming for him a hypertrophy of
appetite for culture which he shares with Joyce, Stravinsky and Picasso.[33]
Godard's fondness for American kitsch (his redeployment of gangster-film
motifs in *Bande à Parte* (1964), for instance, or of comic-strip plotting in
Alphaville (1965)) parallels Wilde's own taste for popular theatrical forms:
in particular his use of the tired conventions of West-End farce in *The
Importance of Being Earnest*. (Kerry Powell, in *Wilde and the Theatre of the
1890s*, identifies many of the specific plays Wilde was indebted to, both in
The Importance and the 'society comedies' but makes the mistake of seeing
Wilde as a prisoner of these conventions and formulae, and not as consciously reworking them to deliberate effect.[34]) Wilde outlined this tactic –
the 'canonisation of the junior branch' as Russian Formalists would have it
– in *The Soul of Man* when he observed that 'delightful work may be produced under burlesque and farcical conditions, and in work of this kind the
artist in England is allowed very great freedom' (1091). Sontag argues that
the self-consciousness of Godard's work 'constitutes a formidable medita-
tion on the *possibilities* of cinema'; it is metacinema and, I suggest, demonstrates Wilde's central claim in 'The Critic as Artist' that criticism is a creative
act. 'I'm still as much of a critic as I ever was during the time of *Cahiers du
Cinema*', claimed Godard, referring to his journalism of the late 1950s. 'The
only difference is that instead of writing criticism, I now film it.'[35]

Godard's films are, according to Sontag, not so much exercizes in style as
in **stylization**. Stylization 'reflects an ambivalence (affection contradicted by
contempt, obsession contradicted by irony) toward the subject matter. This
ambivalence is handled by maintaining, through the rhetorical overlay that

is stylization, a special distance from the subject.'[36] This 'special distance from the subject' is, in my view, entirely characteristic of Wilde, determining the way he handles morality and melodrama, politics and passion: it is what allows morality to be an element of the dramatic design, rather than the object, of *Dorian Gray*. Tarantino is a self-confessed admirer of Godard (the name of his production company, A Band Apart, is a covert acknowledgement of his debt to the French director) and recognizes in his own work a similar ambivalence and rhetorical overlay. Of both *Reservoir Dogs* and *Pulp Fiction* he says: 'I like the idea that I'm taking a genre and reinventing it, like Leone reinvented the whole Western genre.'[37] Such reinvention of genre is equivalent to what Wilde tried to do with Gothic fiction in *Dorian Gray*[38] and with Victorian melodrama and the French well-made play in the 'society comedies', but perhaps only fully achieved in *The Importance of Being Earnest*; it cannot be fulfilled by a simple, dismissive attitude to the models that are being redeployed. Tarantino wants to 'subvert the Hollywood staples, but with respect, not in a superior or pastichey way.'[39] He draws an instructive distinction between his own work and Stanley Kubrick's *The Shining*: 'I always felt that Kubrick felt he was above the horror genre, above giving the audience a real good scare. Now Godard, I always thought, was at his most engaging when he worked within a genre and ran with it the whole way to the moon. *Breathless* is a good example.'[40] The works of Wilde and Tarantino are camp, not 'campy'; they preserve a delicate balance between the arch and the innocent. Wilde parodies the well-used devices of Gothic fiction in 'The Canterville Ghost', but in *Dorian Gray* his tactic is somewhat different. His use of the Gothic is clearly part of his anti-naturalistic project, matching fictive practice to aesthetic theory. It is a self-conscious deployment of motifs, atmosphere, situations and figures from popular Gothic novels of the 1880s and 1890s by writers like Walter Herries Pollock, Edward J. Goodman and Elizabeth Lysaght, with their generic exploration of pictures, portraits and double-identities.[41] This knowing use of the popular Gothic sanctions his desire to write about the supersophisticated surfaces of urban life at his century's end (and modish notions of cultural and ethical decadence) without simply 'mirroring' them. The generally sensational atmosphere of the book is maintained by Wilde's lurid and frequently overwritten descriptions of Dorian's mounting terror in front of his portrait, and of London (in particular the East End and its denizens) as menacing and murderous. (Wilde confessed – probably with more of an eye to self-advertisement than self-criticism – that the novel was 'far too crowded with sensational incident'.[42]) The relationship between the portrait and its 'subject' provides a Gothic and supernatural twist to the central theoretical paradox of 'The Decay of Lying' (that art is more lifelike than nature – as Baudelaire said, 'A portrait! What could be simpler and more complicated, more obvious and more profound?'[43]). Wilde also uses it to dramatize the fluid relationship between signifier and multiform signifieds, the differing Dorians his novels presents us with. And he tries to give his readers a real good scare too.[44]

A crucial element of the stylization in Godard's films is his treatment of violence. The pervasive quality of Godard's work, claims Sontag, is its 'coolness': 'the films have a muted, detached relation to the grotesque and painful as well as to the seriously erotic. People are sometimes tortured and often die in Godard's films – but almost casually.'[45] Tarantino has clearly borrowed the casualness of the violence in his movies from the slick, postmodern, style-obsessed 'pulp' novels of Elmore Leonard,[46] whose *Rum Punch* (1992) he adapted for the screen as *Jackie Brown* (1997); and it is this 'coolness' rather than the explicitness of the violence which has won him such notoriety. Perhaps the best example is the scene in *Reservoir Dogs* in which Mr Blonde tortures a hostage cop with a razor-blade, gasoline and Stealer's Wheel. At the moment Mr Blonde slices off his victim's ear, Tarantino pans away to a ceiling-light. The hostage does not die until Nice Guy Eddie arrives and dispatches him with a revolver: Tarantino denying his audience the relief of a reaction-shot of either victim or witness. Such peremptory violence is a feature of *Pulp Fiction* too – as is Tarantino's emphasis on the sheer contingency of urban violence (the accidental, incidental killing and maiming of bystanders adds considerably to the body-count in both *Reservoir Dogs* and *Pulp Fiction*). Tarantino's defence of the violence in his films – which includes his attitude to the larger question of 'moral' content – makes intriguing reading, unconsciously echoing Wilde's own defence of *Dorian Gray*.

Tarantino claims that violence is just another colour for the artist to work with.[47] (A statement which is a direct echo of Wilde's to *The Scots Observer*, apropos of *Dorian Gray*: 'Virtue and wickedness are to [the artist] simply what the colours on his palette are to the painter'.[48]) Indeed, he could be described as applying with uncompromising literalness Wilde's insistence that bad people add variety, strangeness, colour: the gangsters of *Reservoir Dogs* are called Mr Orange, Mr White, Mr Pink, Mr Blonde, Mr Blue and Mr Brown (played by Tarantino himself). Similarly, Tarantino echoes the way Wilde turned the tables on his attackers by welcoming the prospect of censorship by a Tory government and the inevitable rush to read *Dorian Gray* this would excite. Tarantino is conscious of the same irony in the UK's refusal to grant his movie a licence for video release: 'I like that. It's done better in cinemas in Britain than anywhere else in the world, so the ban has been kinda cool in one way.'[49] Furthermore, Tarantino is as adept as Wilde when it comes to the subject of 'moral' content. 'I'm not trying to preach any kind of moral or get any kind of message across,' he claims, 'but for all the wildness that happens in my movies, I think they usually lead to moral conclusions.'[50] However, he conceives of the 'morality' of his movies in the same dramatic terms as Wilde does in respect of *Dorian Gray*. It realizes itself not at the level of general principle, but in the lives of individuals: 'I find what happens between Mr White and Mr Orange at the end of *Reservoir Dogs* very moving and profound in its morality and its human interaction.'[51] The violent, sacrificial denouement provides a dramatically and aesthetically satisfying conclusion to the movie's '12-gauge pump-action homo-erotic love-story.'[52] In the original screenplay of *Pulp Fiction*, supercool Jules Winnfield simply blows away Honey Bunny and Pumpkin as they attempt to hold up the coffee-shop: in the movie this ending is replaced by one in which Jules spares them, deciding to leave the gangster-life and walk the Earth like Caine in *Kung Fu*. This allows Tarantino to claim that '*Pulp Fiction* is ultimately a film about forgiveness and mercy, albeit in a hard and brutal world.'[53] (After all, *Pulp Fiction* does feature a motorbike – sorry, **chopper** – called Grace, so how could it be otherwise?) However, elsewhere Tarantino admits that his 'moralistic' conclusions are, in reality, shaped by the pressures of genre rather than the abstractions of what Wilde called 'general principle': 'In some ways,' he says, 'my films go by the old Hays code. You can do anything you want in the first 88 minutes so long as in the last two minutes there's some retribution for what the characters have done. I never set out to do that. I always thought if I wrote a heist film, I'd do one where they all got away. But it didn't quite work out that way.'[54] Tarantino is obliged by the demands of genre and aesthetics to provide a moralistic conclusion – working within audience expectations in order to stretch and extend them – just as Wilde's narrative needs to visit retributive justice upon Dorian Gray and his dedication to a life of pleasure-seeking.

Tarantino has been accused of applying 'style to sheer slaughter'[55] and in this respect his work may seem a long way from Wilde's drawing rooms. (Even if the voracious appetite of Tarantino's drug-dealers and killers for junk food like hamburgers and tacos is recognizably the same as Algy's 'callous' consumption of muffins and cucumber sandwiches.) In fact, Wilde's world is one of violent potential, a potential that is distanced, ironized, refracted through the stylistics of wit. (Except, tellingly, in *Dorian Gray* where the passages describing Dorian's murder of Basil and the disposal of the body show Wilde enjoying the over-heated conventions of Gothic fiction.) *Lord Arthur Savile's Crime* is perhaps the best case in point: his *fin-de-siècle* London is one in which international terrorists can be consulted on matters of domestic violence, poisoned bon-bons and dynamite-laden clocks are available at a price, and (as in the fate of Podgers) execution is summary and contingent. Lady Bracknell speaks prophetically of acts of violence in Grosvenor Square and enquires if, the fiction of Algy's double-life having

been 'exploded', Bunbury has been the victim of a revolutionary outrage.
The Importance of Being Earnest must, as Wilde says, 'go like a pistol shot'[56]
– but not just in terms of pace. A good production should drive towards a
climax in which the principals confront each other in an aristocratic version
of what Tarantino calls a 'mexican standoff': Lady Bracknell, Algy and Jack
hold pistols to each other's heads over the question of marriage. Wilde was
playing Russian Roulette for Lady Bracknell and her ilk, and was soon to hit
a loaded chamber.

Tarantino's denouements, his Leone-style standoffs, are self-consciously
and deliberately theatrical. Indeed, the 'stagey' quality of his work is insistent. The long takes and involved dialogue of *Reservoir Dogs* and *Pulp Fiction*
are clearly indebted to Godardian, European art-house cinema, but they
also have a theatrical dimension: Jules and Vincent, for instance, torment
their victims in a discussion of hamburgers that is Pinteresque in its comic
menace. *Reservoir Dogs* with its bleak warehouse setting and 'real-time'
action is a clear nod in the direction of the unities of classical drama. More
explicitly, some of Tarantino's *dramatis personae* call attention to themselves
and their theatrical existence, in much the same way as Gwendolen in *The
Importance of Being Earnest*: 'This suspense is terrible,' she announces, as
Jack crashes around upstairs in search of the handbag that bred him, 'I hope
it will last' (379). 'Let's get into character,' counsels Jules as he and Vincent
go to work. The Wolf wants to know the 'principals' names' in The Bonnie
Situation. He tells Raquel that 'just because you are a character doesn't
mean you have a character'.[57] Tarantino's movies thus combine the theatrical with the pervasively metacinematic. *Pulp Fiction* does not refer just to
the hard-boiled narratives of *Black Mask* writers such as Dashiell Hammett,
Eric Stanley Gardner and Raymond Chandler – and their successor, Elmore
Leonard: it is also a compendium of implicit and explicit references to other
movies, such as *Deliverance*, *The Untouchables*, *The Texas Chainsaw Massa-
cre*, *Superfly T.N.T*, *The Guns of Navarone*, to name but a few. Here Tarantino
is clearly following the example of Godard, whose films Sontag describes as
'casually encyclopedic, anthologizing, formally and thematically eclectic, and
marked by a rapid turnover of styles and forms.'[58] In this respect, the movies
seem to conform to Wilde's belief in 'Pen, Pencil and Poison' that 'in a very
ugly and sensible age, the arts borrow not from life but from each other'
(1001). Tarantino is as wary as Wilde of the prison-house of realism, preferring self-referentiality to representational authenticity: 'My movies obviously
take place now, but they also seem to take place in a never-never world.'[59]

Interviewers and journalists have constantly emphasized Tarantino's borrowings from 'pop' or 'junk' culture: he is, according to *Sight and Sound*,
a 'pasticheur and pop-cultural relativist' and to *The Guardian* a 'Movie
Junkie'.[60] Such claims can be turned against him. According to James Wood,

Tarantino suffers from the 'cultural anorexia of our age; and education sheared of anything but popular media-forms'.[61] However, this is not only to perpetuate a dubious distinction between 'high' and 'low' culture – one which, as we have seen, Wilde would not have recognized – it is also to ignore the cultural inclusiveness of Tarantino's work, hinted at in a rather camp remark which collapses cultural distinctions with some aplomb: 'If ever I see Tennessee Williams's play *Orpheus Descending,* I think Elvis would have been the best person to play that part.'[62] The crucial point here though is that the inclusiveness of Tarantino's cultural appetite is based on the desire to discriminate rather than simply to absorb. He says, for instance, of the 1970s blaxploitation films that influenced him: 'I was going to see all those movies, and they weren't put under any critical light, so you made your own discoveries, you found the diamonds in the dustbin.'[63] Sontag says the connoisseur of Camp sniffs the stink and prides himself on his strong nerves, but in Tarantino's case the image needs revizing: like Wilde – and the Baudelairen *flâneur* – he never abandons the dandy's desire to discriminate, to sift the patterns amongst what others might think of as cultural debris. Central to this discriminatory project is the distinction Tarantino draws between films and movies. Films, claims Clarence Worley in Tarantino's screenplay for *True Romance* (1993), are for people who don't like movies. Films are summed up as Merchant-Ivory claptrap, 'safe, geri-atric, coffee-table dogshit.' However, '*Mad Max,* that's a movie. *The Good, the Bad and the Ugly*, that's a movie. *Rio Bravo*, that's a movie. *Rumble Fish*, that's a fuckin' movie.' Clarence's excited exposition elicits the puzzled re-sponse, 'What's this guy doin'? Makin' a drug deal or getting a job on the New Yorker?'[64] Movies are stylized, distinguished by a Godardian rhetorical overlay and a Wildean perspective on 'content'. Their use of music is man-nered and slick, and has nothing to do with the creation of simple 'period' feel along naturalistic lines; it is closer to the operatic excesses in Morricone's embellishment of Leone's Spaghetti Westerns. Tarantino displays all the con-tempt for Oscar-winning films like *Sophie's Choice, Kramer vs. Kramer* and *Gandhi* that Wilde reserves for the moralizing Victorian three-volume novel and the respectable contents of Mudie's circulating library in *The Import-ance of Being Earnest* – a play about the necessity of being the exact oppos-ite. In *The Soul of Man* Wilde neatly sums up his attitude to the safe, geriatric, coffee-table dogshit of his age: 'No country produces such badly-written fiction, such tedious common work in the novel form, such silly, vulgar plays as England' (1091).

One of the most telling examples of Tarantino's cultural inclusiveness, and of the rhetorical overlay and stylization that he shares with Wilde, is his reworking of biblical motifs and allusions in *Pulp Fiction*. Jules quotes a pastiche of Ezekiel 25:17 before going to work, but in finding grace (not the

motorbike) at the end of the movie he struggles to interpret its significance
– rather than using it as 'just a cold-blooded thing to say to a motherfucker
'fore you popped a cap in his ass.'[65] The original screenplay has an exchange,
cut from the movie, in which Vincent calls Jules Pontius Pilate for not
helping to put Marvin out of his misery after he has been shot. When
Vincent is asked to squire Mia by Marcellus Wallace while he is away on
business in Florida, he finds himself in a situation out of *film noir* and out of
the Bible – with Mia Wallace in the role of Potiphar's wife and Vincent cast
as Joseph (see Genesis 39: 70–23). Indeed, the Mia-Vincent relationship also
echoes Wilde in that it replays that between Salome and John the Baptist
(Wilde having refracted the biblical Salome through a series of continental
artists: Flaubert, Mallarmé, Huysmans, Moreau). When Mia dances alone to
Urge Overkill's version of Neil Diamond's 'Girl, You'll be a Woman Soon'
(Tarantino mercifully spares us the original), she is virtually indistinguish-
able from Wilde's Salome, the predatory adolescent dancing for herself (rather
than Herod) in an act of auto-erotic self-definition. Wilde imprisons John
the Baptist in a cistern; Vincent Vega acts out his drama of sexual temptation in a toilet: 'so, you're gonna go out there, drink your drink, say
"Goodnight, I've had a very lovely evening," go home and jack off. And
that's all you're gonna do.'[66] Like Wilde's, Tarantino's handling of the Bible
is essentially camp: according to Sontag's definition, ideas are held in a
playful way in an atmosphere of failed seriousness.[67] In a sense, the urge
overkill at work in both cases is a deconstructive one; the Bible – the Book
of books, the Text of texts – is split apart, and new, provisional, momentar-
ily satisfying patterns assembled from its shards. This deconstructive energy
is evident in Wilde's five-finger exercise, *La Sainte Courtisane*, and his oral
tales – such as 'The Woman taken in Adultery', 'The Miracle of the Stigmata' and 'The Useless Resurrection' – which revise the Bible in ironic,
playful, stylized fashion.[68] (During the 1890s he considered compiling his
own Gospel: 'Useless Miracles'.[69]) *Salome* was banned for its presumption.

A hundred years ago *Dorian Gray* was, as we have seen, attacked for
failing to supply readers with moral coordinates. Tarantino is now con-
demned in much the same terms for being a product of a new decadence
and *fin-de-siècle* uncertainties: James Wood claims, for instance, that 'Sometimes one doesn't have to look very hard for symptoms of the age we live in
– they squat like visible toads in our postmodern pond. Quentin Tarantino
is one of them.' According to this analysis, Tarantino is both symptom and
victim: 'He represents the final triumph of postmodernism, which is to
empty the artwork of all content, thus voiding its capacity to do anything
but helplessly *represent* our agonies (rather than contain or comprehend).'[70]
There is an interesting elision here as Wood assumes – rather like Carson in
cross-examining Wilde – a simple passage from artwork to author: Tarantino

is offered as a symptomatic individual in the way Nordau constructed Wilde, and Wood's critique is premised on a 'direct simplicity' of reading which tries to crack the nut in search of a moral kernel. True, neither Wilde nor Tarantino offer us the certainties that Wood, and others before him, feel art should embody; instead, their achievements embrace 'the intelligent gratification of consciousness' which, for Sontag, is the 'moral pleasure' inherent in the aesthetic experience.[71] By nourishing consciousness, in other words, art can create the conditions for genuinely moral choice – rather than action and opinions learned by rote, the failure of forming habits. Further, Sontag identifies the moral potential of the aesthetic experience with the agency of style. Shadowing Wilde's Preface to *Dorian Gray*, she claims that 'A work of art, so far as it is a work of art, cannot – whatever the artist's personal intentions – advocate anything at all' (Wilde: 'An ethical sympathy in an artist is an unpardonable mannerism of style' (17)) and goes on to assert unequivocally – in a formulation that is identical with Wilde's own – that 'In the final analysis, "Style" is art'. As the dominant aesthetic category, it is 'the principle of decision in the work of art, the signature of the artist's will'.[72]

Comparing our turn-of-the-century with Wilde's, Terry Eagleton concludes that what we are left with is 'something of the culture of the previous *fin de siècle* shorn of its politics.'[73] The 1880s and 1890s were, he argues, a period of extraordinary spiritual **and** material ferment: 'We are speaking of the period of Aubrey Beardsley *and* the Second International; of aestheticism and anarchism; of decadence and the Dock Strike.' Wilde championing socialism and Yeats veering between theosophy and the Irish Republican Brotherhood are, to Eagleton, symbolic figures marrying experimental aesthetics with revolutionary politics. Today, he continues, the capitalist system 'approaches the millenium, as it did the last, in grave disarray; but the political forces which mustered around the turn of the century to offer an alternative polity to this failed experiment have been temporarily scattered and diffused.'[74] Eagleton thus finds himself in curious agreement with James Wood: our own turn-of-the-century is more concerned with endings than with beginnings. However, Eagleton's critique can be partly refuted if the relationship between Wilde and Tarantino is properly understood, if we accept that style is politics, shaping our world, the ways we represent it and the ways we present ourselves to it. Sontag is surely wrong to conclude that Camp is apolitical: its gestures are a refusal of the limiting, the normative, the authentic, and as such the style of a liberatory politics which is both engendered by and critical of (late? advanced?) capitalism. As Wilde shows, the distance from aesthetic choice and gesture, from the signature of the artist's will, to a material politics is easily traversed. Antony Easthope says of Tarantino's movies that 'people recognise the world of sympathetic gangsters because it echoes our own – intense local consumerism accompanied by long-term anxieties.'[75] It is because Wilde's sensibility lives on as we enter a new century in the work of Tarantino and others that – whether or not its practitioners subscribe to Eagleton's specific political agenda – 'brooding facticity' and material conditions seem capable of refabrication, and we can confront those anxieties with laughter, exhilaration and style.

While Sontag is prepared to acknowledge the moral dimension to stylization, Dick Hebdige has argued for its political potential – particularly when associated with the transgressive and transformative practices of subcultures. He begins by claiming that Jean Genet 'more than most has explored in his life and work the subversive implications of style' and identifies Genet's major themes as the 'status and meaning of revolt, the idea of style as a form of Refusal, the elevation of crime into art' and sees these as central to his own analysis.[76] I would argue that Wilde's own life and work are at least as instructive as Genet's, and that Hebdige's list is equally descriptive of Wilde's major preoccupations. Hebdige focuses on Genet's *The Thief's Journal* and his description of how a tube of vaseline, found in his possession, is confiscated by the Spanish police during a raid – and how it is thus transformed by Genet into a badge of his 'otherness', and his refusal of the heterosexual norm. For Hebdige, Genet's example provides a way of beginning to understand post-war youth subcultures: 'Like Genet also, we are intrigued by the most mundane objects – a safety-pin, a pointed shoe, a motor cycle – which, none the less, like the tube of vaseline, take on a symbolic function, becoming a form of stigmata, tokens of a self-imposed exile.'[77] Much the same might be said of Wilde's significant ephemera such as the green carnation buttonhole and the dandy's cravat, waistcoat and rings. For Hebdige, the process whereby objects signify in subculture begins with a crime against the natural order, 'though in this case the deviation may seem slight indeed – the cultivation of a quiff, the acquisition of a scooter or a record or a certain kind of suit.'[78] However, the process ends with the construction of a style which issues an oblique challenge to hegemony on behalf of a specific subculture: a challenge displayed at 'the profoundly superficial level of appearances: that is, at the level of signs.'[79] Wilde's own manipulation of profound superficiality was an attempt to maintain a kind of 'exile' within society – an increasingly precarious attempt to enjoy celebrity, wealth and position while interrogating them (Wilde commodified himself for a society he was simultaneously contradicting). In this respect, he foreshadowed the paradoxical relationship of post-war subcultural style to the social and political hegemonies it successively tried to undermine; Hebdige points to the continual processes of recuperation by which the 'fractured order' is repaired and the 'subculture incorporated as a diverting spectacle within the dominant ideology from which it in part emanates.'[80] I shall return, in the final chapter, to Wilde's significance for contemporary 'popular' style, with a particular emphasis on dandyism and its complex relationship to stardom. But for the moment I want to concentrate on the relevance to Wilde of one particular technique which Hebdige regards as constitutive of a politically charged subcultural style: *bricolage.*

Hebdige uses a phrase from Umberto Eco to define *bricolage*: 'semiotic guerilla warfare'.[81] Borrowed from anthropology, the term is used to describe the subversive process by which subcultures seize upon and appropriate commodities in order to ascribe to them new meanings, shaking them free from their 'authentic' associations. Hebdige gives as examples the way Teddy Boys stole and transformed the Edwardian style of dress revived in the early 1950s by Savile Row tailors for privileged young urban sophisticates, and the way Mods took the familiar insignia of the business world (the suit, collar, tie, short hair, etc.,) and stripped them of their original connotations by making them newly, oddly visible when combined with parkas emblazoned with Union Jacks. The subcultural *bricoleur* has something in common, for Hebdige, with the Dadaists and Surrealists, creating radical aesthetic effects through the apparently chance combination of objects, commodities, details of dress and décor which the 'natural' order insists on keeping separate. In this respect, it is the violent collage aesthetic of Punk which best exemplifies the subversive impulses of subcultural *bricolage.* What I want to suggest is that something of the *bricoleur's* sensibility and techniques shape Wilde's style – and I am interested here less in the way he deployed fashion in constructing his public personae, than in the way he handles genre, objectifying it, making it visible, subverting its meaning through a process of stylization which is at once knowing, innocent, admiring, critical: in short, camp. This is most clearly the case with the Society Comedies which evince, successively, an increasing degree of stylization. This process culminates in *The Importance of Being Earnest* which is at once Wilde's most stylized, most playful, and most political play.

I am not arguing that we can draw easy or direct comparisons between Wilde and the individual members of post-war, working-class, youth subcultures. As Hebdige acknowledges, the semiotic guerilla warfare may be waged 'at a level beneath the consciousness of the individual members of a spectacular subculture'. In this way, a Mod, for instance, might see business regalia as '"empty" fetishes, objects to be desired, fondled and valued in their own right'[82] rather than congratulate himself on the dexterity with which he has transformed their original connotations of efficiency, ambition and compliance with authority. For Wilde, as we have seen, style is unremittingly selfconscious, as is its articulation with a complex of radical political attitudes. My own view is that it is in the Society Comedies – and the way he remakes genres and specific pre-texts, giving the mundane and well-worn a new, cutting edge – that Wilde most successfully displays and employs the processes of stylization which give his work such a modern look. In some respects, *Salome* is Wilde's most anti-naturalistic drama, and to that degree further evidence of the way his aesthetic theories inform his dramatic practice, but in this context it makes an instructive comparison. On the brink of commercial West End success with his first Society Comedy, *Lady Windermere's Fan*, Wilde wrote *Salome* (in French) in a clear attempt to align himself with the European avant-garde theatre: in retrospect, he described it to Bosie as trying to enlarge the drama's 'artistic horizon'.[83] The result is a play, which – paradoxically – for all its apparently innovative intentions now looks his most dated (I am not including his 'prentice pieces *Vera* and *The Duchess of Padua* in this comparison). As Lady Markby observes in *An Ideal Husband*: 'Nothing is so dangerous as being too modern. One is apt to grow old-fashioned quite suddenly. I have known many instances of it' (514).

Salome is a deliberately heady concoction of continental influences. Wilde draws on Flaubert, Huysmans, Moreau, Mallarmé, Heine, Laforgue, Klimt, in portraying his eponymous heroine – and on Maeterlinck's *La Princesse Maleine* in deploying the atmosphere and devices of an emergent Symbolist drama. Regenia Gagnier and Peter Raby have both argued that the play anticipates in its determined anti-naturalism some of the most important developments in experimental twentieth-century drama: in particular Artaud, Jarry and the Theatre of Cruelty.[84] (Katharine Worth further suggests that this continental bloodline connects Wilde with the later chamber plays of Yeats, and with the radical anti-naturalism of Beckett. From this angle, then, Wilde is paradoxically realigned with his Irish successors by a shared affinity with European experimentalism.[85]) The first production of the play was in Paris, at Lugné-Poë's Theatre de l'Oeuvre on 11 February 1896 – which the imprisoned Wilde saw as a helpful gesture of solidarity from the European 'art' theatre he regarded himself as an honorary member of.[86] The play's treatment in England confirmed Wilde's view that he ought to be addressing a more sophisticated European audience: it was banned while in rehearsal with Sarah Bernhardt's company in 1892, by a censor who invoked the ancient interdiction against portraying Biblical characters on stage and who described it privately as semi-pornographic.[87] The play's notoriety did not end there. It became the centre-piece of a bizarre libel case in 1918 in which the rabidly right-wing Noel Pemberton-Billing was sued by the producer J.T. Grein and the dancer Maud Allan for publishing an article which damned their production of *Salome* as part of the 'Cult of the Clitoris'. (Pemberton-Billing used the trial to publicize his belief that the British establishment was being eaten away from within by 47,000 sexual deviants who were also German sympathizers.[88]) In a sense, Wilde's ghost was on trial too, as Pemberton-Billing's defence deployed the same accusations against the corrupting influence of art and artists as had bedevilled *Dorian Gray* a generation before. The jury acquitted him. (Pat Barker uses the trial as part of the historical backdrop to her 1993 novel, *The Eye in the Door*, noting that Bosie appeared as a witness for the defence and blamed 'England's poor showing in the war on the plays of Oscar Wilde'.[89]) However priggish the objections of the censor, and paranoid and plain daft the fantasies of Pemberton-Billing, they are testament to the provocative, subversive potential of Wilde's evocation of female sexuality as a powerfully destabilizing force.

There is a curious irony here. Of all Wilde's plays, *Salome* – with its narcotic atmosphere, its trance-like stichomythic dramatic language, its central symbolic moments such as the heroine's dance, its verbal arias – could be seen to apply with most consistency (and self-consciously and deliberately) the anti-naturalistic premises of his aesthetic theories. However, Lawrence Danson sees the relationship between theory and practice rather differently: 'Wilde's critic-as-artist', he claims, 'reads (*inter alia*) Flaubert, Baudelaire and Mallarmé, and in response writes an essay called *Salome*.'[90] The implication is that, for all Wilde's attention to putative details of costume and set-design, the play perhaps lends itself rather better to reading than to performance – it is an artistic manifesto rather than a fully achieved, compelling dramatic event. Despite the relative popularity of the play with European audiences[91] – and particularly in its reworking as opera by Richard Strauss – *Salome* has rarely been performed on the English stage. (Indeed, the Lord Chamberlain's ban on public performances of the play was not lifted until 1931, and there seems more than a touch of naïvety in Wilde's assumption that it would be granted a licence in the first place.) Max Beerbohm's fascinated disbelief at the appearance of a cardboard severed head in a private 1905 production hints at some of the problems the play sets performers and audiences.[92]

Recently, however, *Salome* has been resurrected as directors and performers have responded to its erotically-charged content – with Lindsay Kemp's production at the Roundhouse in 1977, Ken Russell's 1987 film *Salome's Last Dance*, and Steven Berkoff's successful and popular revival which opened at the Gate theatre in Dublin in 1988 and then transferred to the National Theatre in London.[93] Russell's film – which imagines a private performance of the play put on for Wilde's delectation by a motley collection of aristocrats and rough trade at a male brothel – combines originality and vulgarity in proportions he does not, apparently, suspect. Salome strips to Grieg's 'In the Hall of the Mountain King' and is played by a serving-girl who, at the climax of the dance, is revealed as having male genitalia; Jokanaan is played by Bosie and is imprisoned in a dumb-waiter. Characteristically, Russell seems unsure whether to take the play seriously at all (if camp art treads the thin line between the serious and the frivolous, Russell trips spectacularly over it) and, equally characteristically, Kemp saw it as a score for his own

luridly androgynous production-style which aimed to 'restore to the theatre
the glamour of the Folies Bergères, the danger of the circus, the sexuality of
rock 'n' roll and the ritual of Death.'[94] Given Kemp's own influence on
'glam-rock', his production is an important example of Wilde's part in the
development of a dandyism, from Baudelaire to Bowie, elements of which I
shall explore in the final chapter. Kemp himself played a transvestite Salome
in his bravura, all-male 'variation on' Wilde's play in which only about a
third of the original text survived: the production has been characterized as
'an assault on the senses, with deafening drumming, green and blood-red
lighting, joss sticks in the hair of the slaves, incense burning in braziers, a
live snake and a live dove, smoke, feathers, snatches of Wagner and Mozart
and more besides.'[95] According to one commentator, Kemp's 'febrile min-
gling of Symbolist decadence, powdered androgyny and blood-soaked
poetics' forged a link between '*fin-de-siècle* and *fin-de-millenium* notions of
decadence.'[96] Berkoff's approach is much the most interesting and revealing,
however. He strips the play of its modish 1890s bric-à-brac: Charles Ricketts
recalled that the design for Wilde's original production was to be organized
around masses of colour, with the Jews all in yellow and Herod and his wife
in blood-red; the stage floor was to have been black, the sky a rich turquoise
blue 'cut by the perpendicular fall of gilded strips of Japanese matting, forming an aerial tent above the terraces.'[97] (Bernhardt, with splendid hauteur,
disregarded Wilde's carefully orchestrated colour scheme and insisted that
she would play Salome with blue hair and in one of her favourite gold
Cleopatra dresses, complete with breastplate and triple crown.[98]) Instead,
Berkoff 'decided that the stage should be bare and allow the words to bounce
off the hard surfaces without being softened or cushioned "by carpets and
ivory tables"'.[99] He also develops a powerful acting and performance-style
by utilizing the vitality of contemporary popular forms, just as Wilde had
counselled in *The Soul of Man*. Berkoff collapses Wilde's minor characters
into a 'protean' chorus 'able to be and reflect whatever you wished', which –
decked out in 1920's evening dress – moves as if trapped in a thick, viscous,
suffocating medium: a perfect physical correlative to Wilde's engorged language, and the smothering atmosphere of Herod's court. Berkoff took his
inspiration from Parisian street-performers he watched outside the Pompidou
Centre, 'moving very slowly to music and impersonating those slow-motion
shoot-outs one sees in Hollywood westerns when the bad guy bites the dust
ultra-slow and the blood spurts.'[100] This blow-torching of Wilde's text and
inflated dramatic conception emphasizes the degree to which the play is
about ways of seeing (witness, for instance, the different ways in which the
moon is seen and described by the Young Syrian, the Page of Herodias, and
by both Herod and Salome themselves) and of the dangers in the desiring
gaze which devours both Jokanaan and, finally, Salome. Berkoff implicates

the audience in this 'active seeing' by having his Salome mime her slo-mo striptease, and by using an imaginary head instead of the frequently ridiculous conventional stage-prop – one of the many problems with the play which led Berkoff to understand 'why few would be bothered to stage it at all'.[101] Berkoff thus succeeds by dint of a radical re-styling of Wilde's text: one which avoids the contempt for its original material which characterizes Russell's film. *Salome* requires such an approach if it is to seem anything but a theatrical curiosity, trapped in its innovative pretensions as in amber.

Nevertheless, *Salome* can be seen as central to some of Wilde's most insistent thematic concerns. Regenia Gagnier argues convincingly that when imagining his play on stage, Wilde paid most attention to the figure of Salome: 'he first wanted her to be costumed in shades of yellow, then green like a lizard, then as unadorned as Victorian stages would permit'. This was to ensure that she – rather than Herod, Herodias or Jokanaan – was the focus for the audience.[102] (In this respect, his intentions were perhaps ill-served by Berkoff's characteristically overheated and bullying performance as Herod, one of the few weaknesses of his version of the play. Alan Stanford had been much more low-key in the role at the Gate before Berkoff took over when the production transferred to the National Theatre. It should be noted, though, that in the first English production of the play, at the Bijou Theatre in 1905, Robert Farquharson's Herod seems to have similarly dominated proceedings.[103]) Wilde reportedly said he could not conceive of a Salome 'who is unconscious of what she does, a Salome who is at best a silent and passive instrument'.[104] She dances for herself, not for Herod or for her mother. Wilde's Salome is clearly a distinctive, unsettling version of the assertive New Woman whose cause we have seen him championing elsewhere.[105] However, she is not just pure, crystallized individualism, but is another complex, multiform personality capable of shifting, oscillating desires (Jokanaan is at once the object of uncontrolled attraction and repulsion). Her dance is an attempt to anchor herself centre-stage, to centre herself in a moment of fixity, self-definition, authenticity. Salome tries to define herself in terms of desire, and to deny its decentering force. In so doing, in stripping veil after veil to expose the 'real' Salome, she destroys herself in the same way as Dorian Gray. In effect, she simplifies herself out of existence, provoking in Herod the disruptive desires which threaten the social order he represents and which must crush her.

Significantly, Wilde was much impressed by Loie Fuller's Salome, who danced the role 'in her characteristic swirling greens and blues, using mirrors to multiply the image of the dancer.'[106] Surfaces encounter surfaces: this performance of Salome's dance does not distil her to the essence of individualism, or authenticate her as naked desire, but instead it distributes her across and around the stage in a compellingly dramatic evocation of multiplicity and inauthenticity. (The stage-mirrors become a means both of representing Salome's narcissism and of replicating it to nullity.) Wilde had carefully balanced the ending of *Dorian Gray* on a similarly graphic evocation of multiformity, which thwarts the protagonist's attempt to authenticate himself with the slash of a knife: Dorian is simultaneously present 'in all the wonder of his exquisite youth and beauty' (the portrait) and as 'withered, wrinkled and loathsome of visage' (the body) and is identified by the transferable, empty signifier of his rings (167). Fuller's dance embodied the unattainability, the elusiveness, the 'lack' which arouses Herod. (Herod himself knows the power of the pose, the act, the inauthentic: 'Neither at things, nor at people should one look. Only in mirrors should one look, for mirrors do but show us masks' (571).) Salome is the dancer as subject to, and of, desire. Opposites cancel each other out. Jokanaan tries to authenticate himself through denial of desire, Salome through personifying it; both are killed: 'all excess, as well as all renunciation, brings its own punishment'.

The problem is this: in seeking to dramatize the conflict between desire and the law Wilde does not so much reinvent and stylize genre as leave it behind. *Salome*'s self-consciously radical dramaturgy operates in something of a vacuum. By dispensing with the 'braziers of perfume wafting scented clouds before spectacular sets'[107] which Wilde saw as integral to his play on stage, Berkoff returns to *Salome* its cutting edge by relocating it in contemporary street-theatre and Peckinpah-style, slo-mo, aestheticized violence. In the Society Comedies Wilde demonstrates a clear sense of audience, and of how far its expectations can be stretched and ambushed. The playwright as *bricoleur* makes visible the processes by which genre is appropriated, assigned new meanings. But in *Salome* that process of appropriation is evident only in the way he rewrites the Biblical Salome, transforming her from the passive instrument of others' will, and at the level of language, in what Owen Dudley Edwards calls his 'professional linguistic use' of the Authorized Version of the Bible, a skill he had already demonstrated in his story 'The Young King'.[108] It is to tracing the specific and increasing stylization of the Society Comedies, and its culmination in his masterpiece, *The Importance of Being Earnest* that I shall now turn.

REFERENCES

[1] Sontag, *A Sontag Reader*: 106, 118.
[2] *A Sontag Reader*: 143. Julia Prewitt Brown argues that the distinction between ethics and aesthetics shaped a series of binary oppositions which were deeply ingrained in late nineteenth century 'cultural criticism'. It was present, she argues, in Carlyle's

categories of the 'mechanistic' (the ethical) and the 'dynamic' (the aesthetic or spiritual) and in Arnold's emphasis (in *Culture and Anarchy*) on the conflict between Hellenism (founded on spontaneity of consciousness) and Hebraism (strictness of conscience). See Julia Prewitt Brown, *Cosmopolitan Criticism: Oscar Wilde's Philosophy of Art*, University Press of Virginia, Charlottesville and London, 1997.

3   Stuart Mason, *Oscar Wilde, Art and Morality*, Haskell House, London, 1971: 65. Mason (who usefully summarizes the debate around the publication of the novel in this book, first published in 1907) is here quoting a review of *Dorian Gray* in *The Daily Chronicle* which continues by claiming that it is 'heavy with the mephitic odours of moral and spiritual putrefaction'.

4   *Art and Morality*: 35.

5   Baudelaire, *Selected Writings*: 7.

6   *Selected Writings*: 42.

7   *Selected Writings*: 43.

8   *Selected Writings*: 44.

9   See also Wilde's amusingly self-obsessed letter to Arthur Fish, who had been his assistant editor on *Woman's World*: 'I am very glad to hear that you are going to be married, and I need hardly say I hope you will be very happy. Lord Henry's views on marriage are quite monstrous, and I highly disapprove of them. I am delighted you like *Dorian Gray* – it has been attacked on ridiculous grounds, but I think it will be ultimately recognised as a real work of art with a strong ethical lesson inherent in it. Where are you going for your honeymoon?' *Selected Letters*: 83.

10   Mason, *Art and Morality*: 72.

11   See Christopher Norris, *Deconstruction*: xiii.

12   Mason, *Art and Morality*: 72–3.

13   *Art and Morality*: 115.

14   Joseph Conrad, *Heart of Darkness*, Penguin, Harmondsworth, 1973: 8.

15   Quoted in H. Montgomery Hyde, *Oscar Wilde*, Methuen, London, 1976: 74.

16   *The Complete Tales of Henry James*, Vol. 9, 1892–1898, Rupert Hart-Davis, London, 1964: 289.

17   Arata, *Fictions of Loss*: 58–9, 67. See also, William A. Cohen, *Sex Scandal: the Private Parts of Victorian Fiction*, Duke University Press, Durham and London, 1996: 217–225.

18   *Letters*: 352.

19   Mark Currie, *Postmodern Narrative Theory*, Macmillan, London, 1998: 2–3.

20   *Postmodern Narrative Theory*: 17.

21   See, for instance, Philip K. Cohen, *The Moral Vision of Oscar Wilde*, Associated Universities Press, New Jersey, 1978. Cohen argues that the novel puts the theories of *Intentions* to the test: '*Dorian Gray* provides the crucible of experience into which these theories must pass. There they prove to be dross not gold' (108). For Cohen, then, the portrait is a supernatural register of the evils of a life of untrammelled individualism which renders 'unwavering judgement against Dorian' (118).

22   Arata, *Fictions of Loss*: 60.

23   *Fictions of Loss*: 64.

[24] *Selected Letters*: 142.

[25] Mason, *Art and Morality*: 73.

[26] *Art and Morality*: 40–1.

[27] *Art and Morality*: 44.

[28] Tom Stoppard, *Lord Malquist and Mr Moon*, Faber, London, 1980: 79.

[29] *Lord Malquist*: 189.

[30] *Lord Malquist*: 79.

[31] Walter Pater, 'A Novel by Mr. Oscar Wilde', in *Oscar Wilde; A Collection of Critical Essays*, ed. Richard Ellmann, Prentice Hall, Englewood Cliffs, N.J., 1969: 36.

[32] Sontag, *A Sontag Reader*: 117.

[33] *A Sontag Reader*: 235.

[34] Kerry Powell, *Wilde and the Theatre of the 1890s*, Cambridge University Press, Cambridge, 1990.

[35] Quoted in *A Susan Sontag Reader*: 236.

[36] *A Sontag Reader*: 141.

[37] Quoted by Sean O'Hagan in 'X Offender', *The Times Magazine*, 15 October 1994: 10.

[38] Neil Cornwell describes *Dorian Gray* as an exercize in the 'synthetic fantastic'; the intense self-consciousness with which it engages with the conventions of the Gothic issuing in an amalgam of the Faustian bargain and the *doppelgänger* motif 'plus strong sub-concerns with science, Darwinism, aesthetics and psychology, a touch of mysticism (including astrology and metempsychosis), underscored by a somewhat aristocratic brand of social rebellion and a sub-text of homo-eroticism.' This self-conscious eclecticism means that, for Cornwell, the novel is 'a monstrous synthesis of foregoing works.' *The Literary Fantastic: from Gothic to Postmodernism*, Harvester/Wheatsheaf, Hemel Hempstead, 1990: 103.

[39] 'X Offender': 14.

[40] 'X Offender': 14.

[41] See Walter Herries Pollock, *The Picture's Secret*, Remington & Co., London, 1883; Edward J. Goodman, *His Other Self*, Ward & Downey, London, 1889; Elizabeth Lysaght, *The Veiled Picture: or, The Wizard's Legacy*, Simpkin, Marshall & Co., London, 1890.

[42] Mason, *Art and Morality*: 50.

[43] Baudelaire, *Art in Paris*: 189.

[44] It may be worth noting here that Wilde manipulates the Gothic narrative in much the same way as his fellow-Irishman J. Sheridan Le Fanu in his stories of the supernatural, one of which, 'Strange Event in the Life of Schalken the Painter' (1839) may have had an influence on his own novel. The alias Wilde adopted on his release from prison, Sebastian Melmoth, is a reference to his favourite saint combined with a typically paradoxical statement of both his exile and his nationality. Charles Maturin was a distant relative of Wilde's, and by adopting the name of the wandering 'hero' of Maturin's *Melmoth the Wanderer* (1820), thus casting himself to Gothic type, Wilde acknowledged both his rootless outcast status and, obliquely, his Irishness. His connection with the Irish Gothic tradition is

completed circumstantially: as a young man he had courted Florence Balcombe, who later married Bram Stoker. It has been suggested that the London prostitutes who danced in provocative celebration of Wilde's conviction provided Stoker with the inspiration for his representation of female vampires.

[45] Sontag, *A Susan Sontag Reader*: 261.

[46] Leonard is as fascinated as Wilde with constructions of masculinity in terms of poise, style, cool. His work is a refraction of the continuing literary interest in dandyism, in which Wilde's buttonhole and green carnation are replaced by the particular angle of a Kangol cap, or the way Chili Palmer lights his cigars. See, for instance, *Be Cool*, Viking, London, 1999.

[47] Quoted in O'Hagan, 'X Offender': 13.

[48] Mason, *Art and Morality*: 80.

[49] *Art and Morality*: 80.

[50] Quoted in Graham Fuller, 'Quentin Tarantino, Answers first, Questions later', *Reservoir Dogs*, Faber, London, 1992: xv.

[51] *Reservoir Dogs*: xv–xvi.

[52] Quoted in Clancy Sigal, 'Killing Jokes?', *The Guardian*, 11 September 1993: 30.

[53] Quoted in O'Hagan, 'X Offender': 13.

[54] Quoted in Jim McClellan, 'On the Run: Tarantino', *Observer*, 3 July 1994: 29–30.

[55] Stanley Kauffmann, quoted by R. Guilliat, 'QT', *Sunday Times*, 3 October 1993: 32.

[56] Quoted in Ellmann, *Oscar Wilde*: 399.

[57] *Pulp Fiction*, Faber, London, 1994: 2, 152, 170.

[58] Sontag, *A Susan Sontag Reader*: 236.

[59] Quoted by Andrew Pulver, 'The Movie Junkie', *The Guardian*, 19 September 1994: 9.

[60] Manohla Dargis, 'Pulp Instinct', *Sight and Sound*, 4: 5 (1994): 6–9. Andrew Pulver, 'The Movie Junkie': 9.

[61] James Wood, 'You're sayin' a foot massage don't mean nothin', and I'm sayin' it does', *The Guardian* Supplement, 19 November 1994: 31.

[62] Tarantino, quoted in 'Rock 'n' Reel', *The Guardian*, 14 April 1995: 9.

[63] 'Quentin Tarantino on Pulp Fiction', *Sight and Sound* 4: 5 (1994): 10.

[64] *True Romance*, Faber, London, 1995: 116–17.

[65] *Pulp Fiction*: 186–7.

[66] *Pulp Fiction*: 69.

[67] Sontag, *A Susan Sontag Reader*: 115–16.

[68] For a discussion of the specific context in which these tales were improvized and noted down, see Deirdre Toomey, 'The Story-Teller at Fault', in MacCormack, ed., *Wilde the Irishman*: 29–32. Toomey argues that these tales are expressive of Wilde's profoundest conceptions and beliefs.

[69] See John Stokes, *Oscar Wilde: Myths, Miracles and Imitations*, Cambridge University Press, Cambridge, 1996: 24.

[70] James Wood, 'A Foot Massage': 31.

[71] Sontag, *A Susan Sontag Reader*: 145.

[72] *A Susan Sontag Reader*: 146, 150.

[73] Terry Eagleton, 'The Flight to the Real', in *Cultural Politics at the Fin de Siècle*, ed. Sally Ledger and Scott McCracken, Cambridge University Press, Cambridge, 1995: 11.

[74] 'The Flight to the Real': 12, 11.

[75] Antony Easthope, *The Guardian*, 23 November, 1994: 10.

[76] Dick Hebdige, *Subculture: the Meaning of Style*, Routledge, London, 1989: 2.

[77] *Subculture*: 2.

[78] *Subculture*: 3.

[79] *Subculture*: 17.

[80] *Subculture*: 94.

[81] *Subculture*: 105.

[82] *Subculture*: 105.

[83] *Letters*: 589.

[84] Regenia Gagnier, *Idylls of the Marketplace*: 166; Peter Raby, ed., *Oscar Wilde: Lady Windermere's Fan, Salome, A Woman of No Importance, An Ideal Husband, The Importance of Being Earnest*, Clarendon Press, Oxford, 1995: xi.

[85] Katharine Worth, *Oscar Wilde*, Macmillan, London, 1983. Worth says (72) that although Yeats professed to dislike Wilde's play, he in fact rewrote it twice: as *The King of the Great Clock Tower* (1934) and *A Full Moon in March* (1935).

[86] See *Letters*: 558.

[87] See Raby, ed., *Oscar Wilde*: xii.

[88] See Philip Hoare, *Wilde's Last Stand: Decadence, Conspiracy and the First World War*, Duckworth, London, 1997.

[89] Pat Barker, *The Regeneration Trilogy*, Penguin, Harmondsworth, 1998: 340.

[90] Lawrence Danson, *Wilde's Intentions: The Artist in his Criticism*, Clarendon Press, Oxford, 1997: 142.

[91] Robert Ross claimed, less than a decade after Wilde's death, that *Salome* had become 'a household word wherever the English language is not spoken'. See *Salome, A Tragedy in One Act Translated from the French of Oscar Wilde*, John Lane, London, 1907: xiii.

[92] Beerbohm's review appeared in the *Saturday Review*, 13 May 1905 and is reprinted in his *Around Theatres*, Heinemann, London, 1924: 140–44.

[93] Berkoff's productions managed to cause a hiccup in Anglo-Irish cultural relations. He claimed, when transferring from Dublin and changing the cast, that he'd had trouble getting the Irish actors out of the pub and that the only way he could make them grasp the narcotic acting-style he required was to ask them to imagine drinking a pint of Guinness. See William Tydeman and Steven Price, *Salome*, Cambridge University Press, Cambridge, 1996: 105–112; this book is also the fullest account of the play's stage history and critical reception.

[94] David Haughton, quoted in William Tydeman and Steven Price, *Salome*: 99. Haughton played Jokanaan in Kemp's production.

[95] Tydeman and Price, *Salome*: 99.

[96] Michael Bracewell, *England is Mine: Pop Life in Albion from Wilde to Goldie*, HarperCollins, London, 1997: 196.

[97] See Katharine Worth, *Oscar Wilde*: 65.

[98] See Robertson, *Time Was*: 125–127.

[99] *Salome*, with an introduction by Steven Berkoff, Faber, London, 1989: xii.

[100] *Salome*: xi–ii.

[101] *Salome*: xiii.

[102] Gagnier, *Idylls of the Marketplace*: 165. In *Sexual Anarchy: Gender and Culture at the Fin de Siècle*, Bloomsbury, London, 1991, Elaine Showalter gives a useful account of various stage and film versions of the play, focusing on the differing interpretations brought to the role by actresses such as Maud Allan and Ida Rubinstein ('a kind of fin-de-siècle Cher') playing Salome. Of particular note is Alla Nazimova's 1922 silent film which drew heavily for design on Beardsley's drawings but also decked out the male supporting cast in spangled tights and heavy make-up. Critical comment was not unanimously approving. See 144–168.

[103] Max Beerbohm claimed that 'he played all the other people off the stage, figuratively. Literally, they remained there, I regret to say.' *Around Theatres*: 142.

[104] Gagnier, *Idylls of the Marketplace*: 166.

[105] Wilde's Salome has been particularly unsettling for feminist critics. I have already noted Kate Millett's transference of anxiety in *Sexual Politics* (1977), in which she says the play incarnates Wilde's fear of female sexuality. She also argues that Salome is really Wilde himself and her sexual voracity not female but homosexual. Jane Marcus sees Salome as rejecting the authority of Herod, but finds her striptease a degrading form of self-expression – if the only one available to her ('Salome: the Jewish Princess Was a New Woman,' *Bulletin of the New York Public Library*, (1974): 104.

[106] Katharine Worth, *Oscar Wilde*: 64.

[107] Gagnier, *Idylls of the Marketplace*: 165.

[108] Owen Dudley Edwards, 'Impressions of an Irish Sphinx' in MacCormack, ed., *Wilde the Irishman*: 55. Dudley Edwards says that Wilde was, after all, the nephew of three Protestant Episcopalian priests and related to several others.

4

THEORY INTO PRACTICE:
THE SOCIETY COMEDIES

Wilde claimed to Herbert Beerbohm Tree apropos of *A Woman of No Importance* that he had taken the plot of the play from the *Family Herald*, 'which took it – wisely, I feel – from my novel *The Picture of Dorian Gray*. People love a wicked aristocrat who seduces a virtuous maid, and they love a virtuous maiden for being seduced by a wicked aristocrat. I have given them what they like, so that they may learn to appreciate what I like to give them.'[1] This self-conscious willingness to employ well-used theatrical forms and motifs has fostered a critical approach to Wilde's commercially successful West End comedies which is premised on a surface-depth model of analysis, neatly summed up in Richard Ellmann's verdict on *The Importance of Being Earnest*: 'amusing as the surface is, the comic energy springs from the realities that are mocked.'[2] According to this enduring model, Wilde is variously seen as either a 'serious' playwright beneath the merely entertaining surface, or as failing to struggle free of conventions that imprison him: both viewpoints begin with an attempt to strip away the carapace of theatrical borrowings and traditions in order to get at the 'real' Wilde underneath. For instance, a recent study which claims to revise our view of Wilde as a dramatist, constantly emphasizing the radical potential of his plays, remains fixated with this paradigm. Sos Eltis says of *Lady Windermere's Fan* that 'beneath the surface of the play' Wilde subtly remoulded the substance of French boulevard theatre and that the play's doctrine of individualism was 'subtly disguised by the surface melodrama of the work'. His process of continuing revision, argues Eltis, resulted in a highly complex piece: 'on the surface it remains reassuringly conventional, but underneath this veneer, unnoticed by most audiences, lies a very different play.'[3] (Even when the terms are reversed, the model persists, as in Epifanio San Juan's comments on *Lady Windermere's Fan*: 'If one strips the play of its verbal pyrotechnics, and such "mindless chatter" as that of the Duchess of Berwick, one gets the residue of cheap melodrama.'[4]) What I want to suggest is that these plays are **all** surface. For Wilde, playwright and *bricoleur*, generic and specific dramatic pre-texts are appropriated and displayed: they are figures in the carpet, not the shell that hides the kernel in the nut. That process of display is a matter of Style. Wilde enjoys the same relation to popular 1890s melodrama, comedy and farce as that claimed by Tarantino for Sergio Leone and the Western. What lies beneath the surface of *Once Upon a Time in the West*?

Inevitably, Wilde himself is quite capable of obscuring the issue. Of *An Ideal Husband* he told a journalist that, 'I have been considerably amused by so many of the critics suggesting that the incident of the diamond bracelet in Act 3 of my new play was suggested by Sardou. It does not occur in any of Sardou's plays, and it was not in my play until less than ten days before production. Nobody else's work gives me any suggestion.'[5] This declaration of originality and implied artistic 'earnestness' is cancelled, however, by a repeatedly throwaway attitude to the playwright's craft: a reaction which sometime looks like Wilde getting his retaliation in first. When approached by George Alexander to write a Society Comedy – which eventually became *Lady Windermere's Fan* – he is reported as saying to Frank Harris, 'I wonder can I do it in a week, or will it take three? It ought not to take long to beat the Pineros and the Joneses.'[6] He struck a similar note when Alexander asked him to make cuts to *The Importance of Being Earnest*: 'This scene you feel is superfluous cost me terrible exhausting labour and heart-rending nerve-wracking strain. You may not believe me, but I assure you that it must have taken me fully five minutes to write!'[7] Wilde's reasons for turning to the theatre in the wake of disappointing royalties from *Dorian Gray* and the escalating expense of his private life were unashamedly financial. He anticipated much 'red gold' from *The Importance of Being Earnest*,[8] having earned about £7,000 from *Lady Windermere's Fan* in 1892. This has encouraged critics to regard his commercial success as the result of studied compromise, the plays characterized principally as 'a misalliance° of trash and wit'.[9] In fact, recent scholarship – such as Eltis's – has established that Wilde worked meticulously through many drafts in refining and polishing his plays, and continued to make changes through production and into publication. Further, it is my contention that Wilde's deployment of commercially successful formulae is not a matter of compromise or laziness, but rather of assiduous and increasing stylization, and is wholly consistent with the theoretical thrust of the essays we have already examined.[10]

Wyndham Lewis characterized Wilde's dramatic methods in exclusively negative terms: 'when he was engaged in stealing from foreign authors, or pillaging less well-known English ones, no doubt [he] got some kick out of the "criminal" character of these acts of literary "dishonesty", on the same principle that *anything* that flew in the face of vulgar, or *bourgeois*, prejudice was to be enthusiastically indulged in.'[11] To do so is to miss the point. Wilde does not 'steal' so much as 'sample' in a fashion that is recognizably the same as rock musicians and DJs with their 'dance mixes' in our own time:

his, like their, acts of appropriation are performative, referential, transformational, on display. Wyndham Lewis wants to root Wilde – to him, a case of
arrested development, frozen in a sort of adolescent posture of defiance and
refusal – in the 'socially snobbish' Naughty Nineties, when '*all* the moral
values, of "honest" or of "good", necessarily came into contempt, as belonging to a vulgar order of servant-girl superstition, as it were.'[12] I want to argue
that – paradoxically – it is by understanding Wilde's relationship to the
theatrical conventions and successes of his time that we can grasp his affinity with our own.

Kerry Powell's researches into the hitherto lost world of 1890s London
theatre have done much to reconstruct the context in which Wilde's plays
were first performed. He argues that Wilde aspired to be the English Ibsen,
but that his work was heavily reliant not only on the French 'sources' critics
have always noted – such as Scribe, Sardou and Dumas *fils*, upon a pile of
whose 'well-made' plays Wilde was pictured as leaning in a famous *Punch*
cartoon – but also on a host of indigenous playwrights whose names have
been long forgotten and whose work, never published, has survived only in
the copies submitted to the censorship office of the Lord Chamberlain. Powell
sees Wilde as engaged in a continual struggle: to overcome the 'anxiety of
influence' he feels for Ibsen's achievements in modernizing the stage by
making it a forum for social and political debate, and to resist drawing too
heavily on the popular but artistically inferior work of less illustrious names
such as W. Lestocq, Pierre Leclerc, R.C. Carton, Haddon Chambers and
others. Arthur Symons had described *Dorian Gray* as 'a mosaic hurriedly
made by a man who reached out in all directions and took and used in his
book whatever scraps of jasper or porphyry or broken flint were put into his
hand.'[13] Powell's thesis rests on a similar view of Wilde as artistic magpie,
attracted by glittering if basically worthless finds. From this perspective,
Wilde's drama is an uneven and unconvincing achievement. At times he
succeeds in his struggles, says Powell: 'one frequently finds that the popular
playwrights who Wilde repeats are ultimately ambushed in some larger matter of substance or style.' At others he himself is overwhelmed: the early acts
of *Lady Windermere's Fan* 'transcribe the theatrical past as much as rewrite
it'; *A Woman of No Importance* 'never really establishes mastery over the
well-traveled ground where it trespasses'; *The Importance of Being Earnest*
frequently 'sinks to the level of the genre in which [Wilde] is writing.'[14] This
argument also hinges on Powell's notion that, when successful, the plays
operate with something of the force and structure of a Wildean epigram:
audience expectations are pandered to, then rounded on in a final act which
rewrites convention, as in *Lady Windermere's Fan* when the 'woman with a
past', Mrs Erlynne (Mrs Alwynne in early typescript versions), not only gets
away with it but prospers.

Valuable though Powell's scholarship is, his argument falls down in two respects. First, his emphasis on the intended whiplash effect of Wilde's endings makes the earlier parts of the plays seem thoroughly pedestrian, as if he is merely laboriously, and at times rather uncertainly, assembling the building blocks only to kick them over at the end. Secondly, he believes that when Wilde manages to resist the 'oppressive presence of the source', a 'new voice emerges'.[15] There are two suppositions operative here: that Wilde's authentic expressive voice struggles to be heard, and that this struggle is symptomatic of his being on the cusp of modernity. Indeed, to push the argument further than Powell does, modernity can be identified with that new voice, untrammelled by social, sexual or artistic convention and thus powerfully expressive of a new subjectivity. What Powell clearly regards as Wilde's equivocal and mediated artistic success is thus directly reflective of the contradictions in his particular historical moment, as the new pushes hard to break through the shell of the old. 'I became engrossed in writing it,' Wilde told Charles Ricketts about *An Ideal Husband*, 'and it contains a great deal of the real Oscar.'[16] This seems to confirm Powell's point, that Wilde's authentic voice can be located beneath the surface of the plays but, as I shall try to show, the 'real' Oscar is distributed across their surface. His modernity lies not in the degree to which he dispenses with the old, but in the designs he fashions from it – the style he holds it in. To return to my notion of sampling and the analogy with contemporary music: Wilde is present in the mix.

Lady Windermere's Fan was first produced on 20 February 1892 and enjoyed the longest run of any of Wilde's plays: 197 performances. Henry James rather sniffily noted its 'candid and primitive simplicity' and its 'perfectly reminiscential air.'[17] Reminiscential it may be – of Sardou and Haddon Chambers's *The Idler* in particular, while Sydney Grundy accused Wilde of plagiarizing his own *The Glass of Fashion* – but primitive and candid it most certainly is not. At the beginning of the final act, with the play having come full circle to the Windermeres' morning room, we find Lady Windermere in an agony of self-recrimination and fear of discovery: has Mrs Erlynne come clean in Darlington's rooms and told the men of Lady Windermere's plan to leave her husband and child? 'Perhaps,' she soliloquizes, '[Mrs Erlynne] told them the true reason of her being there, and the real meaning of that – fatal fan of mine' (420). Lady Windermere, however does not know the 'true' reason (she never learns that Mrs Erlynne is her mother) and Wilde is at pains to prevent any 'real' meaning adhering to the fan as we follow its narrative trajectory, passed from hand to hand, through the play. The fan, the fashion accessory designed at once for display and concealment, floats free of fixed, authentic signification as it acquires shifting, multiple meanings in the course of the drama. It is an example of the way significant ephemera (Hebdige's safety-pin, pointed shoe, motorcycle and tube of vaseline) come to exercize a symbolic function, operating on 'the profoundly superficial level of appearances: that is, at the level of signs.' Despite Henry James, *Lady Windermere's Fan* has all the complexity of the fan itself. Indeed, the fan – which in the original production 'sported sixteen white ostrich feathers fixed to a handle of yellow tortoiseshell', and replicas of which, in a shrewd piece of merchandizing, audiences were told they could acquire from Duvelleroy's of Regent Street[18] – signifies nothing so much as the nature of the play which bears its name. In short, the fan is subjected to that process of *bricolage* which defines Wilde's working methods in the Society Comedies.

Darlington notices the fan straight away in the opening moments, where it is offered as a token of the relationship between Lady Windermere and her husband: it carries her name and is a present for her twenty-first birthday, thus representing her coming of age and passage into experience. It connotes the domestic and the normative. The first act ends with Lady Windermere promising to strike Mrs Erlynne with the fan if she dares to accept her husband's invitation to the ball: it now signifies her unbending puritanism and is a weapon of recrimination. During the neatly choreographed second act, the fan undergoes further transformations. It is handed to Darlington when Lady Windermere confronts her husband: 'A useful thing, a fan, isn't it? . . . I want a friend tonight, Lord Darlington; I didn't know I would want one so soon' (400). It thus signifies her shifting allegiances, and at the crucial moment when – in what she herself sees as an act of moral cowardice – Lady Windermere fails to strike Mrs Erlynne, she first clutches the fan then drops it to the floor. In Act 3, Cecil Graham spots the fan in Darlington's rooms and interprets it as an index of his hypocrisy: 'Darlington has been moralising and talking about the purity of love, and that sort of thing, and he has got some woman in his rooms all the time' (418). At this point in the play the fan also serves the conventional purpose of the 'significant' stage prop by bringing the action to the crisis of discovery: it signifies self-consciously the kind of play we are watching. At the act drop, Mrs Erlynne coolly picks up the fan and leaves – now it simultaneously signifies the self-cancelling confluence of deceit (Lady Windermere has slipped away and Mrs Erlynne allows herself to appear as Darlington's mistress) and self-sacrifice (Mrs Erlynne seems to have thrown away any chance of getting back into society and of snaring Lord Augustus). When, in Act Four, Mrs Erlynne comes back to return the fan, Lord Windermere sees it as a sign of her moral degeneracy: 'I can't bear the sight of it now. I shall never let my wife use it again. The thing is soiled for me. You should have kept it and not brought it back' (424). As the play moves towards its denouement the fan becomes a gift from Lady Windermere to Mrs Erlynne.

It signifies both the latter's complicated motherly feelings (she continues to protect her daughter from painful knowledge), the daughter's new-won tolerance and sense of indebtedness, and further multiple concealments: Lady Windermere is keeping the truth from her husband, who is also keeping it from her. Finally, Lord Augustus is allowed to carry the fan – he has been instrumental in the deceit, and is now being duped into marriage by the 'clever' Mrs Erlynne. So, the fan is appropriated, displayed, passed on and variously transformed as a sign. By the end of the play its multiformity issues a direct challenge to the domestic normativity it connoted at the beginning. Indeed, it enjoys the same relationship to that normativity as the Mod's business-suit does to the world of the city banker.

The fan, of course, is a literal example of the stylish object: it is a desirable commodity which connects directly with the fashionable world of the audience, but which acquires new and everchanging significances according to the way it is appropriated and displayed. The fluidity of meaning which Wilde ascribes to the fan is matched by the indeterminacy of his principal characters. They are opened out, displayed, snapped shut, one surface reversed flamboyantly to reveal another. Lady Windermere is at once the uncompromising puritan and the obverse: a sort of aristocratic Nora Helmer prepared to leave her husband and child. The opening scene brings her into contact with the dandy Lord Darlington who begins as a predatory opportunist (he and the Duchess of Berwick circle Lady Windermere like social sharks), acts as the spokesperson of a high-octane individualism when he tries to persuade Lady Windermere to run off with him ('You said once you would make no compromise with things. Make none now. Be brave! Be yourself!' (404)) and who disappears from the play as a confirmed and heart-broken sentimentalist. Lord Windermere begins as surrogate-father and protector, warning his wife against judging Mrs Erlynne too hastily, and in the final act adopts the rhetoric of puritanism in his condemnation of the 'worthless, vicious' (423) Mrs Erlynne after she is found in Darlington's rooms (he cannot contain his horror at this 'divorced woman going about under an assumed name' (423) and it is hard not to feel this is a bathetic example of self-consciously Wildean rhetorical overlay). Mrs Erlynne – the female dandy who, in Act Two, displaces both Darlington and Lord Windermere as the locus of 'male' wit and control – is the amoral adventuress, the 'woman with a past' who 'wins all' at the end. She is also the mouthpiece for a social and emotional conventionalism when, in Act 3, she tries to persuade her daughter to return to her doll's house: 'if [Lord Windermere] was harsh to you, you must stay with your child. If he ill-treated you, you must stay with your child. If he abandoned you your place is with your child' (413). This is not a case of Wilde revealing hidden psychological depths beneath surface appearances, but rather of his creating *dramatis personae* defined by verbal and theatrical styles, which cancel each other out. As Mrs Erlynne says, 'there is a great deal of good in Lord Augustus. Fortunately it is all on the surface. Just where good qualities should be' (407). Her remark neatly collapses that distinction between surface and depth which so much analysis of the play is predicated upon. Part of what defines the stylization at work in the play is the rapidity and emphatic theatricality with which the characters swap one posture, one surface, one signification for another. This is characterization as *bricolage*, and it is entirely consistent with Wilde's theoretical assertion that language is the parent and not the child of thought. Styled by language and literary form, his characters are dramatic examples of the post-structuralist subject, dispersed and decentered by the processes of signification which simultaneously bring it into being.

Structurally, *Lady Windermere's Fan* neatly replicates the 'well-made' plays of Scribe and Sardou (whose *Odette* (1881) it closely resembles in terms of situation and narrative): its four acts tracing the anticipated formal development from exposition through complication and crisis to denouement. Similarly, Lord Windermere's private bank book, the letter written by his wife explaining why she is leaving him which is stolen by Mrs Erlynne and the fan itself would have been, for 1890s audiences, strongly reminiscent of the manifold documents and misplaced objects which helped to further the plots of French boulevard theatre. Indeed, Lady Windermere knows exactly what kind of play she is in. When Mrs Erlynne throws the incriminating letter into the fire, she asks: 'How do I know that was my letter after all? You seem to think that the commonest device can take me in' (411). *Lady Windermere's Fan* simultaneously employs the most familiar of motifs and characters, the commonest of devices, and distances itself from them in that ambivalent movement which Sontag has identified as stylization: affection contradicted by contempt, obsession contradicted by irony. In this respect, Powell's judgement that the play merely transcribes the theatrical past before ambushing it in the final act is wide of the mark. It would be more accurate to say that the entire play is in scare quotes. It is a 'Society Comedy' rather than a Society Comedy, and its effects are much more subtle than the mechanistic reversals identified by Powell.

In an early draft of the play Wilde had amplified this note of self-reflexivity in Mrs Erlynne's spirited dismissal of Lord Windermere: 'I suppose, Windermere, you would like me to retire into a convent, or become a hospital nurse, or something of that kind, as people do in silly modern novels and silly French plays.'[19] Powell speculates that Wilde probably had in mind *Frou-Frou* (1869) by Meilhac and Halèvy, at the end of which the 'woman with a past' turns to nursing the sick and contemplates entering a convent, begging forgiveness from the husband she has deserted after wrongly suspecting him of adultery. For Powell, Mrs Erlynne thus voices Wilde's 'modernity', and her fate is shaped by his decision not to make his 'woman with a past' repent and pay for her sins. For Sos Eltis this modernity is evidenced in the radicalism of Wilde's decision to have Mrs Erlynne repudiate motherhood – which her theatrical predecessors never would have done. Interestingly, Wilde excised the reference to 'silly French plays' from the published version of the text, presumably because he realized that it unbalanced the delicate relationship of affection and contempt which characterizes *Lady Windermere's Fan*: though Dumby describes Mrs Erlynne during the ball scene as 'an edition de luxe of a wicked French novel, meant specially for the English market' (402). Interestingly, however, *Frou-Frou* makes a telling appearance in the play Wilde never wrote: *Mr and Mrs Daventry*, the treatment for which Wilde sold to Frank Harris and which the latter wrote up for production in October 1900. The last act was to begin with the runaway wife reading *Frou-Frou* and then discussing it with her new lover; Harris's *Mr and Mrs Daventry* then goes on to reverse the conventional morality of its precursor.[20] It is significant that *Lady Windermere's Fan* doesn't point up its references as explicitly as this. Wilde is partly colluding with his audience in a game of recognition, and doesn't need to highlight his 'samples' so directly. Further, as his 'Society Comedies' succeed each other, the degree of stylization he brings to bear on his material increases, preparing the ground for the meta-dramatic self-reflexivity of *The Importance of Being Earnest*. In short, the direction he was moving in as a playwright is confirmed by the appearance of *Frou-Frou* in the play he never wrote.

The crucial point is that Wilde's political and social concerns are not compromized by the camp manner of the way he handles the formulae of the society drama, but are, rather, exercized by it. Mrs Erlynne clearly provides a focus for Wilde's feminist sympathies, for instance. As female dandy she effects a reversal of gender power-relations (on the public stage of the ball, her re-entrance into 'respectable' society, she tells Lord Windermere that she can manage the men, though confesses to being afraid of the women). By refusing the role of mother and escaping to Europe with a rich husband she achieves a victory of sorts, for 'cleverness' over morality and the sexual double-standard in particular. Wilde is aware of the contradictions this resolution implies. Mrs Erlynne is both the play's most consistent individualist and an example of the kinds of compromizes society exacts. Yet, because Wilde eschews naturalistic characterization in favour of characterization as *bricolage* (he strips the 'woman with a past' of conventional connotations, substituting new and challenging ones), and holds the situations and resolutions of society drama in such a particular style, the play claims for itself the kind of transformation of normativity which Wilde's aesthetic theories argue a self-conscious and critical art is capable of.

Interestingly, in this play in which, fan-like, everything has another sur-face to display and so further significations to acquire, the 'oppressive normativity' which Mrs Erlynne struggles against is represented by another version of the feminine: the society dowager, the Duchess of Berwick, whose political and social conservatism prefigures the sinister humour of Lady Bracknell. She arrives in Lady Windermere's morning room from tea at Lady Markby's: 'Such bad tea, too. It was quite undrinkable. I wasn't at all surprised. Her own son-in-law supplies it' (389). Wilde spreads the fan, then snaps it shut to display the other side. It soon becomes clear that the Duchess's aristocratic snobbery is cancelled by her financial concern to marry off her little 'chatter-box' Agatha to the Australian Hopper, who is also in trade: 'His father made a great fortune by selling some kind of food in circular tins – most palatable, I believe – I fancy it is the thing the servants always refuse to eat' (393). In the second act, Wilde shows how aristocratic women police the sexual double-standard which makes Mrs Erlynne un-acceptable, and Lord Darlington 'a charming wicked creature!' (390). The Duchess is similarly trying to control one of her own sex, her daughter Agatha, during the public drama of Lady Windermere's birthday ball. She literally marks her card for dances ('I'm so glad Lady Windermere has re-vived cards – They're a mother's only safeguard. You dear simple little thing!' (397)). However, Wilde shows how the Duchess's scheming can be thwarted. Her aristocratic pretensions are repeatedly undercut by Hopper's Paul Hogan-like, antipodean cool. Productions which insist on playing Hopper as a rather dim suitor miss the point. His dry subversion of the Duchess's imperialist prejudices neatly stylize Wilde's own colonial status as an Irish 'outsider' making his way in the metropolis. Hopper and Agatha negotiate their own deal and the Duchess is faced with the prospect of her daughter escaping her control to 'that dreadful vulgar place' (405) Australia. It is a small enough victory, and one not yet fully won because the Duchess clearly intends to dig in, but it prefigures Mrs Erlynne's flight from an English society dominated by an ideological 'false consciousness' in which powerful women control others in the name of respectability. Hopper and Agatha's alliance thus brings together Wilde's feminism and his anti-imperialism.

It is, of course, the Duchess who warns Lady Windermere about her husband and Mrs Erlynne, adding to that rhetorical counterpoint between puritanism and cynicism (already introduced in the opening exchanges between Lady Windermere and Lord Darlington) which characterizes the verbal style of *Lady Windermere's Fan* and which is neatly captured when Lady Windermere says she married for love and the Duchess responds, 'Yes, we begin like that' (392). Lady Windermere prides herself on being old-fashioned ('You look on me as being behind the age – Well, I am! I should be sorry to be on the same level as an age like this' (387)), but it is important to see that Wilde's modernity lies not simply in silencing that voice with the cynicism and wit of the dandy, but in the stylistic effects he achieves in bringing the two into contact. Wilde does not just give the audience the sentimentality and melodrama they like, in order that they may learn to appreciate what he likes to give them, forging a 'misalliance of trash and wit'. Rather, he manages to preserve that ambivalent and delicate balance of affection and contempt, obsession and irony, which characterizes the camp transformation of popular and well-worn artistic forms and rhetoric. Wilde finds a winning way with winning formulae in *Lady Windermere's Fan*, and in his next play, *A Woman of No Importance*, he takes that stylization a step further.

That *A Woman of No Importance*, which opened on 19 April 1893, was in some respects a deliberate attempt to outdo its predecessor, is clear in Wilde's claim to Gilbert Burgess that he wrote the first act 'in answer to the critics who said that *Lady Windermere's Fan* lacked action. In the act in question there was absolutely no action at all. It was a perfect act.'[21] The remark signals, in part, Wilde's oft-proclaimed lack of interest in plot: the significant events in *A Woman of No Importance* amount to little more than an off-stage attempt at a kiss in Act Three and the final sensational moment when the puritan, Mrs Arbuthnot, outstrips Lady Windermere and her fan, and strikes Lord Illingworth across the face with his glove. This is a play in which talk all but entirely displaces action, as Wilde constructs a dramatic dialogue characterized by the constant undercutting of sentimental puritan rhetoric and the mannered, competitive flirtation between the two dandies, Lord Illingworth and Mrs Allonby. It is also a 'perfect act' in another sense. In that anticipation of postmodernity's denial of the distinction between the natural and the cultural which we have already noted, and examined in Wilde's enculturation of the natural world in the artful opening to *Dorian Gray*, in *A Woman of No Importance* the 'real', the simple and the genuine are cancelled by the artificial, the sophisticated and the theatrical. Philip Prowse's acclaimed 1991 production – which rescued this least-performed of Wilde's society comedies from relative obscurity – accentuated this aspect of the play in its mannerist approach to the text. Prowse's staging of Wilde's 'perfect act' began as the audience was still taking its seats in the auditorium and the louche young aristocrat Lord Alfred played a game of barefoot croquet. The opening exchanges between Sir John, Lady Caroline and Hester Worsley took place as they strolled in front of an eighteenth-century-style landscape painting in a huge gilt frame. The stage was dominated by a lily pond and ornamental urns. According to Robert Gordon, Prowse's design was of an English countryside 'completely landscaped, nature transformed utterly into art.'[22] At the opening of Act Two, the curiously upholstered lily pond was transformed – entirely in keeping with the logic of Wilde's play

– into a massive round sofa covered in artfully clashing striped, spotted and checked fabrics and giant cushions in eye-bruising colours. The exterior landscape painting was replaced as a backdrop by a wooden, gold 'curtain'. In the final act, the landscape of Hunstanton Chase in Act One could be seen through the windows of Mrs Arbuthnot's house with its minimalist décor and deep blue curtains.

What Prowse, as director and designer, had recognized was that Wilde's play, like so much of his other work, deploys the distinction between the natural and the artificial only to deny to it. That distinction is established in the opening dialogue between Lady Caroline and Hester. The young American (played by a black actress in Prowse's production, to emphasize her 'separateness') is asked if she has ever stayed in an English country house before. When she says that she has not, Lady Caroline asks, 'Have you any country? What we should call country?' Hester replies 'We have the largest country in the world, Lady Caroline. They used to tell us at school that some of our states are as big as France and England put together' (431). What Lady Caroline would call country is glaringly there for all to see and is a neat cancellation of Hester's rather smug faith in the great outdoors: 'You must find it very draughty', she says (431). As the play progresses, Hester's attachment to the 'natural world' becomes synonymous with a naïve belief in the pure, the authentic, the unspoiled. Gerald Arbuthnot, she announces, 'has a beautiful nature! He is so simple, so sincere. He has one of the most beautiful natures I have ever come across' (432). In the second act, she interrupts the cynical observations of the aristocratic women on men in general, and husbands in particular, by announcing that American society consists 'simply of all the good women and good men we have in our country.' 'What is that dreadful girl talking about?' asks Mrs Allonby. 'She is painfully natural, is she not?' comes Lady Stutfield's reply (448–9). However, Hester's understanding of what is natural, and the values she attaches to it, is repeatedly undercut. Lady Hunstanton recalls that Lord Illingworth balked at marrying Lady Kelso because her family was too large (or was it her feet?), though she would have made an excellent ambassador's wife. Lady Caroline agrees that 'She certainly has a wonderful facility of remembering people's names, and forgetting people's faces.' 'Well, that,' responds Lady Hunstanton mysteriously, 'is very natural' (433). Mrs Allonby sweeps in and compliments the hostess on her wonderful trees, 'But somehow, I feel sure that if I lived in the country for six months, I should become so unsophisticated that no one would take the slightest notice of me.' 'I assure you dear,' says Lady Hunstanton, recalling the elopement of Lady Belton and Lord Feathersdale which prompted the former's husband to die of joy, or gout, 'that the country has not that effect at all' (434). The exchange neatly cancels the literary distinction between the innocent countryside and the wicked town which

Wilde was to subject to further comic deconstruction in *The Importance of Being Earnest*.

Lord Illingworth's entrance in the first act signals a further rejection of Hester's notions about the natural. He immediately detaches the signifier 'America' from the signifieds Hester cements it to and so claims for herself: candour, simplicity, genuineness, moral straightforwardness. 'The youth of America is their oldest tradition,' he observes, after a few derogatory remarks about its literary achievements, 'It has been going on now for three hundred years. To hear them talk one would imagine they were in their first childhood. As far as civilisation goes they are in their second' (436). But this is not mere xenophobia. His contempt for the politically-correct MP, Kelvil (who is preparing a speech on what is no doubt Hester's favourite subject, Purity), is palpable, as it is for the concatenation of 'natural', 'health' and 'Englishness'. 'Health', he opines, is the silliest word in our language, 'and one knows so well the popular idea of health. The English country gentleman galloping after a fox – the unspeakable in full pursuit of the uneatable' (437). He and Mrs Allonby are hot-house flowers. She tells Lady Hunstanton that she will take a walk as far as the conservatory: 'Lord Illingworth told me this morning that there was an orchid there as beautiful as the seven deadly sins' (438). Mrs Arbuthnot, on the other hand, associates herself with the 'natural simplicity' Hester so approves of. 'It looks quite the happy English home' (470), notes Mrs Allonby sardonically, when she enters Mrs Arbuthnot's house in the final act. Lady Hunstanton points out that 'Most women in London, nowadays, seem to furnish their rooms with nothing but orchids, foreigners and French novels. But here we have the room of a sweet saint. Fresh natural flowers, books that don't shock one, pictures that one can look at without blushing'. 'But I like blushing,' says Mrs Allonby. 'Well, there *is* a good deal to be said for blushing,' confesses Lady Hunstanton, 'if one can do it at the right moment' (470). What is clear is that the visitors from Hunstanton Chase allow of no such thing as a natural reaction. To them all behaviour is studied, mannered, part of the social language of flirtation, control, power. Everything is in scare quotes. They also recognize that Mrs Arbuthnot is carefully designing her own stage-set in which she can play the starring role of penitent sinner. Indeed, she possesses an admirable theatrical sense. Her first entrance '*from the terrace behind with a lace veil over her head*' is artfully timed to coincide with the climax of Hester's tirade against sexual misdemeanour in Act Two: 'Let all women who have sinned be punished' (449). Mrs Arbuthnot's is indeed a perfect act.[23]

Kerry Powell is damning on the subject of *A Woman of No Importance*: 'a victim of influence, it represents the failure of Wilde's method as a playwright.' He identifies the specific influences on Wilde from among the usual French suspects: Dumas's venerable *Le Fils naturel* (1858); Albert

Delpit's *Le Fils de Coralie* (1880); Eugene de Brieux's *Monsieur de Reboval* (1892); Edouard Plouvier's *Madame Aubert* (1865). He also notes influences that are rather closer to home: Henry Arthur Jones's *The Dancing Girl* (1891), for instance. For Powell, *A Woman of No Importance* more or less implodes beneath the weight of borrowings. He claims that, in Mrs Arbuthnot's refusal to marry the father of her son and thus to take her place in the doll's house, Wilde was attempting an Ibsenite conclusion which would reverse the familiar morality and politics of the plays upon which he was drawing but that this potentially radical reversal – unlike the successful whiplash at the end of *Lady Windermere's Fan* – 'is not assimilated to the design of the play as a whole, if a play of so many undigested influences can be said to have a design.' In this respect, Wilde struggles, but 'in the end surrenders to tradition when he silences Lord Illingworth's wit and allows Mrs Arbuthnot the old-fashioned satisfaction of striking her seducer in the face.'[24] What Powell misses – but what Philip Prowse captured so compellingly in his styling of the play – is that rather than having no design, *A Woman of No Importance* has a superabundance of it, and is peopled with a variety of 'designing' characters. Part of Wilde's design is to call attention to the 'sampled' nature of his play, and that self-reflexivity is heightened by a thread of allusion to two novels. Hawthorne's *The Scarlet Letter* (1850) explores the histrionic satisfactions of puritanism;[25] Laclos's *Les Liaisons Dangereuses* (1782) hinges on the 'decadent' aristocrat's acceptance of the challenge to try and 'corrupt' innocent youth. Wilde seems to be self-consciously adding 'high', 'literary' culture to his predominantly popular mix. Another element of the design is the cancellation – by means of the critical running commentary above, and by the heightened theatricality with which Mrs Arbuthnot presents herself and her situation – of that opposition between manners and morals which Hester insists upon and which is focused in the relationship between Mrs Arbuthnot and Lord Illingworth. The whole point of her melodramatic reaction in slapping him across the face is that it is melodramatic. Wilde is not surrendering to tradition but, rather, deploying it to a specific end: to show that Mrs Arbuthnot's 'natural' behaviour is 'a perfect act', that Life imitates Art as it struggles for expression. Mrs Arbuthnot, in other words, is as much a part of this self-conscious, artificial world as Mrs Allonby. She just chooses a different role to play. Her penitence and moral sense are as authentic as Prowse's lily pond and English landscape in the manner of Claude.

In the world of Hunstanton Chase the 'violent hierarchy' of the natural and the unnatural, the authentic and the inauthentic, the ethical and the aesthetic, is repeatedly overturned: the first movement of the deconstructive process. In this sense, *A Woman of No Importance* can be said to conform to the artistic credo Wilde both outlined and demonstrated in his public

defence of *Dorian Gray*. It begins by elevating the mannered and the artificial, the codes by which this society organizes itself, above the 'painfully
natural' (it is hard for any audience not to share the characters' irritation
with Hester, for instance) and ends by collapsing them into each other. This
deconstructive denial of difference is captured in Mrs Allonby's verdict on
Patagonia: 'Savages seem to have quite the same views as cultured people on
almost all subjects. They are exquisitely advanced' (463). However, it is Lord
Illingworth who gives it the most elegant and telling expression in his earlier
sartorial advice to Gerald:

> People nowadays are so absolutely superficial that they don't understand the
> philosophy of the superficial. By the way, Gerald, you should learn how to tie
> your tie better. Sentiment is all very well for the buttonhole. But the essential
> thing for the necktie is style. A well-tied tie is the first serious step in life.

> (459)

So, Illingworth neatly distinguishes between two kinds of superficiality. The
first accepts the 'violent hierarchy' of surface and depth and the associated
valorization of the ethical above the aesthetic. The second, the profoundly
superficial, purports to recognize a distinction between sentiment (depth)
and style (surface), valorizing the latter above the former. At the profoundly
superficial level of signs, this distinction appears to be legitimated by the
difference between the natural (the flower) and the artificial (the knotted
tie). However, both are signs within the field of sartorial meaning and their
relationship to what they signify is entirely arbitrary, as Illingworth well
knows – otherwise his fine discrimination would have no comic effect.
Illingworth inverts the value-laden relationship between style and sentiment,
only to collapse the distinction. The 'ethical beauty' of the play is that
Illingworth's stylish pragmatism is vanquished by a moral code which has all
the authenticity and purity of a buttonhole.[26]

Therein lies the real radicalism and modernity of *A Woman of No
Importance* – not in any attempt to apply Ibsenite conclusions to intractable
material. Wilde evokes an English upper-class society which is profoundly
superficial in a double sense. He makes no attempt to minimize its casual
cruelties, snobbery and general lassitude, but his satirical critique is tempered by his knowledge that it has at least got something right. In its understanding of the importance of fashion and self-consciousness, it contains a
powerful antidote to the posturing, punitive Old Testament morality of
Hester and Mrs Arbuthnot. It realises the vital importance of being inauthentic. (When Lord Illingworth reads the letter of rejection from Gerald
he sees it in terms of an overwrought '*fin-de-siècle*' style (480).) In a sense,

this allows Wilde both to criticize and to flatter his fashionable audience – a useful shift for a writer with radical aims and credentials who, nevertheless, is trying to make a living from the theatre.

Illingworth loses the tug-of-love over Gerald and suffers the indignity of a slap across the face with his own glove, but will presumably gather himself easily enough. For Wilde the real loser is Gerald who is consigned to a future of dim prospects and unrelieved tedium in the company of his mother and his wife-to-be. In Illingworth Wilde creates a complex and challenging figure. He is far from simply the 'mustache-twirling villain of traditional melodrama' which Eltis argues was his original type.[27] 'Taking sides,' he warns Kelvil, 'is the beginning of sincerity and earnestness follows shortly afterwards, and the human being becomes a bore' (437): a dictum which rephrases the assertion in the preface to *Dorian Gray* that an ethical sympathy in an artist is an unpardonable mannerism of style, and which Wilde clearly followed in allowing Mrs Arbuthnot a triumph of sorts. Here, Illingworth sounds very like Lord Henry Wotton, as he does in the way he tries to woo his son away from his former lover (Lord Henry, of course, succeeds in instilling a heightened degree of self-consciousness in Dorian, hence seducing him away from a conventional life-style). Seconds later, Illingworth appears to have been reading Wilde's *The Soul of Man Under Socialism*. He counters Kelvil's insistence that the House of Commons has always shown great sympathy for the sufferings of the poor by claiming that is its special vice: 'It is the special vice of the age. One should sympathize with the joy, the beauty, the colour of life.' In another echo he goes on to admit that the East End is a problem, but it is the problem of slavery 'and we are trying to save it by amusing the slaves' (437). Kelvil becomes rather dimly aware of the potentially subversive implications of Illingworth's remarks: 'He gives the impression of a man who does not appreciate the beauty of our English home-life. I should say that he was tainted with foreign ideas on the subject' (439). He has certainly been tainted with Wilde's ideas on many subjects – Illingworth's claim that 'Discontent is the first step in the progress of a man or a nation' (456) is a more or less direct echo of *The Soul of Man* and its insistence that disobedience is man's original virtue. 'All thought is immoral,' he tells Lady Hunstanton, 'its very essence is destruction' (464): another version of the epigrammatic contention in *The Soul of Man* that an idea that is not dangerous is not worthy of being called an idea at all. There is a peculiarly Wildean, self-referential joke at work here as he puts some of his socialist beliefs, and equally importantly their paradoxical expression, into the mouth of a peer of the realm with no apparent interest in politics whatsoever. It is also a significant stratagem: an example of Wilde's idiosyncratic politicization of the Baudelairean dandy which I shall examine in the final chapter, and which has important consequences for the way we understand Wilde Style.

Wilde told Beerbohm Tree, who played Illingworth in the first production, that 'this witty aristocrat whom you wish to assume in my play is quite unlike anyone who has been on the stage before. He is like no one who has existed before.' When Tree asked if that meant he was supernatural, Wilde replied 'he is certainly not natural. He is a figure of art. Indeed,' he added, clearly warming to the subject, 'if you can bear the truth, he is MYSELF.'[28] We have already seen Frank Harris dismiss Wilde's political beliefs and prejudices as those of the English governing class, claiming them to be all in favour of individual freedom or anarchy under the protection of the policeman – so he, for one, would not have been surprised by this apparent ventriloquism. However, the crucial point is this: style is the dominant aesthetic category which unites Illingworth's aristocratic insouciance and Wilde's elegant socialism in a radical rejection of a 'very ugly and sensible age' in which 'the arts borrow not from life but from each other' (1001). It is a studied denial of authenticity, whether manifest as representational realism or the ethically normative.

Nevertheless, there are moments in *A Woman of No Importance* when Wilde's camp transformation of well-worn characters and situations seems less like rhetorical overlay than rhetorical overdrive. Hester's excesses are nearly always comically undercut by the onstage audience. 'You are unjust to women in England,' she proclaims, as Mrs Arbuthnot enters behind in a lace veil and composes herself into a suitably dramatic image, 'And till you count what is shame in a woman to be infamy in a man, you will always be unjust, and Right, that pillar of fire, and Wrong that pillar of cloud, will be made dim to your eyes, or be not seen at all, or if seen, not regarded.' 'Might I, dear Miss Worsley,' interjects Lady Caroline, 'as you are standing up, ask you for my cotton that is just behind you. Thank you' (450). Later, Gerald provides a similarly bathetic, if this time unintentional, note in response to one of his mother's more lurid outbursts. She returns to her favourite subject, herself, the woman with a past:

> She is a woman who wears a mask, like a thing that is a leper. The fire cannot purify her. The waters cannot quench her anguish. Nothing can heal her! no anodyne can give her sleep! no poppies forgetfulness! She is lost! She is a lost soul! That is why I call Lord Illingworth a bad man. That is why I don't want my boy to be with him.

(469)

'My dear mother,' Gerald chips in, 'it all sounds very tragic, of course . . .' However, Wilde also gives her too much latitude, as in the fourth act when she embarks on an interminably overwrought tirade against Illingworth, her past and Gerald's demand that she marry his father: 'It is my dishonour that has made you so dear to me. It is my disgrace that has bound you so closely to me. It is the price I paid for you – the price of soul and body – that makes me love you as I do. Oh, don't ask me to do this horrible thing. Child of my shame, be still the child of my shame!' (475). I don't think this is a case of Wilde being overpowered by the melodramatic material he is deploying, as Kerry Powell might have it, but rather of the point at which camp becomes, to return to Sontag's analysis, 'campy'. Wilde is clearly enjoying himself, at the expense, I suspect, of those audiences who do not benefit from the producer's blue pencil. But in so doing he tips the play over into kitsch.

An Ideal Husband, which opened on 3 January 1895, also treads the thin line between camp and kitsch. Gertrude Chiltern, for instance, is constantly in danger of finding herself on the wrong side of it: 'Oh', she implores her husband, faced with the prospect of his no longer wishing to occupy the moral high-ground on the subject of the Argentine Canal Scheme, 'be that ideal still. That great inheritance throw not away – that tower of ivory do not destroy' (501). Wilde is clearly deliberately pushing her over the line here and his point is the same as with Mrs Arbuthnot: moralism is a style among others, but rather less aesthetically pleasing than most. 'How silly to write on pink paper!' notes Mrs Cheveley of Gertrude's letter to her husband. 'It looks like the beginning of a middle-class romance.' She then goes on to deliver a suitably damning verdict on the handwriting: 'The ten commandments in every stroke of the pen, and the moral law all over the page' (527). Mrs Cheveley thus neatly reduces her enemy's moralism to a matter of prose-style. In so doing, she echoes the kind of judgement Wilde's stage directions have already made against **her**. When she enters in the first act, we are told that she is in heliotrope, with diamonds, that she has thin and highly-coloured lips, a pallid face, Venetian red hair, an aquiline nose and a long throat: 'a work of art, on the whole, but showing the influence of rather too many schools' (484). This latest version of the 'woman with a past' is thus judged in aesthetic rather than ethical terms. Her criminality is a matter, principally, of bad taste. But is her taste any worse than Lady Chiltern's?

Wilde added his unusually elaborate stage directions when revising the text for publication during 1898 and early 1899, and he clearly put much effort into this process, telling his publisher Leonard Smithers that 'Corrections are a great trouble – worse than a new play. I am quite exhausted.'[29] The stage directions are an attempt to establish the manner of An Ideal Husband, and reinforce the point made to Charles Ricketts that it was 'written for ridiculous puppets to play.'[30] The touchstone is not the real, but the artificial. Wilde's *dramatis personae* are each introduced by reference to works of art; character is displayed as surface. Ladies Marchmont and Basildon are '*types of exquisite fragility. Their affectation of manner has a delicate charm. Watteau would have loved to paint them*' (482). Lord Caversham is '*a fine Whig type. Rather like a portrait by Lawrence*' (483). Mabel Chiltern is described as '*a perfect example of the English type of prettiness, the apple-blossom type*' and has '*the fragrance and freedom of a flower*'. However, she is no more 'natural' than those around her, she is just maintaining a rather different pose: '*She is really like a Tanagra statuette, and would be rather annoyed if she were told so*' (483). Sir Robert Chiltern's entrance seems to provoke an attempt at psychology. We are told that he appears to suffer '*an almost complete separation of passion and intellect, as though thought and emotion were isolated in its own sphere through some violence of will-power*'. However, Wilde is not really concerned with interiorization, but with establishing it only for the purpose of cancelling it: '*It would be inaccurate to call him picturesque. Picturesqueness cannot survive the House of Commons. But Vandyck would have loved to have painted his head*' (485). The backdrop to this first act, suitably enough, is another work of art: '*a large eighteenth-century French tapestry – representing the Triumph of Love, from a design by Boucher – that is stretched on the staircase wall*' (482).

Lady Markby suspects that Mrs Cheveley may be one of the Dorsetshire Cheveleys: 'But I really don't know. Families are so mixed nowadays. Indeed, as a rule, everybody turns out to be somebody else' (486). This echoes Lord Illingworth's tart observation that the peerage is 'the best thing in fiction the English have ever done' (461). It is also an accurate description of the world of Wilde's Society Comedies in which everyone is engaged in a 'perfect act'. The plays do not insist, as Richard Ellmann suggests, on collective unmasking,[31] but rather that those characters most voluble in their adherence to the ethically authentic (Lady Windermere, Hester, Mrs Arbuthnot, Gertrude Chiltern) are also wearing masks, playing roles, though they lack the capacity for varied self-creation which marks the dandies from the dowdies. What Wilde's stage directions to *An Ideal Husband* seek to establish is that a production wedded to a naturalistic acting-style will miss the point. What is required is a style of layered mannerism, because *An Ideal Husband* is as inauthentic as its characters. Among the pre-texts Wilde samples are Ibsen's *The Pillars of Society* (1877) and *Ghosts* (1883), Sardou's *Dora* (1877), Dumas's *L'ami des femmes* (1864) and Pinero's *The Cabinet Minster* (1890). In its focus on insider-dealing at the heart of the imperial metropolis; its acute recognition that information is a commodity; its exploration of the relationship between public and private morality (prompted, no doubt, by Wilde's interest in the Parnell divorce case); its sceptical view of political correctness, *An Ideal Husband* looks in some respects the most topical and contemporary of Wilde's society comedies. (Indeed, Peter Hall's productions in 1992 and 1996 emphasized this topicality and were instrumental in leading the revival of interest in Wilde's society dramas.) However, I want to suggest that *An Ideal Husband* feels compellingly modern not just because of the topicality of its political content but because of its fascination with style and fashion.

The nature and importance of fashion and the fashionable are almost obsessive subjects of comment in *An Ideal Husband*. Mabel Chiltern defends Lord Goring's busily fashionable existence to his father: 'Why, he rides in the Row at ten o'clock in the morning, goes to the Opera three times a week, changes his clothes at least five times a day, and dines out every night of the season. You don't call that leading an idle life, do you?' (483). However, it soon becomes apparent that fashion embraces more than the need to be seen in the right places, doing the right things with the right people, and wearing the right clothes. 'Ah, nowadays people marry as often as they can, don't they?' says Lady Markby when she learns that Mrs Cheveley has married for a second time. 'It is most fashionable' (484). Her sentiments are echoed by Lord Caversham in Act Three when he pursues Goring on the subject of marriage and tells him that 'Bachelors are not fashionable any more. They are a damaged lot' (524). Sir Robert – before his polite flirtation with her turns sour – asks Mrs Cheveley if she is an optimist or a pessimist: 'Those seem to be the only two fashionable religions left to us nowadays' (487). Mrs Cheveley responds by saying that politics are her only pleasure: 'You see, nowadays it is not fashionable to flirt till one is forty, or to be romantic until one is forty-five, so we poor women who are under thirty, or say we are, have nothing open to us but politics and philanthropy' (487). When, in Act Two, Sir Robert says he intends to find out if there is anything known against Mrs Cheveley at the Embassy in Vienna, Lord Goring settles his buttonhole and says, 'Oh, I should fancy Mrs Cheveley is one of those very modern women of our time who find a new scandal as becoming as a new bonnet, and air them both in the Park every afternoon at five-thirty' (508). Sir Robert insists that she looks like a woman with a past, to which Goring replies, 'Most pretty women do. But there is a fashion in pasts just as there is a fashion in frocks. Perhaps Mrs Cheveley's past is merely a slightly *decolleté* one, and they are excessively popular nowadays' (509). 'Fashion' thus erodes the difference between the 'serious' (marriage, religion, criminality, emotional engagement of any kind) and the 'trivial' (the rituals of the social season, clothes). In this context, 'fashion' describes the codes by which a self-consciously disabused society organizes itself. It is a way of keeping *ennui* at bay ('Horribly tedious!' is Lady Basildon's verdict on the Hartlocks' parties. 'Never know why I go. Never know why I go anywhere!' (482)) and of conforming, of ensuring membership of a privileged and powerful elite.

However, *An Ideal Husband* also explores another – and in some respects contradictory – notion of fashion. Act Three opens with an instructive exchange between Lord Goring and Phipps, as he puts the finishing touches to his costume. Goring's buttonhole, silk hat, Inverness cape, white gloves and Louis Seize cane are '*the delicate fopperies of fashion*'. Their signification is spelled out: '*One sees that he stands in immediate relation to modern Life, makes it indeed, and so masters it. He is the first well-dressed philosopher in the history of thought*' (522). We are back to Illingworth and his distinction between those who are so 'absolutely superficial that they don't understand the philosophy of the superficial' and those, like Goring, who are capable of deploying and interrogating the profoundly superficial language of appearances. 'Rather distinguished thing, Phipps,' he pronounces, 'I am the only person of the smallest importance in London at present who wears a buttonhole'. He then formulates a new and challenging definition: 'You see, Phipps, Fashion is what one wears oneself. What is unfashionable is what other people wear.' Fashion, for Goring, is the dominant term in a philosophy of individualism. 'Just as vulgarity is simply the conduct of other people', he continues, 'and falsehoods the truths of other people' (522). For the dandy, 'fashion' embodies the opposite of the conformism it entails for others. This is fashion as self-conscious and deliberate style. In discussing *A Woman of No Importance* I said that Wilde's critique of English aristocratic society was tempered by his knowledge that it had got at least one thing right – that in its understanding of the importance of fashion it contained a powerful antidote to the punitive moralism personified in Hester and Mrs Arbuthnot. In *An Ideal Husband* Wilde takes his analysis of 'fashionable society' a step further.

Ironically, fashion can both sustain that privileged elite and act as its solvent. Lord Caversham announces that he never goes anywhere now: 'Sick of London Society. Shouldn't mind being introduced to my own tailor; he always votes on the right side. But object strongly to being sent down to dinner with my wife's milliner. Never could stand Lady Caversham's bonnets' (484). It is a crucial, if throwaway, remark. Caversham's objections to his wife's milliner are clearly not confined to the hats she makes, but to the fact that her presence represents a potentially threatening social mobility. The charmed circle of the aristocratic elite is being infiltrated by the members of a social class it depends upon to supply the 'delicate fopperies of fashion' by which it identifies, sustains and attempts to seal itself. Style is indeed politically charged in this context. Those responsible for producing the material signifiers of style represent a new social dynamic, one which is corrosive of traditional hierarchies. We have already seen, in discussing *The Soul of Man Under Socialism*, that Wilde drew a connection between individualism, art and style as 'disturbing and disintegrating' forces. Here he gives us a specific example of style at work in a highly paradoxical way: the conditions of its material production threaten the exclusivity and stability of the powerful elite which consumes it. In *A Woman of No Importance*, Lord Illingworth had announced that 'A man who can dominate a London dinner-table can dominate the world. The future belongs to the dandy. It is the exquisites who are going to rule' (459). Caversham has seen the future and he doesn't like it. The dandy lives as if the exquisite aesthetic utopia he yearns for, and is attempting to fashion, has already come into being. For Wilde, that is a socialist future in which hereditary wealth and privilege have been disturbed by a social mobility propelled by the excitements of style, and in which an exclusive and exploitative social structure has disintegrated in the process.

Nevertheless, one of the difficulties of *An Ideal Husband* is the instability of Lord Goring as dandy, who ends by marrying Sir Robert's sister and thus integrating himself fully with the society he comments upon. The detailed stage directions at the beginning of Act Three, and the revealing exchange with Phipps, read like an attempt by Wilde to reestablish Goring as the '*flawless dandy*' (488) we meet in the first act, after a second act in which he has appeared as anything but. In the long, confessional dialogue with Robert Chiltern which opens Act Two, Goring begins with the poised individualism of the dandy ('Everything is dangerous, my dear fellow. If it wasn't so, life shouldn't be worth living' (504)) but modulates through several different changes of register when faced with the politician's *apologia pro vita sua*. Chiltern insists that every man of ambition has to fight his century with its own weapons, and that 'The God of this century is wealth. To succeed one must have wealth. At all costs one must have wealth' (504). Goring responds with the strangely sanctimonious 'Robert, how could you have sold yourself for money?' (505). As the scene progresses, Goring sounds less and less like the dandy, dismissing Chiltern's as 'A thoroughly shallow creed' (505) and more and more like an English version of Ibsen's Gregers Werle, insisting that Chiltern confront his wife with the truth. A Wildean dandy makes an unlikely champion for such notions of authenticity, as he does for the kind of self-congratulatory note Goring strikes when defining Englishness: 'The English can't stand a man who is always saying he is in the right, but they are very fond of a man who admits that he has been in the wrong. It is one of the best things in them' (507). At the same time, Sir Robert takes on some of the dandy's characteristic rhetoric. He sounds like Henry Wotton when claiming that 'there are terrible temptations that it takes great strength to give into' (506). It is tempting to suggest that there is some consistency at work here, that Goring's sniffy reaction to Chiltern's financial skulduggery is prompted by the fact that he fought his century with wealth, rather than its other weapon, style. (After all, Baudelaire declared that, however necessary money is to the dandy's life-style, the dandy does not aspire to wealth as an object in itself: 'he leaves that squalid passion to vulgar mortals'.[32]) However, this rapid relinquishing and assumption of conflicting roles is very similar to that we have already seen in *Lady Windermere's Fan*. It is also what happens to the two main female characters. Mrs Cheveley is both the pragmatist whose sole concern is financial gain, and the vindictive agent of retribution whose face is 'illumined with evil triumph' at the end of Act Three. She is also the sententious moralist who tells Chiltern that no man is rich enough to buy back his past (497). Gertrude is both the unbending puritan and the liar who, at the end of the play, follows Lady Windermere in the art of concealment. As in *Lady Windermere's Fan* and *A Woman of No Importance*, Wilde is deliberately avoiding any attempt at psychological realism, preferring instead to present 'character' as a series of theatrical effects and rhetorical styles, displayed with bewildering speed.

Interestingly, Mrs Cheveley tells her enemy's husband that if he doesn't do what she asks 'the whole world shall know the origin of Sir Robert Chiltern' (520). Yet Wilde's methods of characterization deliberately undermine such notions of origin and authenticity. Like Mabel Chiltern, who announces that 'I am just off to rehearsal. I have got to stand on my head in some tableaux' (514), the play's principal characters are all capable of turning themselves upside down. As Lady Markby had predicted, everybody turns out to be someone else: but is released into a new role rather than being unmasked (Lord Goring acquires a splendid new buttonhole to signal his intention of playing the 'ideal' husband). In this way, Wilde clearly signals the contrived and theatrical nature of his 'happy ending', with marriage – one reconfirmed, another about to be embarked upon – as the conventional sign of comic resolution. Yet the society that reassembles is one which has been sceptically examined. Moralism has been exposed as just another rhetorical style among others; politics, for all the high-sounding rhetoric about the mission of Empire, as riddled with criminal activity. However, the political force of the play lies as much in its examination of style – and indeed, in its own processes of stylization – as in its explicit political commentary. In other words, the manner of the play is as important as its matter: a point forcefully made by George Bernard Shaw in his review of its first production.

For Shaw, the most important characteristic of *An Ideal Husband* is its 'subtle and pervading levity'. Wilde, he declares, is England's 'only thorough playwright. He plays with everything; with wit, with philosophy, with drama, with actors and audience, with the whole theatre.' This playfulness he characterizes as an offensive tactic. Wilde is counted by Shaw as an ally in subversion, emphasizing their shared status as aliens. 'Ireland,' he claims, 'is of all countries the most foreign to England.' England's colonial relationship to John Bull's Other Island is thus redefined. The arrogant assumption of assimilation is replaced by an insistence on foreignness, on 'otherness'. Wilde's playfulness is thus an expression of that politically charged 'otherness', and its principal target is 'earnestness' and 'sincerity'. To the Irishman, declares Shaw, 'there is nothing in the world quite so exquisitely comic as an Englishman's seriousness'.[33] Certainly, Wilde finds Gertrude Chiltern's high-principled rhetoric more than a little amusing and, notwithstanding his own feminism, her attempt to bring a feminized moral and political correctness to bear upon her husband's public and private behaviour is cancelled by the comic rapidity with which she performs an ideological *volte face* in order to save his career: 'A man's life is of more value than a woman's. It has larger issues, wider scope, greater ambitions. Our lives revolve on curves of emotion. It is upon lines of intellect that a man's life progresses. I have just learnt this, and much else with it, from Lord Goring' (549).[34] Wilde's target is not Lady Chiltern's beliefs – in higher education and political rights for women, as evidenced by her involvement with the Women's Liberal Association, for instance – but the style (or perhaps lack of it) in which she holds them.

What Shaw describes as pervading levity I characterize as stylization: the playfulness with which Wilde deploys his pre-texts, and the deliberateness with which he fashions the clash of genres. This is particularly so in Act Three when the conventions of 'strong' drama are mixed with those of farce. Goring's habitual cool is severely tested as he tries to keep apart his father, Sir Robert and Mrs Cheveley, and the action revolves around a series of opening doors, unexpected appearances and mistaken identity. To these farcical devices Wilde adds those of the 'well-made play'. With considerable panache he gives us not one, but two stolen letters. This all needs to be played at high-speed for maximum effect, as in Hall's 1992 production[35] and the 1998 film, directed and adapted by Oliver Parker. One of the results of this farcical action is to foreground the agonizing of Sir Robert Chiltern as overblown sentimental rhetoric: his particular style stands out sharply in this deliberately incongruous context. In *The Soul of Man* Wilde said that delightful work could be done under burlesque conditions, drawing on popular forms, and his deployment of farce in *An Ideal Husband* puts that theory into practice. It also points to the central stylistic tactic of his next play, *The Importance of Being Earnest*, which of all Wilde's works is his most playful, most stylish and most political.

Curiously, though, this was lost on Shaw. Although he grudgingly admitted that *The Importance of Being Earnest* was 'extremely funny', Shaw felt it 'essentially hateful'. Ironically, he found himself in strange alliance with Wilde's conservative critics who were determined, as we have seen, to read his writings as symptoms of Wilde's decadence and depravity. 'I had no idea that Oscar Wilde was going to the dogs,' he said of a meeting at the Café

Royal, 'and that [*The Importance of Being Earnest*] represented a real degeneracy produced by his debauches.'[36] These comments echoed Shaw's review of the first production – which opened at the St James's on 14 February 1895, the play having been drafted and revised by Wilde over the summer and autumn of the previous year. Writing in the *Saturday Review*, Shaw said he could not sympathize with the characters and that the play failed to move him, eliciting instead a 'miserable mechanical laughter'. 'On the whole,' he continued, pointing to the much-used devices and situations of 'rib-tickling' farce, 'I must decline to accept *The Importance of Being Earnest* as a day less than ten years old.'[37] Again ironically, the reviewer of the *New York Times* made exactly the same claim for the connection between the play's levity and Wilde's Irishness which Shaw had insisted on for *An Ideal Husband* but which he refused to acknowledge in *The Importance of Being Earnest*: 'It is a pure farce of Gilbertian parentage, but loaded with drolleries, epigrams, impertinencies, and bubbling comicalities that only an Irishman could have ingrafted on that respectable Saxon stock.'[38] Shaw admired *An Ideal Husband* because it seemed to be doing what he was attempting at the same time with plays like *The Philanderer* (1893) and *Arms and the Man* (1894): bringing a modern 'Ibsenite' preoccupation with social issues to bear upon 'respectable' dramatic conventions, and conveying the political critique with a mocking, paradoxical sense of humour. Shaw's drama is driven by argument, his paradoxes are systematic attempts to reveal the 'irrational' bases to the 'rational' assumptions of capitalist society. This is what he means by laughing at seriousness: exposing its illogicality and proposing instead a new socialist logic of his own. He plays in order to **score**. For Wilde, playfulness is a matter of style rather than argument, but is no less political for that.

Shaw was clearly thrown by Wilde's change of gear. The previous three plays had sampled 'strong drama', recycling stock characters (the puritan, the woman with a past, the dandy) and themes (the hidden secret, the sexual double-standard, parent-child relations) from play to play. With *Salome* he had varied this deployment of commercially successful, 'middle-brow' formulae by writing in an antithetical mode: that of the continental avant garde. Now, in *The Importance of Being Earnest*, he seemed to be breaking with all artistic decorum, refusing the only two alternatives apparently available to a 'serious' dramatist, by turning to 'low-brow' popular entertainment for his models. Shaw may have taken the use of tried-and-tested farce motifs at face-value, condemning the play as old-fashioned, but other contemporaries reacted differently. For St John Hankin, writing in 1908, the play's technique showed in certain details 'a breaking away from the conventional well-made play of the 'seventies and 'eighties in favour of the looser construction and more naturalistic methods of the newer school.'[39] Hankin is right to emphasize the play's newness. It demonstrated a freshness of approach which, even more sharply than Wilde's own previous plays, made the style of 'strong drama' look tired and dated, and its claims to representational authenticity appear no more convincing than Wilde's hyper-self-reflexivity. It is only that last comparison which could make *The Importance of Being Earnest* look 'naturalistic', as Hankin struggles to define precisely the play's radicalism.

In the final act of *The Importance of Being Earnest*, Jack attempts to establish Cecily's identity by appealing to official documents: 'certificates of Miss Cardew's birth, baptism, whooping cough, registration, vaccination, confirmation and the measles; both the German and the English variety' (373). He also insists on her respectable origins by adducing her grandfather's addresses in London, Surrey and Scotland. Lady Bracknell's response is significant: 'That sounds not unsatisfactory. Three addresses always inspire confidence, even in tradesmen. But what proof have I of their authenticity?' Jack's reply that he has carefully preserved the Court Guides of the period elicits a grimly sceptical response: 'I have known strange errors in that publication' (373). It is an important exchange because it neatly highlights the play's obsessive concern with public and private documents, and with their fallibility as means of establishing 'authenticity', whether of person or incident. This concern is a vital aspect of the play's hyper-self-reflexivity. *The Importance of Being Earnest* is a text among other texts, and it shares the principal characteristic of all the texts and documents (certificates, letters, diaries, etc.) it enfolds. It is a fiction, a lie, a work of art.

Wilde's play is obsessed with fictions. To an extent, Wilde is parodying the reliance of the 'well-made play', and indeed his own three previous society dramas, on letters, legal documents, etc., in propelling the plot. Even the principal motor of Wilde's narrative, Jack's cigarette case, is a text: 'It is a very ungentlemanly thing to read a private cigarette case' (324). Further, each of the main characters is directly associated with a document (or documents) which counters the fictions of others and is used in an attempt to shape and control the fictional world in which they live. In the opening scene of the play the relationship between Algy and his servant is defined by Lane's book in which he keeps the household accounts. This, it quickly transpires, is a fictional account of Algy's expenditure: a cover for Lane's plundering of the Moncrieff wine-cellar. It is also, incidentally, the occasion of the first of many pejorative comments on marriage. Algy asks why in bachelors' establishments the servants always drink the wine. Lane says he has often observed that 'in married households the champagne is rarely of a first-rate brand' (321). Cecily has two sets of fictions: her love-letters and her diary, both of which give fictional accounts of her relationship with the equally fictional Ernest. She also brings to her fictionalizing a secure sense of style. 'You see,' she tells Algy of her diary, 'it is simply a very young girl's record of her own thoughts and impressions and consequently meant for publication. When it appears in volume-form I hope you will order a copy' (377). Indeed, the conflict between Cecily and Gwendolen is bolstered by their mutual appeal to documentary evidence for verification of their respective relationships with Ernest. The announcement of their engagement will, Cecily insists, be made in 'Our little county newspaper', while Gwendolen notes, calmly, that the news of hers will 'appear in the *Morning Post* on Saturday at the latest'. When Cecily waves her diary to prove that Ernest proposed to her only ten minutes before, Gwendolen produces hers to show that she has, as it were, the prior engagement: 'It is certainly very curious, for he asked me to be his wife yesterday afternoon at 5.30. If you would care to verify the incident, pray do so.' 'I never travel without my diary,' she declares. 'One should always have something sensational to read in the train' (363). Her mother, Lady Bracknell, is inseparable from her list of eligible young men – a document which threatens to seal Jack's fate – and Jack himself has recourse to the Army Lists to prove his assumed identity. In the earlier four-act version (Alexander insisted on cuts so that it could be played in three acts, the most famous and substantial of which excised the 'Gribsby' episode when Algy is threatened with arrest for Jack's, or rather Wilde's, debts with the Savoy) this obsession with documents reaches a dramatically explicit climax when all the characters are handed a volume by Jack in order to track down his father's name in the army records. The Lists prove not to be what was expected of them, in some cases turning out to be handsomely bound catalogues and railway timetables; one, indeed, is a copy of Hichens's satirical attack on Wilde, *The Green Carnation*, which Lady Bracknell dismisses as 'a morbid and middle-class affair' (383). The documents of private fiction are thus complemented by those of officialdom and neither proves more reliable than the other, the official publications making the claim that Jack is indeed earnest.

When faced with Jack in full mourning for his brother Ernest, Dr Chasuble calmly explains that, armed with his unpublished sermons, he is ready for any eventuality: 'My sermon on the meaning of the manna in the wilderness can be adapted to almost any occasion, joyful, or, as in the present case, distressing. (*All sigh.*) I have preached it at harvest celebrations, christenings, confirmations, on days of humiliation and festal days. The last time I delivered it was in the Cathedral, as a charity sermon on behalf of the Society for the Prevention of Discontent among the Upper Orders' (346). Chasuble's sermon, in other words, has no 'authentic' meaning. His art is entirely self-referential: its signs float free of signifieds, attaching themselves, fleetingly and pragmatically, to whatever 'meanings' are deemed necessary or appropriate. Texts are inherently slippery and indeterminate. When Chasuble finally gives up the unequal struggle with Miss Prism and abandons his plans for a celibate future, he says that 'I have come to the conclusion that the Primitive Church was in error on certain points. Corrupt readings seem to have crept into the text' (381). Yet it is Miss Prism who gives the most dramatic form to the relationship between art and life, signifier and signified, which the play insists upon. We learn that she too has a bent for fiction. Gwendolen and Cecily turn their lives into fiction by means of love-letters and diaries; Algy and Jack indulge their capacity for invention in Bunburying, and their flair for narrative and drama in constructing Ernest. In her few unoccupied hours as a governess, Miss Prism had written a three-volume novel of 'more than usually revolting sentimentality'. By putting the novel in the bassinette and the baby in the handbag she unwittingly replicates that privileging of the sign over the signified, of art over life, which characterizes the behaviour of her social superiors. However, what for her is a matter of confusion, is for them a matter of style.

In effect, the whole play hinges on a privileging of the sign over the signified, or rather, on the insistence that signs are all. Gwendolen tells Jack in Act One that 'We live, as I hope you know, Mr Worthing, in an age of ideals. The fact is constantly mentioned in the more expensive monthly magazines and has now reached the provincial pulpits, I am told; and my ideal has always been to love someone of the name of Ernest. There is something in that name that inspires absolute confidence' (330). The name, the sign, is what matters, and Gwendolen's enthusiasm is, of course, shared by Cecily. Wilde is here parodying his own deployment of idealistic young women like Lady Windermere, Hester Worsley and Gertrude Chiltern, but the larger point is captured by Lady Bracknell: 'We live, I regret to say, in an age of surfaces' (374). Part of the play's radicalism lies in its insistence that identity is not a matter of authenticity or origin (after all, as Lady Bracknell points out, Jack's origin is a Terminus) but of surface, appearance, style. Algy is flabbergasted to hear Jack deny his name: 'You have always told me it was Ernest. I have introduced you to everyone as Ernest. You answer to the name of Ernest. You are the most earnest-looking person I ever saw in my life' (325). It is the fact that Jack **looks** earnest, not that he **is** earnest, which Algy insists upon. When Cecily steels herself to meet Ernest for the first time she voices her fear that 'he will look just like everyone else'. When the 'gay and debonair' Algy enters, she lets out the cry 'He does!' (342). This acute sensitivity to appearances is endemic. Algy dismisses Jack's taste in neckties and tells him that 'I never saw anybody take so long to dress, and with such little result' (353); Lady Bracknell is pointed in her praise for Algy: 'he has nothing, but he looks everything. What more can one desire?' (375). As Gwendolen will have it: 'In matters of grave importance, style, not sincerity, is the vital thing' (371). In the world of Wilde's play, being both Ernest and earnest is a matter of surfaces and style.

What Wilde gives us – in a comic intensification of the way he had explored the issue in his previous plays – is a picture of identity as radically decentered and dispersed. The characters in *The Importance of Being Earnest* all speak in the same way, with that extraterritorial perfection which has nothing to do with naturalism and everything to do with Wilde's assertion that language is the parent and not the child of thought. These are more versions of the poststructuralist subject, defined by what they say rather than what they are, and characterized by indeterminacy and instability. Indeed, the young lovers make a virtue of their changeability, bringing dramatic life to Wilde's assertion in *The Soul of Man* that change is the one quality we can predicate of human nature. 'If you are not too long,' announces Gwendolen proudly as Jack hurries off to ransack his room for the handbag which bred him, 'I will wait here for you all my life' (379). When Jack asks her if her decision on the subject of his name remains irrevocable, she assures him that 'I never change, except in my affections' (382). In effect, Jack and Algy, Cecily and Gwendolen, through the role-playing of Bunburying and the self-fashioning of their letters and diaries, stylize themselves. By putting the lie to the decay of lying, they turn themselves into art. This is most neatly captured in an exchange Wilde dropped from the more frequently performed three-act version of the play, in the interests, presumably, of speed. Miss Prism expresses the sincere hope that Algy will turn over a new leaf in life. 'I have already begun an entire volume,' comes the laconic reply (357).

Wilde releases his characters into a world in which language defines and deconstructs them, a world in which signifiers define the 'meanings' they become attached to, rather than the other way round. 'All women become like their mothers', pronounces Algy. 'That is their tragedy. No man does. That's his.' Jack wonders if this is clever. 'It is perfectly phrased!' claims Algy. 'And quite as true as any observation in civilised life should be' (335). The point is clear: language is not about truth. It is contingent and slippery, its relationship to what it purports to signify is arbitrary: a matter of stylistic effect rather than authenticity. Lady Bracknell asks if Miss Prism is a female of repellent aspect, remotely connected with education. Canon Chasuble replies indignantly that she is the most cultivated of ladies and the picture of respectability. 'It is obviously the same person,' is Lady Bracknell's verdict (378). Miss Prism is both, and neither; the contradictory descriptions multiply and disperse her.

As in *An Ideal Husband*, however, two kinds of style are in conflict. Lady Bracknell uses the notions of fashion and style to police the society she holds sway over. In her interrogation of Jack in Act One she pronounces with instant authority on his house at 149 Belgrave Square: 'The unfashionable side' (333). Russell Jackson notes that in early versions of the text she consulted a red book at this point, but that the omission of this detail is extremely effective in suggesting that her knowledge of street and house numbers is encyclopedic, definitive and immediately accessible.[40] It also suggests that she is the instant and ultimate arbiter of fashion. In the final act, she manages to warm to Cecily when she hears of her fortune: 'Poor child! Your dress is sadly simple, and your hair seems almost as Nature might have left it. But we can soon alter that. A thoroughly experienced French maid produces a really marvellous result in a very brief space of time.' Cecily may be welcomed into the charmed circle, but she must get the signifers of membership right. 'There are distinct possibilities in your profile,' continues Lady Bracknell blithely. 'The two weak points in our age are its want of principle and its want of profile. The chin a little higher, dear. Style largely depends on the way the chin is worn. They are worn very high just at present' (374). Style, as Lady Bracknell knows, is politics: to maintain the style of her society is to preserve its privilege, its power and its exclusivity. Her celebrated remarks on education and democracy, her prophetic warnings about acts of violence in Grosvenor Square, all betoken a deep-seated conservatism, an institutionally-enforced style of normativity, which comes into direct conflict with the pleasure-seeking, liberatory behaviour of the young lovers and is mocked by the play's comic undercutting of the rituals of marriage, mourning and christening.

'You have wonderfully good taste, Ernest,' Cecily tells Algy, 'I have always said that of you. It's the excuse I've always given for your leading such a bad life' (360). The remark is another neat cancellation of the ethical by the aesthetic. Lady Bracknell, however, does not bother to cloak her political prejudices in moralism. The ethical imperative is voiced instead by Miss Prism, who is persistent in reminding us that 'as a man sows so shall he reap'. Of her own novel she says, 'The good ended happily, the bad unhappily. That is what Fiction means' (341). However, for the young lovers fiction does not mean that – it means self-fashioning freedom from the kinds of authority personified by Lady Bracknell, a stylish refusal of her magisterially ordained normativity. For Jack, lying – as for Wilde in his theoretical essays – is a kind of heroism: 'To invent anything at all is an act of sheer genius, and, in a commercial age like ours, shows considerable physical courage. Few of our modern novelists dare to invent a single thing' (375). It is the spirit of playfulness embodied in their Bunburying, the style with which they fictionalize their lives, which acts as a solvent on Lady Bracknell's politics. Interestingly, the early four-act version sketched out a direct alignment between that playfulness and a nexus of radical politics by making Cecily not just assertive but a comic version of the New Woman. Canon Chasuble seeks assurance that she understands the relations between Capital and Labour. She replies by saying that she understands, merely from observation, the relations between Capital and Idleness. Miss Prism is shocked at what sounds like Socialism: 'And I suppose you know where Socialism leads to?' 'Yes,' comes Cecily's reply, which itself recognizes the politics of style, 'that leads to Rational Dress, Miss Prism. And I suppose that when a woman is dressed rationally, she is treated rationally. She certainly deserves to be' (342). Later, Algy asks if she will make it her mission to reform him and she replies, indignantly, that although 'every female' may have a mission, 'no woman' has (344). Cecily is refusing a 'female' role in favour of a politically-charged 'womanly' one and puts Algy firmly in his place when she transcribes his faltering professions of undying love: 'The fact is, men should never try to dictate to women' (358). Wilde excised Cecily's waspishly politicized sense of humour in the interests of economy, but the three-act version retains a challenging of conventional gender-roles. Cecily and Gwendolen assume the traditionally male qualities of the sexual predator; Jack and Algy dedicate themselves to the traditionally feminine interests of clothes and food. It is Cecily who compliments Algy on his hair and asks if it curls naturally. 'Yes, darling', he replies, 'with a little help from others' (360).

This inversion of gender roles has encouraged some critics to see *Earnest* as an exercise in gay politics. Joseph Bristow argues, for instance, that it is a 'privately coded as well as publicly entertaining play.'[41] He cites the currency during the 1890s of 'Ernest' as a carefully coded word for homosexual desire,[42] and points to a series of private 'jokes' about Wilde's homosexual circle: the editor of *The Chameleon* (an Oxford undergraduate magazine of 'uranian' sympathies which published his 'Phrases and Philosophies for the use of the Young') turns up in the name Lady Bloxham; Jack's address, the Albany, was the residence of the 'homosexual emancipationist' George Ives. Bristow's is a basically biographical approach which regards Bunburying as Wilde's comic celebration of the dangers of his sexual double-life (and it is an approach apparently sanctioned by the personal references Wilde makes in his text: to his debts at the Savoy, for instance, and the revenge he takes on *The Green Carnation*). It is also premised, once again, on the surface-depth model of analysis. *Earnest* is a 'gay' play 'underneath'; it is a code to be cracked.[43] This is an attempt to locate the text's originary meaning: to stabilize and fix it. Bristow and Bracknell are curiously at one: he wants to authenticate *Earnest* in the same way as she wants to authenticate Jack. However, the radicalism of the play is not to be found by excavating it and returning it to an authentic and specific homosexual politics, but in recognizing the way it counters and dissolves a pernicious authoritarianism, personified by Lady Bracknell, with a deliberate and self-conscious emphasis on the liberatory potential of style.[44] *Earnest* is not just about the politics of style, its politics are all style.

In this respect, the play's ending is artfully poised. Jack announces that his name is Ernest, after all: 'I mean it naturally is Ernest.' With a respectable family history, a 'name' and position, he is in Lady Bracknell's eyes no longer the rich but threatening 'outsider'. Jack has been respectable 'underneath' all along. By marrying her daughter, he will be formally admitted into aristocratic society and appears to embrace Lady Bracknell's values by declaring that he has finally realized the vital importance of being earnest. This, then, is the unmasking that Ellmann says Wilde's dramas culminate in: Jack must leave his world of 'make believe' behind. However, the conservatism of this conventional ending (signified by the multiple marriages) is deconstructed by the style Wilde holds it in. From another angle, it seems to be not a victory for Lady Bracknell but for Wilde's own theoretical essays. As in 'The Decay of Lying', Life imitates Art as Jack's family history conforms to the role he has been playing. Style, in other words, defines substance. Furthermore, Jack's insistence that his name is 'naturally' Ernest is instantly invalidated because the play has repeatedly undermined the idea of 'the natural' in a way familiar from the three society dramas which have preceded it. Wilde deconstructs the conventional binary opposition between the sophisticated, wicked town and the natural innocence of the country. Lady Bracknell reminds Jack that 'A girl with a simple, unspoiled nature, like Gwendolen, could hardly be expected to reside in the country' (333), and when the action shifts from town to country the movement is hardly that towards the 'pure' and 'simple'.[45] As we have seen, Algy's idea of naturalness involves curling-tongs. Jack's discovery of a 'natural' identity has been cancelled before it is made, because the play denies the difference between the natural (the authentic) and the cultural (the assumed, the constructed, the 'acted'). The final pun celebrates the arbitrary and fluid relationship of sign to signified, deliberately confusing the name with the quality. It is also self-cancelling: Lady Bracknell's 'seriousness' is collapsed into its opposite, the 'triviality' of Jack's role-playing as Ernest. The slipperiness of language allows Wilde and his play to elude Lady Bracknell and the limiting, oppressive normativity she represents.

Powell speculates that Wilde paid a visit to Terry's Theatre in the autumn of 1894 where he saw Lestocq and Benson's *The Foundling*, so striking are the similarities of detail between this long-forgotten farce and *The Importance of Being Earnest*. He goes on to argue that Wilde's play is an act of aggression against the genre of farce as a whole, though occasionally it 'sinks back into the orbit of tradition' and the level of the plays it is parodying.[46] It might be more accurate to say that Wilde employs some of the principal characteristics of farce as an act of aggression against 'respectable' drama and its pretensions to psychological realism, seriousness of content and representational authenticity. The staples of farce – disguise, mistaken identity, gender-bending *à la Charley's Aunt* (1892), cross-talk – are transformed by Wilde into a dramatic exploration of the fluidity and multiformity of social and sexual identity and of the power of language to shape us and the lives we lead. This act of aggression is political as well as stylistic. *Earnest* is not a socialist play 'underneath' but is socialist in its fascination with surface – if not obviously so – and in its manner. Wilde associates socialism with a future that is aesthetically as well as materially satisfying, and one in which authority in all its forms has been deconstructed. The self-conscious playfulness of *The Importance of Being Earnest* is an act of faith in that utopian future in which the exquisites, and not Lady Bracknell, will rule.

REFERENCES

[1] Quoted in Ellmann, *Oscar Wilde*: 359.

[2] *Oscar Wilde*: 399.

[3] Eltis, *Revising Wilde*: 55, 58, 60. Eltis is relentless in applying this model of analysis: *A Woman of No Importance* is 'on one level a successful sentimental play' while 'below the surface lay a far more complex moral pattern' (128); 'beneath the surface melodrama' of *An Ideal Husband*, she argues, 'lies a more subtly contradictory play of social and political satire' (169); *The Importance of Being Earnest* 'is as subtly deceptive as its predecessors, for the light-hearted exterior conceals a more sinister purpose' (171), a radical play 'beneath a smoothly reassuring surface' (175). Eltis also contrasts the explicitness of *The Ballad of Reading Gaol* with the society plays in which 'the politics had lain beneath the surface' (207).

[4] Epifanio San Juan, *The Art of Oscar Wilde*, Princeton University Press, Princeton, 1967: 143.

[5] Gilbert Burgess, '*An Ideal Husband* at the Haymarket Theatre. A Talk with Mr Oscar Wilde', *The Sketch*, 9 January 1895: 495.

[6] Quoted in Peter Raby, 'Wilde's Comedies of Society', in Raby, ed., *The Cambridge Companion*: 143.

[7] Quoted in Eltis, *Revising Wilde*: 176.

[8] *Letters*: 359.

[9] Louis Kronenberger, *The Thread of Laughter*, Alfred A. Knopf, New York, 1952: 222.

[10] The game Wilde was playing was not lost on some of his contemporaries. For instance, P.P. Howe – writing in 1911, perhaps at the kind of near-distance which allowed him to go beyond the usual charges of artistic theft and dramatic larceny – recognized that the anti-naturalism of *Lady Windermere's Fan* was deliberate, rather than the accidental consequence of Wilde stealing from other plays. Although he felt the play dated and badly constructed, Howe recognized the link between it and 'The Decay of Lying': 'What is *Lady Windermere's Fan* but one long, elaborate, self-conscious lie, based throughout on the doctrines of his "new aesthetics"?' In

Outlook, 21 October, 1911: 536. Reprinted in William Tydeman, ed., *Wilde: Comedies*, Macmillan, Basingstoke, 1982: 90.

[11] Wyndham Lewis, *Men Without Art*: 67.

[12] *Men Without Art*: 67.

[13] Arthur Symons, *A Study of Oscar Wilde*, C.J. Sawyer, London, 1930: 56.

[14] Kerry Powell, *Oscar Wilde and the Theatre of the 1890s*, Cambridge University Press, Cambridge, 1990: 6, 8, 57, 140.

[15] *Theatre of the 1890s*: 12, 11.

[16] Quoted by Ellmann, *Oscar Wilde*: 387.

[17] Quoted in Tydeman, ed., *Wilde: Comedies*: 32.

[18] See Joel H. Kaplan and Sheila Stowell, *Theatre and Fashion: Oscar Wilde to the Suffragettes*, Cambridge University Press, Cambridge, 1994: 20.

[19] See Powell, *Theatre of the 1890s*: 26.

[20] George Bernard Shaw remarked of *Mr and Mrs Daventry* that 'If Oscar had written it, it would now be a classic.' Quoted by Eltis, *Revising Wilde*: 205.

[21] Gilbert Burgess, 'A Talk with Mr Oscar Wilde': 495.

[22] Robert Gordon, 'Wilde's "Plays of Modern Life" on the Contemporary British Stage', in George Sandulescu, ed., *Rediscovering Oscar Wilde*, Colin Smythe, Gerrard's Cross, 1994: 161.

[23] Mrs Arbuthnot's stagey entrance was neatly parodied in *Theatre* magazine for June 1893: 'I am a lady with a past tempered by repentance: that is why I am attired in black velveteen.' See Kaplan and Stowell, *Theatre and Fashion*: 188. Kaplan and Stowell also note that Mrs Arbuthnot's costuming in the original production, by Lewis and Allenby, neatly captured the ambivalent style of her penitence: 'The result was an elegant form of anti-fashion that borrowed from the codified chic of Victorian mourning as well as the self-conscious theatricality of mid-century dandies and bohemians' (26). In a sense, Mrs Arbuthnot is also styling herself as Hawthorne's Hester Prynne, who brought a similarly theatrical sense to her status as outcast from the New England puritan community.

[24] Powell, *Theatre of the 1890s*: 56, 72, 7. To Powell's list of plays Wilde 'borrowed from' Sos Eltis adds Sardou's *Les Vieux Garcons* (1865); Augier's *Le Fils de Giboyer* (1862) and *Les Fourchambault* (1878); Jones's *Saints and Sinners* (1884), and Pinero's *The Profligate* (1889). See *Revising Wilde*: 95–6.

[25] Hawthorne's *The Scarlet Letter*, first published in 1850, had been adapted several times for the stage during the previous decade. Its heroine is another puritan, Hester Prynne, who has an illegitimate daughter, Pearl (Mrs Arbuthnot calls Gerald her pearl) and sews a scarlet 'A' onto her dress to signal her outcast status.

[26] For an entirely different reading of Wilde's treatment of moralism in the society comedies see Philip K. Cohen, *The Moral Vision of Oscar Wilde*. He argues of *Lady Windermere's Fan* and *A Women of No Importance*, for instance, that, 'the heroines redeem themselves and regain their authenticity by defying the power of conventional morality and answering to God himself' (193). *An Ideal Husband* and *The Importance of Being Earnest*, on the other hand, reveal a loss of imaginative control and artistic disintegration as they refuse to confront moral considerations (13).

[27] See Eltis, *Revising Wilde*: 111. Eltis compares Illingworth with conventional rakes such as Dumas's Charles Sternay and the Duke of Guisbury in *The Dancing Girl* (a role made famous by Beerbohm Tree before he took on the part of Illingworth in Wilde's play).

[28] Quoted in Ellmann, *Oscar Wilde*: 359.

[29] See Eltis, *Revising Wilde*: 134–5.

[30] Quoted in Ellmann, *Oscar Wilde*: 387.

[31] *Oscar Wilde*: ix.

[32] Baudelaire, *Selected Writings*: 420.

[33] George Bernard Shaw, review of *An Ideal Husband*, *Saturday Review*, 12 January 1895: 44–5.

[34] For an illuminating account of the play in terms of 1890s debates about the 'morally improving' nature of a particularly politicized version of the feminine, and Wilde's attempt to resist the 'feminist police', see Powell, *Theatre of the 1890s*: 89–107.

[35] For a detailed account of Hall's Globe theatre production and its approach to this scene, see Richard Allen Cave, 'Wilde designs; some thoughts about recent British productions of his plays', *Modern Drama*, 37 (Spring 1994): 175–91.

[36] Reprinted in Tydeman, ed., *Wilde: Comedies*: 42.

[37] Reprinted in Margery Morgan, ed., *File on Wilde*, Methuen, London, 1990: 44.

[38] *File on Wilde*: 44.

[39] *File on Wilde*: 45.

[40] Russell Jackson, 'The Importance of Being Earnest', in Raby, ed., *The Cambridge Companion*: 169.

[41] Joseph Bristow, ed., *The Importance of Being Earnest and Related Writings*, Routledge, London, 1992: 19.

[42] See Timothy D'Arch Smith, *Love in Earnest: Some Notes on the Lives and Writings of English 'Uranian' Poets from 1889 to 1930*, Routledge and Kegan Paul, London, 1970: viii.

[43] Nick Hytner's 1993 revival at the Aldwych tried to lay bare a 'gay subtext'. Algy and Jack greeted each other with a full kiss on the lips and John Peter claimed in the *Sunday Times* (2 April, 1993) that 'it is simply understood that marrying enchanting young ladies need only be part of a young gentleman's social and erotic career.' See Joel Kaplan, 'Wilde on the Stage' in Raby, ed., *The Cambridge Companion*: 271–2. Patrick Mason's 1997 production at the Abbey Theatre in Dublin gave this 'gay subtext' a different twist. According to Fintan O'Toole, Mason suggested that the sexual subversiveness of the play lies in the fact that real interactions are between members of the same sex: 'The relationship of Frank McCusker's haplessly bemused Jack to Darragh Kelly's fruity and louche Algy seems much more like a bored marriage than a mere friendship.' See 'Glorious triviality', *Irish Times*, 21 January 1997.

[44] In another attempt to authenticate Wilde, Declan Kiberd also identifies Lady Bracknell as the principal target in *Earnest* and declares that 'the politics and psychology of the play are quintessentially republican.' 'Oscar Wilde: The Artist as Irishman' in MacCormack, ed., *Wilde the Irishman*: 20.

[45] In a manner reminiscent of Prowse's staging of *A Woman of No Importance*, Peter Hall's 1982 National Theatre production emphasized the artificiality of the Manor House setting. *The Guardian* described John Bury's garden set as featuring a 'shimmering blue stage floor backed with a cut-out landscape and pantomime tree'. See Joel Kaplan, 'Wilde on the Stage', in Raby, ed., *The Cambridge Companion*: 270.

[46] See Powell, *Theatre of the 1890s*: 108–43.

5

FROM BAUDELAIRE TO BOWIE

When Sex Pistols Svengali Malcolm McLaren can convince the *Irish Times* (19 July 1997) that he is planning a movie with Stephen Spielberg about how Wilde discovered rock 'n' roll in America, it is clear that his name has acquired a resonance and currency that even Oscar would have been surprised at. 'Wilde' is now a pop-cultural icon, a multiform signifier of youth, rebelliousness, individualism, sexual freedom, modernity. In order to understand the particular fascination Wilde now exercizes, it is necessary first to look back to some of the historical antecedents of that dandyism which Wilde explored in his writings and acted out in his life, and which is now variously interpreted as marking him so graphically as our contemporary.

Once again Baudelaire looms large, both for Wilde and for us. The dominant category in Baudelaire's definition of dandyism is 'attitude'.[1] Nowadays, attitude is all. It is the basic constituent of what is understood as style. Clothes have attitude, music has attitude. (If you don't have attitude, you run the risk of being 'sad': the ultimate insult.) Although Baudelaire claimed for dandyism a long history, citing Caeser, Catilina and Alcibiades as exemplars, he saw it principally as a kind of modern heroism, a way of embodying individualism in an age of increasing conformity and utility ('To be a useful person has always appeared to me something particularly horrible'[2]) and he acknowledged the importance of Jules Barbey D'Aurevilly's *On Dandyism and George Brummell* (1845) in theorizing it as such. The dandy strives to 'create a personal form of originality within the external limits of social conventions', says Baudelaire. That originality is expressed in the 'pleasure of causing surprise in others, and the proud satisfaction of never showing any oneself.'[3] Dandyism is an exercise in 'cool', and, for Baudelaire, 'cool' is both aesthetic and political.

Baudelaire neatly captures the paradox of dandyism, one which is central to Huysmans's treatment of his hero Des Esseintes in *Against Nature* (1884), the novel described by Arthur Symons as the 'breviary' of the decadence,[4] and sampled by Wilde in *Dorian Gray*. Des Esseintes is the type of the aristocratic dandy who withdraws further and further into a luxuriously

artificial world of his own making. He adopts an increasingly uncompromising regime, regarding eating as cheating, and deciding, eventually, to
take nourishment only through elaborately prepared enemas. In the end, he
is forced by ill-health back into the society for which he has developed such
distaste. Huysmans's novel is partly a parable about the difference between
the pursuit of style, and the retreat into solipsism. For Baudelaire, the dandy
is both insider and outsider: he must play tantalizingly with social conventions rather than put himself beyond the pale by ignoring or blatantly transgressing them. The dandy needs an audience to complete the performance,
so his individualism is always mediated. As Baudelaire says, dandyism is 'a
kind of cult of the ego which can still survive the pursuit of that form of
happiness to be found in others.' This ambivalence is embodied in the
dandy's attitude to that most concrete manifestation of modernity: urban
living. City life, for Baudelaire, was 'rich in poetic and marvellous subjects.
We are enveloped and steeped as though in an atmosphere of the marvellous;
but we do not notice it.'[5] The Baudelairean *flâneur* strolls effortlessly through
the Parisian arcades, converting the ephemera of consumerism into the prized
objects of a discriminating aesthetic gaze. That conversion distinguishes the
dandy from the vulgarly acquisitive impulses of those who swirl around
him. It also signals his dependence on the commodity and on those whose
labour produces it. The dandy must treat the crowd with disdain, while
secretly acknowledging its necessity to him. As Benjamin puts it: 'Baudelaire
loved solitude, but he wanted it in a crowd.'[6] Dandyism is thus characterized
not simply by its detachment and *hauteur* but by its doubleness: it is implicated in, has an investment in, the very formations against which it defines
itself. This contradiction is clear when Baudelaire articulates explicitly what
he understands as the political implications of dandyism. At times he links a
dandyesque individualism with social progress in a manner that seems to
anticipate Wilde in *The Soul of Man*: 'in order that the law of Progress could
exist each man would have to be willing to enforce it; for it is only when
every individual has made up his mind to move forward that humanity will
be in a state of progress.'[7] At others his disdain for the vulgarity of the crowd
or mob issues in a virulent anti-democratism which rejects the notion of
political progress: 'Can you imagine a dandy addressing the common herd,
except to make game of them? There is no form of rational and assured
government save an aristocracy.'[8] Indeed, dandies are, for Baudelaire, a threatened species, caught by the filthy modern tide of democracy 'which spreads
everywhere and reduces everything to the same level' and 'is daily carrying
away these last champions of human pride, and submerging, in the waters of
oblivion, the last traces of these remarkable myrmidons.'[9] For Benjamin,
Baudelaire's anti-democratism is cognate with an aestheticization of politics
that is proto-fascistic.[10]

The crucial issue is the degree to which Wilde draws on Baudelaire's formulations in both his presentation and his performance of dandyism, and the way he simultaneously transforms its politics. Ironically, in *The Soul of Man* Wilde cites Baudelaire as an example of those rare personalities who have managed to realize themselves fully, before the advent of that socialist future which, he believes, will extend that opportunity to everyone. The languidly patrician attitudes, the cool detachment, the superfine aesthetic sensibilities, the studied indolence of Wilde's dandies are clearly indebted to Baudelaire. (Des Esseintes's neurotic personality means that his pose of imperturbability is very precariously maintained.) However, Wilde has English practice and precedent as well as French theory to draw upon. Beau Brummell, Dickens, Disraeli, for instance, had all employed the dandy's arsenal of sartorial expertise and insouciant wit as a means of attaining social mobility: all were social 'outsiders' (and, in Disraeli's case, a racial outsider) who moved from margin to centre.[11] It is possible to see this movement as simply confirming power and privilege, and of reinforcing social formations based on exclusivity: dandyism becomes merely a method of social-climbing. John Harvey argues, though, of Beau Brummell's restrained and disciplined dandyism that 'it was the style, conspicuously unflashy, of an impeccable self-respect, of a self-respect not tied to rank. He never aped the aristocrats, and on the contrary the times were such that the aristocrats, and even the prince of the realm, doffed their plumage in order to ape him.'[12] Brummell effects an inversion of social and political relations. Wilde takes the process a step further: those structures are not just inverted, they are collapsed. As I have argued of his presentation in *An Ideal Husband* of the social dynamics of fashion which level the producers and the consumers of style, it can in fact be an important solvent of social hierarchies. Style comes to function not as a means by which the centre defines itself, but as a means by which that same centre is transformed and democratized – by people with attitude.

Baudelaire believed that, although things were going from bad to worse in France, social and political conditions in England in the 1860s (where the aristocracy in his view had not yet been fatally wounded) meant that there would be room for the dandies (the heirs of Brummell and Byron, as he called them) for some time to come.[13] Dandyism thus acquired for him some of the glamour of foreignness, and was also a way of constructing 'Englishness' and of annexing it for his own purposes. For Baudelaire, 'Englishness' became a complex signifier of a radically anti-bourgeois attitude; by sympathizing with it he signalled his own oppositional stance and exotic 'otherness'.[14] For Wilde, both 'Irishness' and 'Englishness' were, as we have seen, forms of discursive play and performance. Indeed, his personal dandyism can be seen as a kind of performed 'Englishness' in which he apparently takes direction from Baudelaire. However, by seeming to identify 'Englishness' with dandyism (in both his life and his writing) Wilde was not following Baudelaire and announcing his allegiance to a beleaguered but still powerful aristocracy which was the repository of political and aesthetic authority. He was, instead, simultaneously parodying those aristocratic attitudes and identifying them with their opposite: with a stylish refusal of social and political hierarchies authenticated by birth and sustained by material exploitation.

Perhaps the most salient example of Wilde's transformation of Baudelaire's dandyism, however, is in their respective gender-politics. Wilde aligns himself with early nineteenth-century English dandies like Brummell, Disraeli and Bulwer-Lytton who were, according to Harvey, pioneers of gender, 'exploring an identity that puzzled contemporaries by seeming at once both manly and feminine.'[15] Baudelaire's theory of dandyism, however, is proudly misogynistic. 'Woman,' he announces, 'is *natural*, that is to say abominable.' Women are the incarnation of appetite and thus inspire horror. They are 'the opposite' of the dandy.[16] (For Baudelaire the dandy is both exclusively male and curiously asexual. Sexual intercourse is an abnegation of individualism, an annihilation of the self: 'To fornicate is to enter into another; the artist never emerges from himself.'[17]) Although Wilde has been accused of similar misogyny,[18] the charge can be refuted not just by reference to his interest in and support of feminism but by the way he self-consciously counters Baudelaire in creating female dandies. Mrs Erlynne, Mrs Allonby and, to a lesser extent, Mabel Chiltern all display the wit and 'cool' which displaces male authority and control. Cecily and Gwendolen, in *The Importance of Being Earnest*, are similarly poised and, like all dandies, alert to the abominations of the natural and the authentic. However, the most instructive and ironic example is Lady Bracknell. She displays a dandy's self-possession, verbal facility and insistence on the importance of appearances and style. In that respect, she is thoroughly 'Wildean'. However, she combines this with an epigrammatic contempt for democracy and is the self-appointed champion of a threatened aristocracy which needs Jack's wealth to survive. In other words, Wilde's most Baudelairean dandy is a woman. It is a pointed and deliberate reversal: a self-consciously paradoxical cancellation of both Baudelaire's misogyny and his belief in the desirability of aristocratic government. After all, Lady Bracknell also represents the stifling normativity which all dandies, both Baudelairean and Wildean, define themselves against.

Wilde recognized in the attitude of Baudelaire's mid-nineteenth-century dandyism a radical potential which ran counter to its declared politics. As we have seen, he plays with this idea in *An Ideal Husband* by putting the paradoxical expression of his own socialism into the mouth of Lord

Illingworth. In this respect, Wilde is a pivotal figure in the history of dandyism: the progressive aspects he chose to develop and emphasize have become powerfully influential upon modern 'pop-cultural' versions of dandyism which are similarly crystallized around notions of style and attitude. Michael Bracewell's *England is Mine: Pop Life in England from Wilde to Goldie* (1997), and his BBC television film 'Oscar' (12 October 1997), are examples of the way Wilde is now reproduced as a kind of Godfather of Rock (the proximity of Wilde's grave to Jim Morrison's in Père Lâchaise gives such an idea a kind of camp morbidity). In the film Bracewell argues that Wilde is the first rock star, that Bosie was the 'ultimate' groupie, and that Wilde initiated a cult of youth which has spawned modern Dorian Grays such as Cliff Richard and Michael Jackson (cut to a black-and-white clip of a quiffed and brylcreemed Sir Cliff singing 'The Young Ones'). In the book, these slick and frequently unconvincing parallels are replaced by a more thoughtful discussion in which Bracewell argues that pop has picked up the cultural baton from literary modernism, in the sense that it is now the most fitting vehicle for that spirit of anti-bourgeois rebellion which he sees as originating at the end of the nineteenth century in the cult of aesthetics. Wilde is thus the seminal figure: 'the first martyr to modern bigotry.'[19]

Bracewell's thesis produces some amusing and occasionally illuminating formulations, such as Wyndham Lewis as a kind of proto-punk and Neil Tennant of the Pet Shop Boys as a latter-day Auden. He also argues that Wilde has passed the baton (a curiously unhurried relay-team, this one) to David Bowie: 'English dandyism reached an apotheosis with Bowie, and dandyism, in England, had always suggested the suburban outsider's subtle revenge on home and high society alike – a mask behind which to advance.'[20] Wilde, unlike Bowie, was no suburbanite, but the central point is an interesting one: as Dick Hebdige puts it, from Mick Jagger in Nic Roeg's *Performance* (1969) to Bowie's 'thin white duke', the spectre of the dandy has 'haunted rock from the wings.'[21] Bowie's sequence of stage-personae from Ziggy Stardust through Aladdin Sane to the thin white duke and beyond spring from a Wildean aesthetic grounded in 'make-believe', in role-playing and the inauthentic: and it is one which he self-consciously culled from artists like Warhol and other avant-garde 'underground' sources. In his television film Bracewell recalls, while sitting on what he claims is the bed in which Wilde died (the hotel room distinguished by some particularly unpleasant flock wallpaper), that as a fifteen year old he had two posters on his wall. Bowie and Wilde stared across at each other. While Bowie was taken down, Wilde stayed, as a more lasting icon for 'those who dared to be different.' Although Bracewell doesn't give his reasons for outgrowing Bowie, they perhaps lie in the way Bowie's career as dandy is trapped in contradiction. In some respects he is the Wildean dandy whose polymorphous sexuality and flair for self-fashioning promises a liberatory future, despite his apparent indifference to the 'real' world of politics. As a rock star he makes Camp available to an audience which would otherwise not experience it, helping to fashion an 'adolescent' rejection of the 'real' world which awaits. In other respects his desire to shock leads to a self-conscious aestheticization of politics which, in a progression Benjamin would have recognized as characteristic of the Baudelairean dandy, issues in designer-fascism: 'Hitler was the first superstar,' Bowie is reported as saying, 'he really did it right.'[22]

Bracewell usefully highlights, as evidence of Wilde's influence on the developing self-image of rock, the promotional film made by The Rolling Stones for their 1967 single 'We Love You'. The film features Mick Jagger as Oscar and his girlfriend Marianne Faithfull as the ultimately treacherous Bosie. As Bracewell notes, 'after the Jagger drug trial, their choice of conceit in an English courtroom (complete with rattling keys and chains) took on an extra frisson of meaning.'[23] The film is certainly a significant cultural text, enacting a series of revealing identifications and transformations. Jagger as rock star is identified in his criminality with Wilde as artist: both are identified as martyrs to personal freedom. Wilde is lifted from his historical context and identified with modern celebrity. Together they embody an androgynous sexuality which attracts a cluster of significations: glamour, marginality, sexual nonconformism, freedom through role-play. Further, Jagger and Faithfull are identified with 'aristocracy'. That is to say, they transform it into an oxymoron: the 'pop-aristocracy'. The film is a neat anatomy of dandyism, laying bare both its oppositional stance and its ambivalent relationship to what it defines itself against and seeks to transform. The film is, after all, an advert: it commodifies the diverting spectacle of revolt and refusal. As Benjamin says: 'Baudelaire knew what the situation of the man of letters was: he goes to the marketplace as a *flâneur*, supposedly to look at it, but in reality to find a buyer.'[24]

Wilde's career as a public personality enacts that same contradiction. He was implicated in, had an investment in, the commercial and commodity culture he critiqued. His 1882 lecture tour of America (Bracewell: 'like all budding rock stars, he had to break in America') was not a simple evangelical mission. Wilde sold himself as a dandy and 'Professor of Aesthetics', and also helped Richard D'Oyly Carte to sell the Gilbert and Sullivan comic opera *Patience* which lampooned the aesthetic movement, and which toured the States in his wake. Such self-commodification is a form of self-fashioning. Wilde undertook it with shameless brashness, with attitude. However, as his celebrity grew it was purloined to sell specific 'luxury' commodities such as Straiton and Storm cigars and Ehrich Brothers Trimmed Hats.[25] Later still he helped – inadvertently, of course – to increase sales of the *Illustrated*

Police Budget. In other words, Wilde struggled to keep control and posses-sion of his most precious commodity: himself. As a writer, I have argued, he was more successful: he invested, metaphorically, in the commercial stage by deploying its conventions, but did so with a style which transformed them. For the playwright, as for the dandy, to ignore conventions – artistic or social – was to risk losing the audience and the public both relied upon. Wilde's struggles in this respect were paralleled by Impressionist painters like Manet and Degas as their work became commercially successful. As T.J. Clark puts it, by the end of the 1880s, 'Market conditions encouraged the dealer to speculate with the long-term "creativity" of those artists he favoured; and artists in turn learnt to market that particular commodity with some skill – nursing and refining it in a steady sequence of shows, interviews and promotional literature, trying to strike the right balance between innova-tion and product reliability, sniffing out the market's approximate wishes while maintaining (to the death) the protocols of individuality and artistic freedom.'[26] There is, then, something fitting in our contemporary fixation with Wilde as a precursor of a dandyism that is inseparable from celebrity and stardom. It recognizes the acute tensions he had to negotiate, and the dandy's involved detachment from the material conditions he comments upon, refuses and needs. This is not a matter of compromise, but of style and attitude. By turning himself deliberately and self-consciously into a commodity, Wilde parodied the relentless logic of the marketplace, trans-forming its material processes into performance art.

By claiming that Wilde discovered rock 'n' roll in America, Malcolm McLaren is not simply retreading the idea that he was the first rock star. He is also adroitly recognizing the importance of Wilde's notion that our first duty to history is to rewrite it. In effect, the deconstructive elements of Wilde's aesthetic are turned back against his own biography. His champion-ing of the inauthentic itself sanctions the self-consciously inaccurate ways in which he is now reproduced: as in Eagleton's *Saint Oscar*, and, more signific-antly here, in Todd Haynes's 1998 film *Velvet Goldmine*, which opens in Dublin in 1854 with Wilde, as infant alien, deposited by spaceship on a doorstep. Haynes's 'history' of glam rock which fictionalizes Bowie as Brian Slade, claims Wilde as its presiding genius: 'there was no more articulate spokesman for that artifice, that informed camp sensibility than Wilde.' Haynes regards Wilde as a symbol of radical otherness and strangeness: 'I decided to align the sexually ambivalent Wilde with aliens – homosexuals and teens are often seen as "alien" – so I opened with the spaceship, which tied in with glam's interest in sci-fi. . . .'[27] (Ziggy's spiders came, after all, from Mars.) The brooch worn by the infant alien is passed on – rather like Bracewell's baton – to Slade and Curt Wild, Haynes's version of Iggy Pop. The film's anti-naturalistic and self-referential style makes it an exercize in

the inauthentic as well as a celebration of it: 'I don't want the film to carry a
notion of objective truth or ultimate psychological meaning,' says Haynes,
explaining in particular his use of *Citizen Kane* as a distancing-frame.[28] Glam
rock fascinates Haynes because of its 'attack on authentic, direct emotional
communication, which is what tends to define music, at least in America.'[29]
(For the American Haynes, as for Baudelaire, dandyism in the persons of
Bryan Ferry and David Bowie has the glamour of foreignness, and 'Englishness' is constructed in terms of its indifference to 'roots'.) The film is also
interesting because of the knowingness with which it shows Slade/Bowie
'selling out': a recognition of the problematic relationships between dandyism and stardom, and between self-fashioning and self-commodification. It
also demonstrates the way subcultural style can be 'incorporated within the
dominant ideology from which it in part emerges.'[30] For Haynes, glam rock
marks the historical high-point of pop-cultural style as subversion. He is
acutely aware of the way such style can turn into its opposite so that the
MTV/Madonna generation now suffers from a saturation with style and
look: 'what was truly interesting about it – the act of looking and reading –
has gone away and we've lost a critical distance, an interrogative relationship
with ourselves and what we're seeing. We're so used to the pose now, we just
take it at face-value.'[31]

Central to our notions of rock-stardom is the narrative of burn-out, of
the life of imperious and heroic excess which, as with Janis Joplin, Jimi
Hendrix, Jim Morrison, Kurt Cobain, Michael Hutchence, extinguishes
itself. As we have seen with his own self-fabrication in *De Profundis*, with
which I opened this book, Wilde's life is easily accommodated to, or seen as
an archetype for, this narrative of overreaching which can be variously seen
as a form of tragedy or martyrdom, or both – and tailored to suit contemporary needs for self-destructive heroes.[32] (Self-destruction is, after all, a
victory of sorts because it denies to the opposition the satisfaction of deliv-
ering the final defeat.) Brian Gilbert's film *Wilde* (1997) with Stephen Fry in
the lead is another attempt to sell him as our contemporary, deploying a
variation of this narrative, but it is one which, in my view, is significantly
less effective and interesting than Todd Haynes's fantasy. This is 'straight'
biography in more than one sense. The film offers itself as 'based' on
Ellmann's researches, as faithful to historical fact, and is thoroughly conventional in format. Stephen Fry says that Gilbert had initially considered using
various framing and distancing devices, such as 'witnesses' explaining what
Wilde meant to them (rather like in Warren Beatty's *Reds*) or of using a
modern figure who has Wilde as a kind of familiar (shades here of Humphrey
Bogart in Woody Allen's *Play it Again, Sam* and of Elvis in Tarantino's *True
Romance*). In the end, these ideas were jettisoned, and any attempt to foreground the film's artifice dispensed with, Fry commenting that 'perhaps

when you have an unconventional story to tell, a good rule of thumb is to tell it in a conventional way.'[33] However, both Gilbert's matter and manner are entirely conventional: this is Wilde as a kind of all-purpose enemy of a vaguely conceived Victorianism that, in its intolerance and bigotry, is inimical to the individual, 'authentic' personality. It is a familiar narrative of persecution, with some pointed contemporary parallels: Gilbert shows Wilde's mother harried by a pack of reporters after the verdict goes against him. Wilde is one of us, the film claims, because he tries to realize his real nature, to go his own way in spite of law and social convention. In this respect, Gilbert's film is very similar to Tom Stoppard's *The Invention of Love* (1997) in which A.E. Housman's inability to face up to, and act upon, his true sexual nature brands him as indelibly Victorian, while Wilde makes his salutary appearance as an example of a modern sexual assertiveness and fidelity to self ('Better a fallen rocket than never a burst of light,' says Wilde's ghost.[34]). Gilbert's film has it both ways. It enlists our sympathy for Wilde by upholding his right to 'deviant' sexual preference, while simultaneously recuperating him as a family man. The film does have some explicit sexual content, but it involves Jude Law's Bosie, while Wilde merely watches. Gilbert locates his film firmly within the genre of Brit-Lit costume drama: this is Wilde as part of the heritage industry, rendered as decorative and unthreatening as a Merchant-Ivory E.M. Forster. In so doing Gilbert negates that replacement of authenticity with style which Haynes effects in *Velvet Goldmine*. *Wilde* may be closer to what we know of historical fact, but it is much less 'Wildean'.

In locating 'some lines of influence' from Wilde's plays to recent British and Irish drama, Richard Allen Cave notes both direct indebtedness (as in Joe Orton, the 'Oscar Wilde of the Welfare State', another subversive dramatist writing for 'middle-brow', West-End audiences) and some more oblique legacies: he claims for instance that Wilde's ghost haunts Frank McGuinness's defence of the gay artist in *Carthaginians* (1988).[35] I would argue that a significant influence can also be seen in Mark Ravenhill's *Handbag* (1998). The play is partly a burlesque prequel to *The Importance of Being Earnest* in which Lady Bracknell appears as an Irish woman in London on the make ('I am not Irish. Except by birth and upbringing. Which I am sure you will agree, are of no relevance whatsoever.'[36]) and Thomas Cardew is a suspected child molester running a refuge for homeless boys. These vaguely historicized scenes are interpenetrated by others set in a sexually predatory but unfulfilled present (attempts at oral and anal sex are repeatedly interrupted by pagers, mobile phones and a crying baby) in which a lesbian couple and a gay male couple decide to have a child which will be 'doubly blessed. There's a positive glut of parents here for you.'[37] Ravenhill is clearly intent on interrogating what we mean by 'natural' behaviour and enlists Wilde in the project. Its final scene counterpoises two self-cancelling images of father-hood. Thomas Cardew cradles, sinisterly, the baby he just discovered in a handbag; and Phil – the thief and drug-addict who has previously acted out Cardew's sexual fantasies in Victorian costume – stubs out his cigarette in another baby's eyes, before wrapping its corpse in a plastic bag and howling that he has done a bad thing. Ravenhill's self-conscious attempts to shock (the play feels on occasions like a cross between Edward Bond and Joe Orton) may seem a long way from Wilde's own elegantly sceptical explora-tion of parenthood and family relations in *The Importance of Being Earnest*. However, Ravenhill's play is as much an act of 'creative criticism' as Tom Stoppard's *Travesties* (1974). Stoppard transforms the explicit burden of literary comment and self-consciousness in *Earnest* into a full-blown debate about the nature of art and the artist, one which is designed to trump the political and aesthetic authoritarianism Stoppard associates with Marxist-Leninism and its legacy.[38] *Handbag*, which is subtitled *The Importance of Being Someone*, is similarly interpretative and transformational. Phil 'travesties' Jack Worthing's search to find out who he is by rejecting re-peated attempts to control him by fathers/lovers: his killing of the baby is a desperate and self-defeating attempt to break the cycle of control and abuse so that Cardew cannot shape the baby's identity as he has tried to shape his. Phil's growing confidence that he is ready to be his own person is cancelled by the play's Wildean insistence on the indeterminacy of identity: the original production at the Lyric Theatre in Hammersmith had the actors doubling-up their roles, and characters who try to 'act' naturally (to summon up motherly feelings, for instance) find themselves staring into a void.

What Ravenhill is in part examining is the contradictory nature of the ways in which we now reproduce Wilde. Gilbert's film, along with David Hare's play *The Judas Kiss* (1998), enlist Wilde in support of a liberal agenda which regards him as an example of tragic individualism: a martyr to free-dom, nonconformity, love. (Hare's play ends, significantly, with Wilde alone on the stage, his voice filling the theatre as the morning sun rises brilliantly over the sea and he speaks the paean to Nature at the close of *De Profundis*. This, the whole force of the dramatic moment insists, is the 'real' Wilde, at last able to feel and love the great primeval simplicity of the natural world.) This conviction that Wilde was trying to live the 'truth' about himself finds expression in the essentially naturalistic 'truth-telling' style in which they tell his story. In *Handbag* that understanding of individualism is incoherently and brutally articulated in Phil's determination to grow up and to take control of his own life. By cancelling Phil's confidence in his authentic self, however, Ravenhill recognizes that for Wilde, the pursuit of individualism will not end in the discovery of natural, simple identity, but will be endlessly deferred into multiplication, fracture and dispersal. So, the radically and self-consciously intertextual and inauthentic style of *Handbag* and *Velvet Goldmine* tells a different kind of truth about Wilde, and one which is closer to both his aesthetic theories and his artistic practice: postmodern versions of postmodern Wilde.

Wilde seems close to us partly because he grapples with contradictions we have yet to resolve. While proclaiming the importance of individualism, he nevertheless recognizes it as problematic and indeterminate. He champions self-fashioning while undermining the sense of self. These contradictions can be seen as reflective of his historical moment, as symptomatic of an emergent Modernism seeking to extinguish a fading Romanticism. But they are also inherent to Postmodernism. The deconstruction of meta-narratives seems to promise release into existential possibility; simultaneously, the dis-solution of meta-narratives of fixed identity denies the existence of a stable self that might exploit that space and freedom. We can see some of these contradictions operative in the ways we now struggle to understand and reproduce him. Thus, insofar as Wilde anticipates and articulates these contradictions we should see him not as simply reflective of his historical moment but as formative of our own. For Wilde the process of contradiction is enabling and exhilarating, because it promises that no ideological or intel-lectual impasse is ever final – it will move on, generating its own opposite. That movement is simultaneously deconstructive, generative and comic: as Baudelaire puts it, 'Laughter is the expression of a double or contradictory feeling'.[39] It is precisely that relish in the proliferation of contradiction which allows Wilde to pursue and enjoy his celebrity: taking pleasure in the para-doxical relationship between self-commodification and self-fashioning, be-tween salesmanship and subversion. Wilde said in 'The Truth of Masks' that a truth in art is that whose contradictory is also true. It is as neat an encap-sulation as any of the way his own writing functions as it seeks to embody the political and aesthetic ideas which inform his theoretical essays, refusing to rest easy with habitual ways of seeing and saying. Wilde also said that 'properly speaking, there is no such thing as style, there are merely styles, that is all.'[40] It is a significant remark because it implies that style might be a contradictory notion, and we have seen how Wilde explores both the radical potential of style, and acknowledges its opposite. Perhaps more importantly, Wilde is here recognizing that style is defined not by essence, or by some approximation to an absolute aesthetic standard, but by its function. It is in the performance and constant renewal of that critical function, in turning the real, the inevitable and the natural into their opposites, that Wilde Style can be liberating, subversive and sustaining.

REFERENCES

1 Baudelaire, *Selected Writings*: 419.
2 Baudelaire, *Intimate Journals*: 57.
3 Baudelaire, *Selected Writings*: 420.
4 Joris-Karl Huysmans, *Against Nature*, Penguin, Harmondsworth, 1959: 13.
5 Baudelaire, *Art in Paris*: 119.
6 Benjamin, *Charles Baudelaire*: 50.
7 Baudelaire, *Intimate Journals*: 95.
8 *Intimate Journals*: 64.
9 Baudelaire, *Selected Writings*: 422.
10 See Walter Benjamin, 'The Work of Art in the Age of Mechanical Reproduction', in *Illuminations*, ed. Hannah Arendt, Fontana, London, 1992: 234.
11 See Ellen Moers, *The Dandy: Brummell to Beerbohm*, Secker & Warburg, London, 1960.
12 John Harvey, *Men in Black*, Reaktion Books, London, 1995: 29–30.
13 Baudelaire, *Selected Writings*: 422.
14 Walter Benjamin puts a different construction on this. He regards dandyism as the invention of the English – a poise cultivated by the leaders in world trade in order to hide their reactions to tremors in the stock market. See *Charles Baudelaire*: 96.
15 Harvey, *Men in Black*: 31.
16 Baudelaire, *Intimate Journals*: 55.
17 *Intimate Journals*: 87.
18 See, for instance, Sally Ledger, 'Oscar Wilde and the "daughters of decadence"', in Hill, ed., *Decadence and Danger*: 109–18, and Victoria White, 'Women of No Importance: Misogyny in the Work of Oscar Wilde', in McCormack, ed., *Wilde the Irishman*: 158–65.
19 Bracewell, *England is Mine*: 13.
20 *England is Mine*: 193.
21 Hebdige, *Subculture*: 28.
22 *Subculture*: 61.
23 Bracewell, *England is Mine*: 84.
24 Benjamin, *Charles Baudelaire*: 34.
25 For reproductions of these firms' trade cards featuring images of Wilde, see Merlin Holland, *The Wilde Album*, Fourth Estate, London, 1997: 92. Holland points out that the New York photographer Nicholas Sarony sued the Burrow Giles Lithographic Co. for using one of his photos of Wilde on the Ehrich Brothers' advert. He won the case and thus established the legal basis for American photographic copyright.
26 T.J. Clark, *The Painting of Modern Life*: 258.
27 Todd Haynes, interview with Geoff Andrew, 'All That Glitters . . .', *Time Out*, 2–9 September 1998: 18.
28 Todd Haynes, *Velvet Goldmine*, Faber, London, 1998: xiv.
29 'All That Glitters . . .': 17.
30 Hebdige, *Subculture*: 94.

[31] Haynes, *Velvet Goldmine*: xxvii.

[32] So compelling is Wilde as an exemplar of this self-destructive, tragic narrative, that disgraced former cabinet minister Jonathan Aitken adopted his mantle while serving eighteen months for perjury, publishing in the summer of 1999 his excruciating *A Ballad from Belmarsh Gaol*.

[33] Stephen Fry in Richard Porton, 'The Actor as Critic: An Interview with Stephen Fry', *Cineaste*, vol. xxiii, no. 4, 1998: 9.

[34] Tom Stoppard, *The Invention of Love*, Faber, London, 1997: 96. Stoppard told Peter Conrad that Wilde 'sacrifices himself to self-fulfilment, if that's an intelligible statement.' In 'Thomas the think engine', *Observer Review*, 1 November 1998: 5.

[35] Richard Allen Cave, ''Wilde's Plays: some lines of influence', in Raby, ed., *The Cambridge Companion*: 219–48.

[36] Mark Ravenhill, *Handbag*, Methuen, London, 1998: 7.

[37] *Handbag*: 3.

[38] For a detailed discussion of the relationship between *Travesties* and *The Importance of Being Earnest*, see Neil Sammells, *Tom Stoppard: the Artist as Critic*, Macmillan, Basingstoke, 1988: 73–86.

[39] Baudelaire, *Selected Writings*: 150.

[40] Review of James Aitcheson's *The Chronicle of Mites*, in Ellmann, ed., *The Artist as Critic*: 97.

BIBLIOGRAPHY

Ackroyd, Peter. (1984) *The Last Testament of Oscar Wilde*. London: Abacus.

Allen, Grant. (1891) 'The Celt in English Art', *Fortnightly Review*, 1 February.

Arata, Stephen. (1996) *Fictions of Loss in the Victorian Fin de Siècle*. Cambridge: Cambridge University Press.

Banville, John. (1997) *The Untouchable*. London: Picador.

Barker, Pat. (1998) *The Regeneration Trilogy*. Harmondsworth: Penguin.

Barry, Kevin. (1996) 'Critical Notes on Post-Colonial Aesthetics', *Irish Studies Review*, 14, Spring.

Barthes, Roland. (1993) *A Barthes Reader*, ed. Susan Sontag. London: Vintage.

Bartlett, Neil. (1988) *Who Was That Man? A Present for Mr Oscar Wilde*. London: Serpent's Tail.

Bashford, Bruce. (1977) 'Oscar Wilde: His Criticism and His Critics', *English Literature in Transition*, vol. 20, no. 4.

——————. (1978) 'Oscar Wilde and Subjectivist Criticism', *English Literature in Transition*, vol. 21, no. 2.

——————. (1985) 'Oscar Wilde as Theorist: The case of *De Profundis*', *English Literature in Transition*, vol. 28, no. 4.

Baudelaire, Charles. (1983) *Intimate Journals*, trans. Christopher Isherwood. San Francisco: City Lights.

——————. (1972) *Baudelaire: Selected Writings on Art and the Artist*, trans. P. Charvet. Cambridge: Cambridge University Press.

——————. (1981) *Art in Paris 1845–1862*, ed. and trans. Jonathan Mayne. Oxford: Clarendon Press.

Beckett, Samuel. (1965) *Proust and Three Dialogues with Georges Duthuit*. London: Calder.

Beckson, Karl, ed. (1970) *Oscar Wilde: The Critical Heritage*. London: Routledge & Kegan Paul.

Behrendt, Patricia Flanagan. (1991) *Oscar Wilde: Eros and Aesthetics*. London: Macmillan.

Bendtz, Ernst. (1914) *The Influence of Pater and Matthew Arnold in the Prose Writings of Oscar Wilde*. London: H. Grevel.

Benjamin, Walter. (1973) *Charles Baudelaire: A Lyric Poet in the Era of High Capitalism*, trans. Harry Zohn. London: New Left Books.

——————. (1992) *Illuminations*, ed. Hannah Arendt. London: Fontana.

Bird, Alan. (1977) *The Plays of Oscar Wilde*. London: Vision Press.

Blanchard, Mary Warner. (1998) *Oscar Wilde's America: Counterculture in the Gilded Age.* London and New Haven: Yale University Press.

Bloom, Harold. (1974) *Selected Writings of Walter Pater.* New York: Signet.

Bowlby, Rachel. (1987) 'Promoting Dorian Gray', *Oxford Literary Review*, no. 9.

Bracewell, Michael. (1997) *England is Mine: Pop Life in Albion from Wilde to Goldie.* London: HarperCollins.

Bradbury, Malcolm and Ian Fletcher, eds. (1979) *Decadence and the 1890s.* London: Edward Arnold.

Bradley, Anthony and Maryann Gialanella Valiulis, eds. (1997) *Gender and Sexuality in Modern Ireland.* Amherst: University of Massachusetts Press.

Brake, Laurel. (1994) *Subjugated Knowledges: Journalism, Gender and Literature in the Nineteenth Century.* Basingstoke: Macmillan.

Brown, Julia Prewitt. (1997) *Cosmopolitan Criticism: Oscar Wilde's Philosophy of Art.* Charlottesville and London: University Press of Virginia.

Buell, Lawrence. (1995) *The Environmental Imagination: Thoreau, Nature Writing and the Formation of American Culture.* Cambridge, Mass.: Harvard University Press.

Bullen, J.B., ed. (1997) *Writing and Victorianism.* London: Longman.

Burgess, Gilbert. (1895) '*An Ideal Husband* at the Haymarket Theatre. A Talk with Mr Oscar Wilde', *The Sketch*, 9 January.

Byrne, Patrick. (1953) *The Wildes of Merrion Square.* London: Staples Press.

Callinicos, Alex. (1989) *Against Postmodernism: A Marxist Critique.* Cambridge: Polity Press.

Calloway, Stephen. (1997) *The Exquisite Life of Oscar Wilde.* London: Orion Media.

Cave, Richard Allen. (1994) 'Wilde designs: some thoughts about recent British productions of his plays', *Modern Drama*, 37, Spring.

Clark, T.J. (1985) *The Painting of Modern Life: Paris in the Art of Manet and his Followers.* London: Thames & Hudson.

Clements, Patricia. (1985) *Baudelaire and the English Tradition.* Princeton: Princeton University Press.

Coakley, Davis. (1994) *Oscar Wilde: The Importance of Being Irish.* Dublin: Town House.

Cohen, Ed. (1993) *Talk on the Wilde Side: Towards a Genealogy of Discourse on Male Sexualities.* New York: Routledge.

Cohen, Philip K. (1978) *The Moral Vision of Oscar Wilde.* London and New Jersey: Associated University Presses.

Cohen, William A. (1996) *Sex Scandal: The Private Parts of Victorian Fiction.* Durham and London: Duke University Press.

Conrad, Joseph. (1973) *Heart of Darkness.* Harmondsworth: Penguin.

Conrad, Peter. (1998) 'Thomas the think engine', *Observer Review*, 1 November.

Cook, Rupert Croft. (1967) *Feasting with Panthers.* London: W.H. Allen.

————. (1972) *The Unrecorded Life of Oscar Wilde.* London: W.H. Allen.

Corkery, D. (1931) *Synge and Anglo-Irish Literature.* Cork: Cork University Press.

Cornwell, Neil. (1990) *The Literary Fantastic: from Gothic to Postmodernism.* Hemel Hempstead: Harvester/Wheatsheaf.

Craft, Christopher. (1994) *Another Kind of Love: Male Homosexual Desire in English Discourse 1850–1920.* Berkeley: University of California Press.

Currie, Mark. (1998) *Postmodern Narrative Theory*. London: Macmillan.

Danson, Laurence. (1997) *Wilde's Intentions: The Artist in his Criticism*. Oxford: Clarendon Press.

D'Arch Smith, Timothy. (1970) *Love in Earnest: Some Notes on the Lives and Writings of English 'Uranian' Poets from 1889 to 1930*. London: Routledge & Kegan Paul.

Dargis, Manohla. (1994) 'Pulp Instinct', *Sight and Sound*, vol. 4, no. 5.

David, Hugh. (1997) *On Queer Street: A Social History of British Homosexuality, 1895–1995*. London: HarperCollins.

Deane, Seamus. (1986) *A Short History of Irish Literature*. London: Hutchinson.

—————, ed. (1991) *The Field Day Anthology of Irish Writing*. Derry: Field Day.

Dellamora, Richard. (1990) *Masculine Desire: the Sexual Politics of Victorian Aestheticism*. Chapel Hill: University of North Carolina Press.

De Man, Paul. (1986) *The Resistance to Theory*. Manchester: Manchester University Press.

Derrida, J. (1998) *The Derrida Reader*, ed. Julian Wolfreys. Edinburgh: Edinburgh University Press.

Dollimore, Jonathan. (1991) *Sexual Dissidence: Augustine to Wilde, Freud to Foucault*. Oxford: Oxford University Press.

Douglas, Lord Alfred. (1914) *Oscar Wilde and Myself*. London: John Long.

—————. (1938) *Without Apology*. New York: Martin Secker.

—————. (1940) *Oscar Wilde: A Summing-up*. London: Duckworth.

Dowling, Linda. (1986) *Language and Decadence in the Victorian Fin de Siècle*. Princeton: Princeton University Press.

—————. (1994) *Hellenism and Homosexuality in Victorian Oxford*. Ithaca and London: Cornell University Press.

Dudley Edwards, Owen. (1995) 'Oscar Wilde: The Soul of Man under Hibernicism', *Irish Studies Review*, 11, Summer.

Eagleton, Terry. (1989) *Saint Oscar*. Derry: Field Day.

—————. (1995) *Heathcliff and the Great Hunger: Studies in Irish Culture*. London, Verso.

—————. (1996) *The Illusions of Postmodernism*. Oxford: Blackwell.

—————. (1996) *Literary Theory: An Introduction*. Oxford: Blackwell (second edn.).

Ellmann, Richard, ed. (1969) *Oscar Wilde: A Collection of Critical Essays*. Englewood Cliffs, N.J.: Prentice Hall.

—————. (1987) *Oscar Wilde*. London: Hamilton.

—————. (1988) *Four Dubliners: Wilde, Yeats, Joyce and Beckett*. London: Cardinal.

Eltis, Sos. (1996) *Revising Wilde: Society and Subversion in the Plays of Oscar Wilde*. Oxford: Clarendon Press.

Fido, Martin. (1976) *Oscar Wilde*. London: Cardinal.

Foldy, Michael S. (1997) *The Trials of Oscar Wilde: Deviance, Morality and Late-Victorian Society*. London and New Haven: Yale University Press.

Foley, Tadhg and Sean Ryder, eds. (1998) *Ideology and Ireland in the Nineteenth Century*. Dublin: Four Courts Press.

Foucault, M. (1986) *The Foucault Reader*, ed. Paul Rabinow. Harmondsworth: Penguin.

Fry, Stephen. (1997) Interview by Eileen Battersby, 'Big Fry', *Irish Times*, 30 October.

Fuller, Graham. (1994) 'Quentin Tarantino, Answers first, Questions later', in *Reservoir Dogs.* London: Faber.

Gagnier, Regenia. (1987) *Idylls of the Marketplace: Oscar Wilde and the Victorian Public.* Aldershot: Scolar Press.

——————, ed. (1992) *Critical Essays on Oscar Wilde.* New York: G.K. Hall.

Galloway, David, ed. (1967) *Edgar Allan Poe: Selected Writings.* Harmondsworth: Penguin.

Gardiner, Juliet. (1995) *Oscar Wilde: A Life in Letters, Writings and Wit.* London: Collins & Brown.

Genet, Jean. (1967) *The Thief's Journal.* Harmondsworth: Penguin.

Gibbons, Luke. (1992) 'Identity Without a Centre: Allegory, History and Irish Nationalism', *Cultural Studies*, vol. VI, no. 3.

Gilbert, Brian. (1997) *Wilde*, Polygram Films.

Goodman, Edward J. (1889) *His Other Self.* London: Ward & Downey.

Goodman, Jonathan. (1988) *The Oscar Wilde File.* London: Allison & Busby.

Graham, Colin. (1994) ' "Liminal Spaces": Post-Colonial Theories and Irish Culture', *Irish Review*, 16.

—————— and Richard Kirkland, eds. (1999) *Ireland and Cultural Theory: the Mechanics of Authenticity.* London: Macmillan.

Guilliat, R. (1993) 'QT', *Sunday Times*, 3 October.

Halperin, David. (1990) *One Hundred Years of Homosexuality and Other Essays on Greek Love.* London: Routledge.

——————, John J. Winkler and Froma I. Zeitlin, eds. (1990) *Before Sexuality: the Construction of Erotic Experience in the Ancient Greek World.* Princeton, N.J.: Princeton University Press.

Hare, David. (1998) *The Judas Kiss.* London: Faber.

Harris, Frank. (1965) *Oscar Wilde: His Life and Confessions.* London: Panther.

Harvey, John. (1995) *Men in Black*, London: Reaktion Books.

Haynes, Todd. (1998) *Velvet Goldmine.* London: Faber.

——————. (1998) Interview with Geoff Andrew, 'All that Glitters . . .', *Time Out*, vol. 2, no. 9, September.

Hebdige, Dick. (1989) *Subculture: the Meaning of Style.* London: Routledge.

Helfand, Michael S. and Philip E. Smith II, eds. (1989) *Oscar Wilde's Oxford Notebooks: A Portrait of a Mind in the Making.* Oxford: Oxford University Press.

Hill, Tracey. (1998) *Decadence and Danger: Writing, History and the Fin de Siècle.* Bath: Sulis Press.

Hichins, Robert. (1894) *The Green Carnation.* London: Heinemann.

Hoare, Philip. (1997) *Wilde's Last Stand: Decadence, Conspiracy and the First World War.* London: Duckworth.

Holland, Merlin. (1997) *The Wilde Album.* London: Fourth Estate.

Holland, Vyvyan. (1954) *Son of Oscar Wilde.* London: Rupert Hart-Davis.

Howe, P.P. (1911) Review of *Lady Windermere's Fan*, *Outlook*, 21 October. Repr. in William Tydeman, ed. (1982) *Wilde: Comedies.* Basingstoke: Macmillan.

Huysmans, Joris-Karl. (1959) *Against Nature.* Harmondsworth: Penguin.

Hyde, H. Montgomery. (1948) *The Trials of Oscar Wilde.* London: Hodge.

————————. (1976) *Oscar Wilde*. London: Methuen.

Hyland, Paul and Neil Sammells, eds. (1991) *Irish Writing: Exile and Subversion*. Basingstoke: Macmillan.

Jackson, Holbrook. (1914) *The Eighteen Nineties*. London: Grant Richards.

Jackson, Russell, ed. (1989) *Victorian Theatre*. London: A. & C. Black.

James, Henry. (1964) *The Complete Tales of Henry James*, vol. 9, 1892–1898. London: Rupert Hart-Davis.

Jullian, Phillippe, trans. Violet Wyndham. (1994) *Oscar Wilde*. London: Constable.

Kaplan, Joel H. and Sheila Stowell. (1994) *Theatre and Fashion: Oscar Wilde to the Suffragettes*. Cambridge: Cambridge University Press.

Kauffman, Moises. (1998) *Gross Indecency: The Three Trials of Oscar Wilde*. London: Methuen.

Kerridge, Richard and Neil Sammells. (1997) *Writing the Environment*. London: Zed Books.

Kiberd, Declan. (1995) *Inventing Ireland: The Literature of the Modern Nation*. London: Jonathan Cape.

Knox, Melissa. (1994) *Oscar Wilde: A Long and Lovely Suicide*. London and New Haven: Yale University Press.

Kohl, Norbert. (1989) *Oscar Wilde: The Works of a Conformist Rebel*, trans. David Henry Wilson. Cambridge: Cambridge University Press.

Kotzin, Michael C. (1979) ' "The Selfish Giant" as Literary Fairy Tale', *Studies in Short Fiction*, vol. 16.

Kristeva, Julia. (1986) *The Kristeva Reader*, ed. Toril Moi. Oxford: Blackwell.

Kronenberger, Louis. (1952) *The Thread of Laughter*. New York: Alfred A. Knopf.

————————. (1976) *Oscar Wilde*. Boston, Mass.: Little, Brown.

Lacan, J. (1977) *Ecrits: a Selection*, trans. Alan Sheridan. London: Tavistock Publications.

Ledger, Sally and Scott McCracken, eds. (1995) *Cultural Politics at the Fin de Siècle*. Cambridge: Cambridge University Press.

Leonard, Elmore. (1999) *Be Cool*. London: Viking.

Lewis, Wyndham. (1987) *Men Without Art*, ed. Seamus Cooney. Santa Rosa: Black Sparrow Press.

Lloyd, David. (1993) *Anomalous States: Irish Writing and the Post-Colonial Moment*. Dublin: Lilliput.

Lodge, David. (1977) *The Modes of Modern Writing*. London: Edward Arnold.

————————, ed. (1988) *Modern Criticism and Theory*. London: Longman.

Lysaght, Elizabeth. (1890) *The Veiled Picture: or, The Wizard's Legacy*. London: Simpkin, Marshall & Co.

McClellan, Jim. (1994) 'On the Run: Tarantino', *Observer*, 3 July.

MacCormack, Jerusha, ed. (1998) *Wilde the Irishman*. London and New Haven: Yale University Press.

Marcus, Jane. (1974) 'Salome: the Jewish Princess Was a New Woman', *Bulletin of the New York Public Library*.

Martin, Robert K. (1979) 'Oscar Wilde and the Fairy Tale: The Happy Prince as self-dramatization', *Studies in Victorian Fiction*, vol. 16.

Mason, Stuart. (1971) *Oscar Wilde, Art and Morality*. London: Haskell House.

Mikhail, E.H. (1978) *Oscar Wilde: An Annotated Bibliography of Criticism.* London, Macmillan.

——————, ed. (1979) *Oscar Wilde: Interviews and Recollections*, 2 vols. London: Macmillan.

Miller, Robert Keith. (1982) *Oscar Wilde.* New York: Frederick Ungar.

Millett, Kate. (1977) *Sexual Politics.* London: Virago.

Moers, Ellen. (1960) *The Dandy: Brummell to Beerbohm.* London: Secker & Warburg.

Moi, Toril. (1985) *Sexual/Textual Politics.* London: Methuen.

Monsman, Geoffrey. (1977) *Walter Pater.* Boston, Mass.: G.K. Hall.

Morgan, Margery ed. (1990) *File on Wilde.* London: Methuen.

Morley, Sheridan. (1976) *Oscar Wilde.* London: Weidenfeld & Nicolson.

Mulvey-Roberts, Marie, ed. (1998) *The Handbook to Gothic Literature.* Basingstoke: Macmillan.

Nandy, Ashis. (1988) *The Intimate Enemy: Loss and Recovery of Self under Colonialism.* Oxford: Oxford University Press.

Nassaar, Christopher S. (1974) *Into the Demon Universe: A Literary Exploration of Oscar Wilde.* London and New Haven: Yale University Press.

Nelson, Walter W. (1989) *Oscar Wilde and the Dramatic Critics: A Study in Victorian Theatre.* Lund: Bloms Boktryckerl.

Norris, Christopher. (1982) *Deconstruction: Theory and Practice.* London: Methuen.

——————. (1991) *What's Wrong with Postmodernism: Critical Theory and the Ends of Philosophy.* Brighton: Harvester.

O'Hagan, Sean. (1994) 'X Offender', *The Times Magazine*, 15 October.

O'Toole, Fintan. (1997) 'Glorious triviality', *Irish Times*, 21 January.

Page, Norman. (1991) *An Oscar Wilde Chronology.* London: Macmillan.

Paglia, Camille. (1992) *Sexual Personae: Art and Decadence from Nefertiti to Emily Dickinson.* Harmondsworth: Penguin.

Pater, Walter. (1986) *Marius the Epicurean*, ed. Ian Small. Oxford: Oxford University Press.

——————. (1986) *The Renaissance: Studies in Art and Poetry*, ed. Adam Phillips. Oxford: Oxford University Press.

Pearson, Hesketh. (1960) *The Life of Oscar Wilde.* London: Penguin/Methuen.

Peckham, Morse. (1962) *Beyond the Tragic Vision: The Quest for Identity in the Nineteenth Century.* New York: George Brazillier.

Pine, Richard. (1983) *Oscar Wilde.* Dublin: Gill & Macmillan.

——————. (1995) *The Thief of Reason: Oscar Wilde and Modern Ireland.* Dublin: Gill & Macmillan.

Pollock, Walter Herries. (1883) *The Picture's Secret.* London: Remington & Co.

Porton, Richard. (1998) 'The Actor as Critic: An Interview with Stephen Fry', *Cineaste*, vol. xxiii, no. 4.

Powell, Kerry. (1990) *Wilde and the Theatre of the 1890s.* Cambridge: Cambridge University Press.

Price, Steven and William Tydeman. (1996) *Salome.* Cambridge: Cambridge University Press.

Pulver, Andrew. (1994) 'The Movie Junkie', *Guardian*, 19 September.

Raby, Peter. (1988) *Oscar Wilde*. Cambridge: Cambridge University Press.

——————, ed. (1997) *The Cambridge Companion to Oscar Wilde*. Cambridge: Cambridge University Press.

Ransome, Arthur. (1912) *Oscar Wilde: A Critical Study*. London: Martin Secker.

Ravenhill, Mark. (1998) *Handbag*. London: Methuen.

Reade, Brian, ed. (1970) *Sexual Heretics: Male Homosexuality in English Literature from 1850 to 1900*. London: Routledge & Kegan Paul.

Reed, John R. (1985) *Decadent Style*. Athens, Ohio: Ohio University Press.

Renier, G.J. (1933) *Oscar Wilde*, London: Nelson.

Robertson, W. Graham. (1931) *Time Was*. London: Hamish Hamilton.

Roditi, Edouard. (1947) *Oscar Wilde*. Norfolk, CT.: New Directions Books.

Said, Edward W. (1975) *Beginnings: Intention and Method*. New York: Basic Books.

——————. (1980) *Orientalism*. London: Routledge & Kegan Paul.

——————. (1983) *The World, The Text and the Critic*. Cambridge, Mass.: Harvard University Press.

——————. (1988) *Nationalism, Colonialism and Literature: Yeats and Decolonization*. Derry: Field Day.

——————. (1994) *Culture and Imperialism*. London: Vintage.

Sammells, Neil. (1988) *Tom Stoppard: the Artist as Critic*. Basingstoke: Macmillan.

—————— and Paul Hyland, eds. (1995) *Irish Studies Review*, no. 11, Oscar Wilde special issue, September.

Sandulescu, George, ed. (1994) *Rediscovering Oscar Wilde*. Gerrard's Cross: Colin Smythe.

San Juan, Epifanio. (1967) *The Art of Oscar Wilde*. Princeton: Princeton University Press.

Satterthwaite, Walter. (1991) *Wilde West*. London: Fontana.

Schad, John. (1999) *Victorians in Theory: from Derrida to Browning*. Manchester: Manchester University Press.

Schmidgall, Gary. (1994) *The Stranger Wilde: Interpreting Oscar*. London: Abacus.

Sedgwick, Eve Kosofsky. (1986) *Between Men: English Literature and Male Homosocial Desire*. New York: Columbia University Press.

——————. (1991) *The Epistemology of the Closet*. London: Harvester/Wheatsheaf.

Segal, Clancy. (1993) 'Killing Jokes?', *Guardian*, 11 September.

Selden, Raman. (1985) *A Reader's Guide to Contemporary Literary Theory*. Brighton: Harvester.

Shaw, George Bernard. (1895) Review of *An Ideal Husband*, *Saturday Review*, 12 January.

——————. (1945) *Major Barbara*. Harmondsworth: Penguin.

——————. (1946) *Arms and the Man*. Harmondsworth: Penguin.

——————. (1946) *The Philanderer*. Harmondsworth: Penguin.

Shewan, Rodney. (1997) *Oscar Wilde: Art and Egotism*. London: Macmillan.

Showalter, Elaine. (1991) *Sexual Anarchy: Gender and Culture at the Fin de Siècle*. London: Bloomsbury.

Sinfield, Alan. (1994) *The Wilde Century*. London: Cassell.

——————. (1995) 'Wilde and the Queer Moment', *Irish Studies Review*, 11, Summer.

Sisley, Maurice. (1892) 'La Salome de M. Oscar Wilde', *Le Gaulois*, 29 June.

Small, Ian. (1979) *The Aesthetes*. London: Routledge & Kegan Paul.

———. (1993) *Oscar Wilde Revalued: An Essay on New Materials and Methods of Research*. Greensboro, N.C., Gerrards Cross: Colin Smythe (distributor).

Sontag, Susan. (1983) *A Susan Sontag Reader*, ed. Elizabeth Hardwick. Harmondsworth: Penguin.

Steinman, Michael. (1983) *Yeats's Heroic Figures: Wilde, Parnell, Swift, Casement*. Basingstoke: Macmillan.

Stokes, John. (1972) *Resistible Theatres*. London: Paul Elek.

———. (1978) *Oscar Wilde*. Harlow: Longman/British Council.

———. (1996) *Oscar Wilde: Myths, Miracles and Imitations*. Cambridge: Cambridge University Press.

Stoppard, Tom. (1975) *Travesties*. London: Faber.

———. (1980) *Lord Malquist and Mr Moon*. London: Faber.

———. (1997) *The Invention of Love*. London: Faber.

Symons, Arthur. (1930) *A Study of Oscar Wilde*. London: C.J. Sawyer.

Tarantino, Quentin. (1992) *Reservoir Dogs*. London: Faber.

———. (1994) *Pulp Fiction*. London: Faber.

———. (1994) 'Quentin Tarantino on Pulp Fiction', *Sight and Sound*, vol. 4, no. 5.

———. (1995) *True Romance*. London: Faber.

———. (1995) in 'Rock 'n' Reel', *The Guardian*, 14 April.

Thornton, R.K.R. (1983) *The Decadent Dilemma*. London: Edward Arnold.

Trilling, Lionel. (1972) *Sincerity and Authenticity*. Oxford: Oxford University Press.

Tydeman, William, ed. (1982) *Wilde Comedies: a Selection of Critical Essays*. Basingstoke: Macmillan.

Varty, Anne. (1998) *A Preface to Oscar Wilde*. London: Longman.

Von Eckhardt, Wolf, Sander L. Gilman and J. Edward Chamberlin. (1987) *Oscar Wilde's London*. New York: Anchor Press.

Walshe, Eibhear, ed. (1997) *Sex, Nation and Dissent in Irish Writing*. Cork: Cork University Press.

Warner, Alan. (1981) *A Guide to Anglo-Irish Literature*. Dublin: Gill & Macmillan.

West, Rebecca. (1983) *The Young Rebecca: Writings of Rebecca West, 1911–1917*, ed. Jane Marcus. London: Virago.

Wilde, Oscar. (1907) *Salome: A Tragedy in One Act Translated from the French of Oscar Wilde*, ed. Robert Ross. London: John Lane.

———. (1912) *The Soul of Man Under Socialism*. London: Arthur L. Humphreys.

———. (1961) *Selected Writings of Oscar Wilde*, ed. Richard Ellmann. Oxford: Oxford University Press.

———. (1962) *The Letters of Oscar Wilde*, ed. Rupert Hart-Davis. London: Rupert Hart-Davis.

———. (1962) *The Happy Prince and Other Stories*, introduced by Michael MacLiammoir. London: Puffin Books.

———. (1966) *The Complete Works of Oscar Wilde*. London: Collins, new edition.

———. (1973) *The Artist as Critic: Critical Writings of Oscar Wilde*, ed. Richard Ellmann. London: W.H. Allen.

—————————. (1979) *Selected Letters of Oscar Wilde*, ed. Rupert Hart-Davis. Oxford: Oxford University Press.

—————————. (1980) *Oscar Wilde: Complete Shorter Fiction*, ed. Isobel Murray. Oxford: Oxford University Press.

—————————. (1982) *The Annotated Oscar Wilde*, ed. H. Montgomery Hyde. London: Orbis.

—————————. (1985) *More Letters of Oscar Wilde*, ed. Rupert Hart-Davis. London: Murray.

—————————. (1988) *Oscar Wilde: The Picture of Dorian Gray*, ed. Donald Lawler. New York: W. Norton.

—————————. (1989) *The Fireworks of Oscar Wilde*, selected, edited and introduced by Owen Dudley Edwards. London: Barrie & Jenkins.

—————————. (1989) *Salome*, introd. Steven Berkoff. London: Faber.

—————————. (1992) *The Importance of Being Earnest and Related Writings*, ed. Joseph Bristow. London: Routledge.

—————————. (1995) *Oscar Wilde: Lady Windermere's Fan, Salome, A Woman of No Importance, An Ideal Husband, The Importance of Being Earnest*, ed. Peter Raby. Oxford: Clarendon Press.

Wood, James. (1994) 'You're sayin' a foot massage don't mean nothin', and I'm sayin' it does', *The Guardian* supplement, 19 November.

Woodcock, George A. (1949) *The Paradox of Oscar Wilde*. London: T.V. Boardman.

Worth, Katharine. (1978) *The Irish Drama in Europe from Yeats to Beckett*. London: Athlone Press.

—————————. (1983) *Oscar Wilde*. London: Macmillan.

Zola, Emile. (1974) 'The Experimental Novel and Other Essays', *Dramatic Theory and Criticism: Greeks to Grotowski*, ed. Bernard Dukore. London: Holt, Rinehart & Winston.

INDEX